Long Time Passing:
Mothers Speak about War and Terror

Long Time Passing: Mothers Speak about War and Terror

SUSAN GALLEYMORE

PLUTO PRESS
www.plutobooks.com

First published 2009 by Pluto Press
345 Archway Road, London N6 5AA and
175 Fifth Avenue, New York, NY 10010

www.plutobooks.com

Distributed in the United States of America exclusively by
Palgrave Macmillan, a division of St. Martin's Press LLC,
175 Fifth Avenue, New York, NY 10010

British Library Cataloguing in Publication Data
A catalogue record for this book is available from the British Library

ISBN   978 0 7453 2829 4   Hardback

Library of Congress Cataloging in Publication Data applied for

This book is printed on paper suitable for recycling and made from fully managed
and sustained forest sources. Logging, pulping and manufacturing processes are
expected to conform to the environmental standards of the country of origin.
The paper may contain up to 70% post consumer waste.

10   9   8   7   6   5   4   3   2   1

Designed and produced for Pluto Press by
Chase Publishing Services Ltd, Sidmouth, EX10 9QG, England
Typeset from disk by Stanford DTP Services, Northampton
Printed and bound in the European Union by
TJ International Ltd, Padstow, England

Where have all the soldiers gone?
Long time passing …
Where have all the soldiers gone?
They've gone to graveyards every one.
Oh, when will they ever learn?

—Pete Seeger, "Where Have All the Flowers Gone?"

Dedicated to my son:
may your experiences of war open your heart
to all that is graceful and true.
And to my daughter,
know that your presence is the blessing of hope.

Contents

Acknowledgements

In recognition of Anwar whose story broke my heart and started the journey to all that follows. Dr. Ali Rasheed Hamid and Harb Muktar—and more than 2 million other Iraqis—may you return from exile to the land you love.

In Israel, Nurit Peled-Elhanan convinced me that sons don't disapprove of mothers forever, and that working for peace may make us mutants in a militaristic world, but it is mutation that will change the world. Amina in the West Bank proves that no mere mountain can stop a mother. Dorothy Naor at the checkpoints is the mother of all persistence. And thank you to all the mothers and families who, in courageously sharing your stories, honor our common humanity.

May peace reign in indomitable Lebanon and for Mary Abu Saba who paved the way to Sara Osseiran who made things happen; Antun and Judith Harik who shared Byblos; Dr. Mary Mikhael and the Near East School of Theology who gave me a home away from home; Josef and Amal who generously offered hospitality in Mieh Mieh; for Karen Button who introduced me to Ra'fat who braved Lebanon's roads. In Beirut Maurice renewed my faith in taxi drivers and Carlos encouraged me to outwait the Syrian border officials in Jdeideh…and he was right!

Kathryn Winogura introduced voices of Afghan women who had immigrated to the United States after the Russian occupation of their country. Jennifer Heath and Marsha MacColl introduced me to voices from Afghanistan.

In San Francisco Bay Area, Elizabeth Bell shared editorial skill and fast turnaround so far beyond the call of duty that I know she respects these courageous mothers as much as I do. (Any errors and omissions here are mine alone.) Joe Woodard always assists when needed. The poets, artists, writers, and readers at Spec's offer encouragement. The folks on the GI Rights Hotline share life-affirming counsel to our youth waking up to the horrors of war and the inevitable conclusions that derive from the logic of capitalism.

In South Africa, thank you to Mike and to my own mother, who give the trees, birds, and other living critters a home amidst the encroaching devastation of industry.

Join in and learn more

View photographs and other collateral related to the stories shared in this book at http://www.mothersspeakaboutwarandterror.org/.

Make your voice heard and challenge the underlying assumptions fueling the leaders and worldviews that bring countries to war at http://mothersspeakaboutwarandterror.blogspot.com.

Stay in touch with like-minded people at MotherSpeak, http://www.motherspeak.org, and Raising Sand Radio, http://www.raisingsandradio.org.

Introduction

I tried to fathom whether human feelings were able to withstand such a vast power machine.... Perhaps the only option was to forget, to not see. To listen to the official version of things, to half-listen, distractedly, and respond with nothing more than a sigh...or to turn my life into a battlefield where you don't hope to survive but merely to go down after a good fight.
—Roberto Saviano, *Gomorrah*

"I'M BACK! I GOT BACK LAST NIGHT." My son sounded buoyant over the phone—our first conversation since he'd deployed to Afghanistan.

"Welcome home! Are you doing okay? Will you get some time off? When can we see you?"

"I'll get a week off soon and come home."

After I put down the phone I remembered the conversation when my son announced he'd enlisted in the U.S. Army. It had been a lovely summer day in 1999 and we'd sat in the garden awaiting the "important announcement," as he put it. After the shock—my kid joining the U.S. military? How could this happen?—my response was unequivocal. "Oh no, you're not! You could be sent to war!"

"Oh, there won't be a war. Anyway, I already signed up."

A year later I dropped him off at the recruiting office in my California town. After months of trying to dissuade him, I'd finally given up. Having immigrated to the States from South Africa in my early 20s, I was naïve about the U.S. military's recruitment and retention processes—I honestly believed that basic training would cure him and he would quickly get out, wiser for the experience. Little did I know that recruits can't simply change their minds. A much deeper understanding lay ahead for me.

After 9/11, I knew President Bush would soon identify perpetrators and send the military after them. Would it have been a different decision with a different president? I doubt it. People all over the world expect their leaders to keep them safe, and Bush capitalized upon—then politicized—this expectation.

1

But now, as I experienced its meaning from the perspective of a mother with an enlisted child, I felt a sudden rush of astonishment and energy: How could we mothers allow this to happen—how could we have allowed it throughout history? How did mothers in other lands—especially those lands ravaged by ongoing conflict—react to their children's deployment? And did Americans really believe that this so-called War on Terror was about spreading freedom and democracy?

While my son was deployed to Afghanistan in 2003 I awoke from nightmares almost every night: the knock on the door, uniformed military personnel on the doorstep, "We're sorry to inform you…," images of my son disabled like the soldier in *Johnny Got His Gun*, bombs raining on a family's home while a mother screamed out her children's names….

My first real encounter with the vast horror that is war was meeting Holocaust survivors when I was a child. Then I had reacted by imagining how I would steel myself for hearing the worst news. But now, try as I might, I couldn't hold for more than a few seconds the thought of my own child's direct involvement: the pain was overwhelming. I couldn't imagine how mothers could—how *I* might have to—adjust to the unthinkable: the death or maiming of a beloved child, the nightmare vision of that child killing or maiming others.

The long way home

Before the War on Terror, I knew nothing about the variety of tactics U.S. military recruiters use to enlist young people into the volunteer military. I'd immigrated to the U.S. after the Vietnam War and the protests against it. Other than an awareness of draftee David Harris's conscientious objection, for which he spent two years in jail, I knew nothing about GI resistance to that war and next to nothing about GI underground networks and newspapers. I had no idea that anti-militarism activists offer free, confidential counseling to military personnel and their families…or that I would train and volunteer as a counselor myself.

My son's six-month tour of duty in Afghanistan had been extended to nine months—the three extra months were harder for him than for me, but my nightmares and obsessive thoughts continued: would he suffer Post Traumatic Stress Disorder? What are the long-term effects of forced anthrax and smallpox vaccines, anti-malarial drugs, and depleted uranium contamination? Would the U.S. military opt out of caring for War on Terror troops the way they'd done after Gulf War I veterans reported illnesses subsequently diagnosed as Gulf War Syndrome?

When he came home on leave, I observed my son carefully but I was almost too frightened of what I might hear to ask him directly about his experiences. Nevertheless, an anecdote he related gave a glimpse into how our troops are systematically desensitized.

Local Afghan dogs sought scraps around the military base and, as people do anywhere, American troops befriended the animals. The well-fed dogs switched allegiances and soon were barking at and harassing Afghan villagers who came too near. But as the troops prepared to return to the United States, the base commander announced that all the dogs must be killed. The soldiers were ordered to shoot the same animals that had been their pets, their companions, their confidants.

What you gotta do

Three months later—on his birthday—my son told me he was deploying to Iraq. When I expressed dismay, he responded, "Well, you gotta do what you gotta do...."

I was numb with a cascade of terrifying images: my son hesitates before shooting—how could he not hesitate?—and is himself shot; my son's body riddled with bullets; my son shooting into a crowd of civilians; my son begging for handouts like the Vietnam veterans on San Francisco's streets....

My fear turned to rage. What was going on over there? Why was news coverage so one-sided, so pro-war, so lacking in balanced information, always reduced to trivial sound bites?

Are mothers supposed to simply sit and wait while their children are imperiled?

Am I overreacting? How do other mothers manage their fears and grief?

Jolted awake by another nightmare, I realized I'd not prepared him for some of the harshest realities of life: I hadn't told him how easy it is for human beings, in certain situations, to observe—or participate in—acts that may haunt them for life. A story my brother related to me decades ago, about events during *his* military service, had jarred my memory. After "terries" (the dehumanizing appellation for "terrorists") were captured and brought into camp, South African Defense Force troops separated the males and females. They took the males out back and executed them. Before executing the females, however, they dusted them with bleached baking flour. Then they raped them. Then they killed them. The prerequisite flouring allowed the troops to joke that they were not contravening apartheid's miscegenation laws—the women were as white as they could be.

My brother did not participate in these floured rapes...nor did he intervene against them. He did learn to self-medicate with alcohol, a coping mechanism he practices to this day.

I knew I must talk with my son...and with other mothers. Perhaps, I thought, I can seek them through the Internet? Perhaps I can interview them and, together, we can highlight the devastating effects of war... perhaps we can effect long-term change and create generative solutions to conflict? Unbeknownst to me, I was tapping into a burgeoning hunger among "military moms" for information, news, stories, anything, that validated our feelings about the war. Many of the mothers I talked to seemed to share my intuition that this so-called War on Terror, unlike the United States' quick military forays into Panama, Somalia, and Kuwait, would take our country on a disastrous trajectory. But, the more I talked to "military moms" the more I realized that few understood what really happened in war. Could Iraqi mothers share their experiences with American mothers?

I asked my friend, a retired Air Force Colonel, if ordinary parents can visit their kids on military bases. He said, "The military discourages it, and they make it difficult, but you do have the right to see your child."

A Code Pink women's delegation was traveling to Baghdad, and I reserved a spot. Then I talked to an NGO worker recently returned from rural Iraq for his perspective on the delegation's proposed overland trip from Amman to Baghdad.

He said, "These days travelers fly into Kuwait and drive to Baghdad. Few use Highway 10 anymore because it goes past Ramadi, Habbaniyah, and Fallujah—restive towns—and since it's harder and harder to find work, highway robbery has become many people's day job. The modus operandi is tailing a convoy at very high speeds, picking off the weakest vehicle, forcing it to stop, and demanding passengers' money. If I were you, I'd choose a different route into Baghdad."

My daughter was worried. How do I tell her, without frightening her, that I believe her brother is in grave danger? Not only from bullets, IEDs, and RPGs[1]—his spirit, too, is in jeopardy. How do I say, without seeming to lecture her, that I feel our country's precipitous rush to war endangers the spirits of all the world's people?

I emailed my plans to my son but heard nothing in return, so I had no idea if he was aware of my intentions. My concerns back then were the same as they are today: I worry about his spirit and I honor his heart as I honor my own. Our activities are not mutually exclusive. He is idealistic and wants to serve his country. He is tenacious in following his own course. How can I not also be tenacious in my belief in a more equitable world, one that actively confronts war, violence, prejudice, domination, and discrimination? He and I hold different assumptions about our country's current course yet we still love and respect one another.

"Don't come to Baghdad!"

I arrived home to a phone message. "What's this I hear about you coming to Baghdad? Don't do it! It's too dangerous for anyone! Or, if I can't convince you to stay home, go to a rifle range and practice shooting before you come. And carry a big gun while you're there." He added, "You won't be able to visit me. Operational security decrees that I can't tell you where I am. The Sunni Triangle is a huge area. There's only the slightest possibility that we can meet if you come. Take my advice: stay home."

I was so rattled by his admonitions that I didn't ask who had told him I was coming. Had he received my email? Or had the military told him to dissuade me? But, if anything, I was more determined than ever. I had two gnawing concerns: my son's safety and psychological health and, if it was that dangerous in Iraq, how were Iraqi mothers managing? A decade of economic sanctions had devastated their social system, and a war would finish it off. If I was fearful for my child, a member of a well-armed force, Iraqi mothers must be terrified for their children, denizens of a failing infrastructure. What did they have to say? Would American mothers do anything to help Iraqi mothers if they knew what was going on?

I pulled together items for the trip: treats for my son, treats for Iraqi kids. Medicine. Following the first Gulf War and subsequent U.N. sanctions, mortality rates for Iraqi children were dire. By all accounts nothing had improved, hospitals hadn't been reconstructed, and sanctions had prevented medicine from entering the country. Spurred by the deep anger that surged through me as I imagined watching my own child become progressively more ill because of a lack of basic health care and medicine, I shopped for chewable vitamins, analgesics, a few bottles of cough syrup. My donations looked so paltry in the face of such overwhelming need that I called local clinics and medical offices and asked for donations. Receptionists sounded incredulous when I explained my mission. They said they'd ask the doctors and "get back" to me. Not a single clinic donated a single thing.

My son had departed the U.S. in a commercial air liner the military leased to transport troops. A wheel fell off the landing gear over Nova Scotia. Then his paratrooper battalion was delayed on an airbase in Spain due to mechanical problems: they took off for Iraq four times and returned three.

I hoped these problems didn't presage a similar lack of organization in Iraq. I'd already heard military moms' stories about the long list of items the military presented their children to purchase out of their own meager salaries before they deployed—everything from underwear and shaving gear to batteries for vision equipment on guns—but I was still surprised when military families raised funds to purchase and send protective armor to troops. Couldn't the richest country in the world afford to equip the troops who had volunteered to defend it?

"Sylvia" told me she was in awe of her child, "Ed," volunteering for the mission. She was proud he was risking his life for our safety yet terrified that he'd come home damaged or would damage others. She reported feeling both close to and distanced from him: close because he was facing danger, distanced because he was doing something she'd prefer he not do. "I swore I'd go to the ends of the earth to keep my son from fighting in a war…now he's in Iraq." Sylvia reported episodes of spontaneous crying while Ed was deployed. I shared that I, too, would burst out crying—usually while driving. Sometimes, I awoke in tears with my jaws clenched and my hands in prayer position under my chin.

The trip

Camp Anaconda is one of the world's largest U.S. military bases, 40 miles north of Baghdad near Balad in Al Anbar province. I went through military channels and emailed the Public Affairs Officer (PAO) the date and approximate time I expected to arrive at this base.

My driver and translator Ahmed, a Shi'a, had never been into the Sunni Triangle and had no idea where the town of Balad or the American base was located. When he stopped along the way to ask directions, he told me my borrowed *hijab* must stay firmly on my head, adding, "You are now a French journalist."

That I hadn't spoken French in 20 years wasn't important to Ahmed: "Just don't speak. I'll do the talking."

Camp Anaconda's PAO had never responded to my emails, but the military guards at the checkpoint seemed to expect me. When they noticed the U.S. passport I waved, they lowered the M16s they'd pointed at me and crowded around, aghast that I, an American, was wearing a *hijab*. Then they escorted me onto the base and Ahmed into the parking lot reserved for Iraqi nationals.

The 80 minutes I spent with my son were worth all the chaos, fear, danger, and sadness of the journey.

When an article about the trip appeared in the *San Francisco Chronicle*[2] the story was quickly picked up by national and international media, and I became a reluctant overnight celebrity. I received rafts of electronic hate mail and fan mail declaring me everything from a patriot to a traitor, as well as "a useless, fucking bitch." Later, when a photograph of me with my son at Camp Anaconda appeared on the front cover of *Le Monde* magazine,[3] my son told me, "You're going to get me killed."

... and the publicity

The increased exposure brought uncomfortable moments. During a nationally televised MSNBC newscast in the spring of 2004, U.S. Army four-star General Barry McCaffrey (ret.) accused me of "a politically motivated act that endangered the troops." I had not been informed prior to the satellite broadcast that McCaffrey would appear with me. If anything, the network had politicized an anxious mother's private action by turning it into a public confrontation with a military spokesperson.

I responded, "General, perhaps you have to be a mother to understand."

The simple fact is that the military is inimical to mothering: mothers are nurturing, the military is authoritarian; mothers encourage sensitivity, the military desensitizes; mothers support uniqueness, the military demands conformity; mothers dialogue, the military pronounces....

As I faced the range of critiques and attention for my action—not easy for a very private person—I began to recognize on a new level that mothering itself is both a personal act and a public responsibility. It is never easy for mothers—or anyone else—to challenge deeply entrenched systems, be they the political status quo or one's own worldview.

Two women's stories illustrate this. The 13-year-old daughter of Nurit Peled-Elhanan of Israel was killed by a suicide bomber in Jerusalem. Today Nurit overtly challenges the militaristic worldview: "It is people against politicians and armies," she declares. "Bush, Saddam, Milosevic, Sharon, and so on, they're all the same...they slash, they burn, and they move on. They don't really care about anything. This is a failure of democracy. These politicians use our kids like chips in a gambling game, and when our children get killed they say, 'Oops, sorry.'"

San Francisco Bay Area mother Lara Dutto challenged her own worldview. "I was overcome with sadness about the war," she says, "and felt like I needed *to do something*...but what? I've never lived in a place with conflict, and I only know how to respond with optimism and something fairly happy and mild." Lara and her friends, with the help of Iraqi Children's Art Exchange founder Claudia Lefko, raised $50,000 in one evening to support a grade school in Amman so that Iraqi refugee children can continue their education during the bloody chaos that is the Global War on Terror. "I'd never before envisioned anything like organizing a fundraiser. I didn't frame it as anti-war, and frankly, I think people wouldn't have responded as well as they did had it been an anti-war event," she observes. "I believe people attended because every human being has the ability to, and down deep wants to, love others...."[4]

Making sense through sharing stories

"Colonization takes people's stories away and assigns them supportive roles in stories that empower others at their expense," says Rev. Davidson Loehr. Make the first word "occupation" and the statement is no less true. Sharing these families' stories allows the storytellers to claim their voices, empowers them as storytellers, develops the capacity to see through propaganda, and enables empathy and unity across artificial dividing lines.

I interviewed dozens of American military moms, Middle Eastern and Afghan mothers, war veterans, and active-duty, wounded, Absent Without Leave (AWOL), stop-lossed,[5] and discharged troops. I approached each interview as an open inquiry and invited each mother to share what she believed was most relevant to her experience of war and terror. I did not define "terror" and avoided the politicized word "terrorism," for which there is no generally accepted legal definition.

Each time I described this project to a mother I made sure that she understood my son was a soldier deployed to the War on Terror. I sought interviews with a range of American mothers, and some refused to share their stories in this public forum. A few stated that if I did not support the troops, the President of the United States, and the war *no matter what*, I was "an unfit mother," even a traitor. I expected Muslim or Middle Eastern women to refuse to talk with me, but none did. Overall, most mothers were voluble and eager to share their stories, which, they said, are solicited infrequently or are co-opted to fit a particular political narrative. Many agreed with Lebanon's Elham, who stated, "My message to Americans, especially American women, is Please, try to feel how Arab women feel."

Every mother's story is presented in her own words, edited only for brevity and, occasionally, clarity. Interviews translated from Arabic by native Arabic speakers are referenced. Requests for anonymity are respected.

That these women's voices are shared here does not imply that they share my perspective or my worldview. For the most part none are celebrities or anti-war spokeswomen. Instead they are, like me, ordinary women with families and everyday duties and jobs. Yet their suffering—both deeply personal and extraordinarily universal—highlights the private tragedies behind the public spectacle of war.

The fallout

Most Americans never experience war—the sounds, the chaos, the blood and broken bodies, the trauma and the mourning—and of those who have, many will not or cannot talk about their experiences. It is as if they have visited an indescribably horrible dimension unimaginable to others in their peaceful American surroundings, and they'd rather avoid the memories. Besides, talking about real terror—not the media-generated variety—in the land with the inalienable right to life, liberty, and the pursuit of happiness is so, you know, "negative," "inappropriate," such a "downer."

But silence denies the rest of the U.S. population the opportunity to examine the individual and cultural assumptions that underlie our domestic and foreign policies. Even war-weary military personnel are complicit in keeping the American public—including their own families—ignorant about what they've seen and done in combat. For that matter, few civilians even want to know how the military turns young people into warriors—and sometimes into suicide statistics—or what happens to those who refuse to fight. But maintaining ignorance keeps the U.S. population from examining the individual and cultural assumptions that underlie our foreign policies.

Testimony at the Winter Soldier Hearings 2008[6] from Global War on Terror veterans and active-duty personnel attempted to break down these walls of silence. One after another, for three days, troops told of superiors instructing them to "soften up" prisoners with illegal and inhumane techniques (sleep deprivation, hunger, cold, terror by mock execution), tacitly encouraging them to think of local people as "dogs," and worse. As veterans rocked the military's "business as usual" stance—despite the initial media blackout of the event a modified version was repeated in Congress—the military's responses to the testimony sounded hollow.

But, where do we go from here? My youth in apartheid South Africa informs my life in the United States and I recognize parallels between the two. The British, then the reigning super-empire, packaged their thirst for resources as "the white man's burden": to civilize the "childlike," "primitive" unfortunates burdened by tribalism and superstition. Today the West, led by the United States as the remaining superpower, packages its thirst for resources as the West's burden: to spread democracy and freedom to "backward," "Islamofascist"-oppressed unfortunates burdened by tribalism and superstition.

While the Islamic world struggles to maintain its unique way of life, the West, confident in its technologies, scientism, and orientation toward change, is not only ignorant of the myriad facets of the Islamic worldview but, more important, arrogantly derisive about it. The West summarily dismisses the Islamic world's desire to maintain a social and religious orderliness and stability as it navigates a cultural shift in adjusting to modernity.

I'm aware that many Americans consider my views hopelessly naïve, downright dangerous, and possibly fundamentally un-American. But, look at the ongoing chaos that is the Global War on Terror: the deaths of more than 5,000 U.S. troops and a million Iraqis,[7] the flight of more than 2 million Iraqis from their country and the internal displacement of over 2 million more, and the cost to U.S. taxpayers of over $720 million per day.[8]

Which is more dangerous and un-American: never-ending war or understanding that, as a society, we can modify our foreign policies so that we can know, respect, and live in harmony with other worldviews?

The stories presented here put a human face on those beyond our borders who suffer the effects of war...and implicitly answer that question.

1—IRAQ

JANUARY AND FEBRUARY 2004—AMMAN (JORDAN)—BAGHDAD – BALAD

Your glass
has destroyed
their stones[1]

ON JANUARY 9, 2004, after serving nine months in Afghanistan, my son deployed to Iraq's Sunni Triangle. I'd spent his tour of duty in Afghanistan fretting about his safety but denying the reality of war. In my limited experience, American troops seldom were committed to prolonged ground wars. Instead, the U.S. military trained and supported militias (such as the Contras in Nicaragua and the Mujahideen in Afghanistan) or carried out sorties before the American people woke up to what was going on (such as the invasions of Grenada under Reagan and Panama under George H. W. Bush, as well as Gulf War I).

My acquaintances expressed condolences: "Don't worry. Your son will be back before you know it." None mentioned what invading troops do...or what happens to the invaded.

I watched the green-tinted television footage of Shock and Awe. I'm not immune to images of overwhelming power, and my body shivered with awe...then shock...and fear: it was a matter of time before my child deployed to Iraq.

I couldn't spend another nine months worrying while he was deployed.

As a child I'd been mesmerized by the flash and mythology of war, but I understood nothing about the U.S. armed forces. Since my son's enlistment made me a military mom, I sought other military moms to learn what this meant. I quickly realized that none among us knew what was really going on, and after three decades of living here, I knew

I wouldn't learn much from our media. I joined a women's delegation and traveled to Iraq for an empirical view.

My son was not pleased that I was bound for Baghdad. "Don't come. It is too dangerous. If you do come, go to a rifle range first and practice shooting. Then carry a big gun while you're here."

I didn't go to a rifle range nor did I carry a big gun. Instead, I talked to GIs and Iraqis....

Half an hour before landing in Amman our aircraft was engulfed in a thunderstorm; rain pelted the portholes and lightning illuminated the darkness we'd disappear into if the plane was struck.

It was the first of many times I asked myself, "What are you doing here?"

I repeated it twelve days later when an IED exploded amid a U.S. convoy on a Baghdad bridge: I believed my son was part of that convoy.

Amman was fresh and clear after the storm, and I was excited to be back in the region after 27 years. I had spent my honeymoon near a small reef cave at Sharm el-Sheik on the confluence of the Red Sea and the Gulf of Aqaba. My son could have been conceived there.

As the delegation milled about Queen Alia International Airport, we learned that the three drivers with vehicles hired to convoy us across the desert hadn't shown up; they'd expected us to arrive the following night.

While the delegation head called around for alternative transportation, delegates introduced ourselves: delegation head Jodie Evans, Frances Anderson, Victoria Cunningham, Linda Durham, Robin Fasano, Anne Hoiberg, Leslie Hope, Kayhan Irani, Kate Raphael, and Roseyanna Yeap. I was the only military mom.

Two hours behind schedule (Baghdad's curfew was 8:00 p.m.) we scrambled into three late-model white SUVs—known locally as "bullet magnets," since so many private military contractors drive them—and departed Amman in the dark.

Soudoun, our driver, had draped blue velvet curtains on all the passenger windows (common in rural Iraq to hide female passengers from view), so Kate, Kayhan, and I were cocooned in the back. Linda sat in the front passenger seat with an elegant scarf hiding her face and blonde hair. We rolled our eyes at what we interpreted as Soudoun's dramatics as he explained that we'd drive "fast, fast, fast!" to avoid Ali Baba (highway robbers) for the next ten hours.

This conjured an image of lions—Ali Baba—picking off the slowest members of a stampeding herd—us! But it wasn't funny when news about terrified Iraqi civilians fleeing their homeland along this same route began circulating in the international press. By then other predators hunted alongside Ali Baba: militias, religious and political fundamentalists, small entrepreneurs, vengeful neighbors, and corrupt officials all wanted a bite of the vulnerable.

At dawn, silver light jabbed through gray clouds and backlit rocks the size of footstools scattered over the patchwork landscape. Kate shared her hummus and pita bread and explained that she'd joined the delegation after being jailed, then expelled from Israel, for working with Palestinians. Kayhan was a theater director in New York. Linda owned and ran an art gallery in Santa Fe, New Mexico.

At Jordanian border control, while two administrators manually checked hundreds of passports, I photographed the array of red-and-white-checked kaffiya headdresses of fellow travelers.

An avalanche of security guards hauled me off to the base commander, who demanded I smash my camera.

Through mime and truncated English—I speak no Arabic—I persuaded him that erasing the offending picture (and all the others I'd taken) was as effective as destroying the camera. We parted with nods, smiles, and iterations of "welcome," "good day," and "thank you."

By then five hours behind schedule, our anxious drivers sped across the desert at 140 to 180 kilometers per hour, the vehicles often within inches of one another.

Western Iraq simmers at midafternoon. Charred patches along Highway 10 suggested burnt vehicles, but otherwise it was as clean as any three-lane American highway. The electric power pylons dotting the landscape, however, had a peculiar cockeyed symmetry: all the tips twisted brokenly in the same direction as if a giant reaper wielding a scythe had trimmed each one 40 feet above the ground.

In Fallujah we lost track of one SUV in our convoy. When it came into view with its headlights flashing, we learned that Ali Baba had forced it off the road at gunpoint and robbed the passengers. No one was badly injured, although the robbers, while tugging Anne's money belt from her waist, had pulled her from the vehicle and she'd fallen onto her hands and knees in the road. Her money, passport, and return air ticket were stolen. Farther on, the same robbers were shaking down a truck driver: he stood with his hands in the air at gunpoint while the thieves searched his vehicle.

After dark, the four-lane freeway suddenly presented headlights coming toward us. Soldiers at an ad hoc checkpoint reported an unexploded IED in the road. Soudoun detoured through Baghdad's side streets to the Aghadeer Hotel, where another surprise greeted us: the hotel managers expected us the following day. We slept on mattresses on the floor.

The Aghadeer, closed now, was a low-budget hotel near Firdos ("Paradise") Square—actually a traffic circle—where a U.S. soldier had draped the stars and stripes over a statue of Saddam Hussein before it was toppled. Beyond the razor wire and the barricades encircling the square are the heavily fortified Palestine and Sheraton Hotels. The Green Zone, housing the largest U.S. embassy in the world, is on the other side of the Tigris River.

A brief history, looting, and other "stuff"

In April, 2003, television images around the world showed U.S. Secretary of Defense Donald Rumsfeld repackaging Baghdad's tragic looting as "Stuff happens." "Freedom's untidy," he continued, "and free people are free to make mistakes and commit crimes and do bad things."

The looting was, he asserted, "not as bad as some television and newspaper reports have indicated...there was no major crisis in Baghdad." After all, as CNN's Sean Loughlin put it, "looting was part of the price for what the United States and Britain have called the liberation of Iraq."[2]

What was the price of this looting "stuff"?

Baghdad dates back at least to the eighth century. It may have been founded on the west bank of the Tigris in 762, although it may be pre-Islamic. The Jewish Talmud mentions a city of Baghdad, whose name may derive from a Middle Persian compound of *Bhaga*, "god," and *dad*, "given," with the sense of "God's gift," or from Middle Persian *Bagh-dad*, "the given garden." Some researchers believe the biblical Garden of Eden was here.

Baghdad's long history includes the sacking of the city in 1258 by Hulagu Khan's Mongols, who massacred most of the inhabitants and destroyed its system of irrigation canals and dykes. Ottoman Turks conquered Baghdad in 1534 and remained in power until 1921 when the British established the kingdom of Iraq. This gerrymandered country gained formal independence in 1932 and increased autonomy in 1946. In 1958, the Iraqi army deposed the grandson of British-installed Faisal II. Ten years later, Saddam Hussein played a key role in the coup that brought the Ba'ath Party to power.

Oil is key to modern Iraq. Oil funds built Iraq's modern sewage, water, and highway facilities and endowed Iraq's citizens with free education and free health care. Oil's potential also brought covetous Western economic interests to Iraq. Saddam Hussein temporarily thwarted these when he nationalized the Iraq Petroleum Company, the West's monopoly on Iraqi oil.

Saddam Hussein's disastrous war with Iran from 1980 to 1988 not only destroyed the lives of hundreds of thousands of Iraqi and Iranian men and boys, it forced Hussein to sell off publicly held assets to raise money to keep the military afloat.

If the economic sanctions applied after Gulf War I destroyed Iraq's social fabric and economy, Operation Iraqi Freedom snuffed out its history.

In April 2003, billions of dollars' worth of history and antiquities housed in museums—as well as more mundane supplies and equipment from shops, government offices, presidential palaces, even hospitals—were carried away in carts and wheelbarrows. Iraq's National Museum had closed at the beginning of the Gulf War in 1991 and reopened to the public six months before Operation Iraqi Freedom. A BBC report summed up the stakes: "Treasures at the museum date back 5,000 years to the dawn of civilization in Mesopotamia [including] items from ancient Babylon and Nineveh, Sumerian statues, Assyrian reliefs, and 5,000-year-old tablets bearing some of the earliest known writing [and] gold and silver items from the Ur cemetery."[3] *The Los Angeles Times* describes the devastation: "A 4,000-year-old inscribed clay tablet...was pulled from eBay's Swiss website [and] a limestone head of a 2nd century BC king had been seized from the home of a Lebanese interior decorator and transferred to a museum for safekeeping. But experts suspect that most of the stolen objects are hidden in warehouses around the world because they are too hot to sell. The museum has recovered nearly 4,000 of the 15,000 pieces lost in looting...some of the thefts spontaneous and some seemingly carefully planned."[4] The deputy director of the Iraq National Museum said, "The Americans were supposed to protect the museum. If they had [deployed] just one tank and two soldiers, nothing like this would have happened."[5] It is as if Hulagu Khan's Mongols had returned. Every member of the human family lost an ancient heritage in a matter of days for the lack of a tank and two soldiers.

But, as Donald Rumsfeld pointed out, "Stuff happens...."

The price is right

After Saddam Hussein invaded Kuwait on August 2, 1990, President George H. W. Bush froze Iraqi and Kuwaiti assets and the U.N. called on Hussein to withdraw.

On January 17, 1991, U.S. presidential press secretary Marlin Fitzwater announced, "The liberation of Kuwait has begun," and U.S. warplanes attacked Baghdad and other military targets in Iraq, inflicting severe damage on Baghdad's transportation, power, and sanitary infrastructure.

On February 26, U.S. aircraft attacked and destroyed retreating Iraqi army units and civilian vehicles caught in a massive traffic jam on Highway 80 (between Kuwait and Basra). The incident and its site became known as the Highway of Death, or as U.S. military personnel described it, the "turkey shoot."[6] Journalist Robert Fisk reported, "I had seen hundreds of dead here; there must have been thousands. Shouldn't we have been referring...not to the Highway of Death, but to the Massacre at the Mutla Ridge?"[7] A number somewhere between Saddam Hussein's figure, 44, and U.S. commanders' estimate of thousands of Iraqi soldiers were buried alive during the assault, which lasted two days, February 24 and 25, 1991.

A *New England Journal of Medicine* article states that U.N.-imposed sanctions following Gulf War I destroyed Iraq's "power plants [and] brought its entire system of water purification and distribution to a halt, leading to epidemics of cholera, typhoid fever, and gastroenteritis, particularly among children...the destruction of the infrastructure resulted in devastating long-term effects on health."

60 Minutes anchor Lesley Stahl, interviewing then U.S. Secretary of State Madeleine Albright, said, "We have heard that a half a million children have died [because of sanctions against Iraq]. I mean that's more children than died in Hiroshima. And—you know, is the price worth it?"[8]

Albright replied, "I think this is a very hard choice, but the price—we think the price is worth it."[9]

According to UNICEF, Iraq had by far the sharpest rise in mortality rate for infants and young children of any nation in the world during sanctions: "It is the only instance of a sustained increase in mortality in a stable population of more than 2 million in the last 200 years."[10]

Reporting from Iraq

I awoke to a dawn explosion followed by the pop-pop of automatic gunfire and helicopters circling overhead. A cable news crew had been attacked, although it wasn't clear how many journalists and civilians had been killed or injured. During the ten days the delegation visited Iraq, many journalists died:

- U.S. cable news network's Duraid Isa Mohammed and his driver, Yasser Khatab, were killed when unidentified assailants fired on their two-car convoy.

- Qulan TV's Safir Nader and Haymin Mohamed Salih, Kurdistan TV's Ayoub Mohamed and Gharib Mohamed Salih, freelance journalist, Semko Karim Mohyideen, and Abdel Sattar Abdel Karim of the Arabic-language daily *Al Ta'akhy* died in twin suicide bombings at the offices of the Patriotic Union of Kurdistan and the Kurdistan Democratic Party.

- On April 8, Spanish Tele 5 cameraman José Couso died and four were injured when a U.S. tank shelled the Palestine Hotel. The same day, Jordanian cameraman Tarek Ayoub was killed when a U.S. missile hit and badly damaged Al Jazeera's offices near the Al Mansour Hotel in the city center. (In 2006, Spain's high court dismissed the Couso family's lawsuit against the three U.S. soldiers directly involved in the attack on the hotel.)

- Reporters Without Borders describes this war as "the bloodiest for the media since World War II."[11] By 2006, more than 200 journalists and media assistants had been killed, 14 had been kidnapped, and two, Frédéric Nérac of ITV News (UK) and Isam Hadi Muhsin al-Shumary of Germany's Suedostmedia, were still missing when this book went to press.

During breakfast at the Aghadeer Hotel, we met a contingent of unembedded, independent reporters, including Dahr Jamail, Mike Ferner, and Rob Eschelman. After breakfast, the delegation set off to talk to Iraqis.

Dr. Ali Rasheed Hamid

Psychiatrist Ali Rasheed Hamid, then of the University of Baghdad, specializes in Post Traumatic Stress Disorder (PTSD) in children. He explained that it was difficult to measure Iraqi children's psychological health since the country's nearly continuous string of conflicts, from the Iran–Iraq war, Gulf War I, and U.N. sanctions to the current war and occupation. Iraq's young parents, themselves victims of war trauma, are often incapable of addressing their children's trauma.

"While Americans and adult Iraqis were jubilant at Saddam's demise, Iraqi children witnessed a mythical figure disappear, someone who loomed larger than life, whose image was everywhere, for whom songs were sung at school, and national holidays celebrated," Dr. Hamid observes. "Filling Saddam's void, children saw TV images of statues toppling, mass graves exhumed, Iraqis huddling in ruined buildings, bombs destroying familiar places, family members wracked with fear, and children like themselves begging in the streets."

Some also experienced foreign soldiers smashing in the doors of their homes at midnight, shining blinding lights, yelling incomprehensible orders, and dragging family members outside in their nightclothes in a futile search for insurgents. Too often they witnessed fathers and grandfathers—the heads of families—humiliated.

Outside their homes, children saw razor wire and barricades in their streets, military tanks, Humvees, uniformed and heavily armed foreigners patrolling their neighborhoods, and arbitrary arrests in which Iraqis were forced to the ground with boots placed upon their necks or nylon bags covering their heads. In extreme cases, they witnessed civilians randomly shot in the streets and car bombs exploding.

Dr. Ali Hamid says, "No child should witness such events."

Prior to the bombing of the U.N.'s Baghdad headquarters and the organization's subsequent departure from Iraq, Dr. Ali worked under a U.N. umbrella group composed of the U.S. military, the Coalition Provisional Authority, UNICEF, and Iraq's Ministry of Health to create a basic PTSD program that included reducing combat stress in troops.

He was skeptical of the program's prospects for success after observing already stressed troops moved from one stressful situation to another with no time to regroup: "Battle-stressed soldiers are likely to overreact to minor incidents involving civilians," he observes.

He approached U.S. military leadership with his concerns and learned that, due to reduced deployment numbers, military officers had no alternative but to use the in-country troops wherever and whenever they were needed.

One month later, as if to prove Dr. Hamid's point, the first of many photographs of U.S. soldiers abusing Iraqi prisoners surfaced. The reports described activities specifically at Abu Ghraib Prison during the last three months of 2003, but Iraqis had been complaining of widespread abuse earlier than that.

"Tell them there is tragedy in Iraq…"

Anwar Kadhun Jeward's daughter, Abir, played with baby Hassan as Anwar described to me how her husband, oldest son, and two other daughters were shot to death by U.S. soldiers in August 2003. (Anwar's full story begins on page 35.)

Victims' families are reimbursed from $100 to $1,000 under the Foreign Claims Act[12] for such random shooting incidents. The Act, however, is void in "combat situations," definitions of "combat" and "noncombat" are elastic, and Rules of Engagement are easily misunderstood.

While variations of Anwar's tragedy have been repeated thousands of times since 2003, no accurate accounting exists of how many have been killed in random shootings, how many families have been reimbursed— or not—nor of how much has been spent on such reimbursements. The American Civil Liberties Union filed suit against the Department of Defense in September 2007, demanding that it comply with a Freedom of Information Act request to release documents regarding civilians killed by coalition forces in Iraq and Afghanistan.[13]

I left Anwar's house in turmoil, then sat in the van and cried. What if my child ever perpetrated such an act? In the chaos that is Iraq, soldiers and civilians lose their bearings and terrible things happen. My own son or the sons and daughters of any American military mom could do such things if a perfect storm of fear, anger, training, and weaponry intersected.

On to a hospital...

Al Mansour Teaching Hospital for Children's Medical City was built in 1986. During my visit, the hospital was poor in resources (understaffed, underfunded, and underequipped) but rich in patients. Unfortunately, the pediatric wing was rich in young patients dying of various cancers; leukemias predominated.

Oncology pediatrician Dr. Faisal al-Jadiry showed delegates around the pediatric oncology wards and talked about the range of cancers striking infants and children: acute leukemia, lymphoma, neuroblastoma, and non-Hodgkin's lymphoma. He reported high incidences of once rare malignancies and solid tumors in infants.

Even though experts understand that rampant malnourishment exacerbates illness, at Al Mansour food was sparse and of poor quality; patients' families brought food from home.

What irony—and implicit violence—in that situation: a military mom from the richest country in the world, touring a pediatric ward where other mothers' children die because her country bans life-saving chemo-therapies that *might* contain substances that *might* aid the manufacture of weapons of mass destruction.

Permitted drugs were so expensive that families sold cars, even homes, to pay for an eight-day chemotherapy treatment. Frequently, two to three years of treatment are required...and there is no guarantee of success.

During sanctions, Dr. al-Jadiry's salary hovered around the equivalent of US $5 per month. "Soon," he said, "my salary will increase...perhaps to as much as US $250 per month."

Fortunately, Dr. al-Jadiry lived with his father and could continue practicing medicine in this very needy place. Without his father's generosity, he'd be driving taxis like his former colleagues to make ends meet. Many competent nurses had left Al Mansour Hospital as their salaries, equivalent to US $3 or less per month, were insufficient. But, with unemployment hovering between 60 and 70 percent, there was little hope of finding better-paid work.

As a professional scientist Dr. al-Jadiry was unwilling to offer opinions on why cancer rates in Iraqi children were skyrocketing, especially in children from northern Iraq. He was seeking funds to conduct a study.

A visit to a police station

At a Baghdad police station to report the hijacking and theft of Anne's travel documents, we talked with a police chief, a supervisor, and their U.S. advisor.

The chief expressed his view of the many bombings in Iraq. "These terrorist attacks, we believe—and we have evidence of this—are committed by foreigners from Kuwait, Jordan, Iran, Saudi Arabia, Syria, Yemen, Pakistan...people from all over. Some of these are Ba'athist Iraqis who lost everything with the downfall of Saddam. Iraq's borders are wide open, and no one is trying to stop these terrorists."

The supervisor added, "The United States is using Iraq to attract terrorists from around the world to take potshots at Americans. The terrorists come, like bees to honey, then the Americans shoot them."

Variations of this "honeypot" view were reiterated throughout the trip.

One delegate asked, "Can you talk about the role of women in Islam...and about the high incidences of physical abuse and rape of women?"

The chief responded, "Islam looks at women with great respect and believes that women have a big role in the family. I have served as a police officer in Baghdad for 32 years and in all this time I have heard of only two cases of rape. Rape is not a crime that occurs frequently in this country."

"Do you think cases of rape are reported to the police?"

"Not often, no."

"So how do you know that rape occurs infrequently?"

"I only know what I see with my own eyes and what comes into my office."

Departing the police station, Jodie Evans said that the American advisor had pulled her aside and reported that police had recently used electrical cord to whip four young women arrested for prostitution. He had told the officers, "You can't do this stuff anymore. We'll charge the women according to the law...and punish them according to the law."

That week an English-language newspaper carried an article on prostitution in Saddam's Iraq. A young woman's typical trajectory into prostitution began when a high-ranking military officer or wealthy businessman set her up in a house or a room. When he tired of her, he handed her over to a lesser colleague or to a brothel. As "damaged goods" she was on a downward spiral, and it was a matter of time before she was servicing as many men as the brothel owners demanded...or she was on the street. Since prostitution contravened both the law and the society's code of honor, it was a matter of time before her life came to an unpleasant end.

In September 2004, Nermeen al-Mufti of *Al Ahram Weekly* reported:

> Rape was uncommon in Iraq. Police records before the occupation cite rape figures at less than a dozen or so per year. Some cases may have gone unreported in a country with strong tribal traditions, but for the figures to climb to dozens per month is something new and painful for Iraqis...Iraqi police sources say that most of the gangs bringing drugs into Iraq, running prostitution networks, and abducting women are operated by non-Iraqis but are helped by some Iraqis who have criminal records or who have failed to find other employment.[14]

By 2007, not only was prostitution and rape commonplace in Iraq, but U.S. troops stood accused of the rape and murder of 14-year-old Abeer Qassim al-Janabi and the murder of three of her family members to hide the first crime. (Charges of murder or of covering up and failing to properly investigate the killings were dropped in June 2008 against six of eight Marines involved; the trial of the last two Marines is pending with murder charges replaced by the lesser offense of manslaughter.)

Confirming Dr. Hamid's words, testimony for this crime during the August 2006 Article 32 hearing (the military's version of a grand jury) painted a picture of a military unit demoralized, drained emotionally after the deaths of comrades, and exhausted after the frequent attacks.

Private First Class Justin Cross testified, "You're just walking a death walk.... It drives you nuts. You feel like every step you might get blown up.... You just hit a point where you're like, 'If I die today, I die.'"

Cross said the unit was "full of despair," and he feared "dying at his post before he could go home. I couldn't sleep mainly for fear we would be attacked." He testified that the deaths of two soldiers at a checkpoint "pretty much crushed the platoon." To cope with the stress, soldiers turned to whiskey—a violation of U.S. regulations in Iraq—and painkillers to ease their fears.[15]

Abeer Qassim al-Janabi's rape and murder reached the public. Many such cases do not.

In October 2007, Dr. Hamid told me in a personal email:

> One pretty young lady, Luma, who was working...as translator [for the United States] was killed by an American soldier in the airport. He wanted to sleep with her...she refused him...he shot her dead. Her naked body was found in a room near the airport. News leaked out that the killer was arrested and will go to trial...but nothing more has been heard about that. Luma was the mother of a 3-year-old child.

A trip to an Internet café

After a week in Baghdad with no word from my son, I ditched a delegation shopping expedition to a local bazaar (why is shopping always on itineraries, despite the dire circumstances?) and departed the Hotel Aghadeer on foot to find an Internet café. A sign pointed down an alley off Saadun Street, and I walked between high concrete walls, rolls of razor wire, and sandbagged lookout towers with armed GIs protecting the Istar Sheraton and Palestine Meridian hotels.

Light poured through dusty windows into a Spanish-style café and reflected from polished terra-cotta tiles. The Internet connection was slow but charges were minimal: US $1 for half an hour, no refund for power outages. With no email from my son, I abandoned the computer and joined a young U.S. soldier sipping coffee. He'd stepped into the café—uniformed, helmeted, and carrying an M16—after I'd arrived, and I'd kept an eye on him in case he attracted the wrong kind of attention. He ordered Turkish coffee like he'd been here before.

I introduced myself as a mother trying to locate a son in the 82nd Airborne.

Staff Sgt. Juan didn't offer advice on how to do that, but he told me both he and his wife were deployed to Iraq: He guarded the Istar Sheraton and she guarded the Baghdad airport. They talked on the phone sometimes but seldom saw one another. Their 2- and 3-year-old children were living with Juan's parents in San Francisco's Mission District.

Juan had been in the military for seven years and in Iraq for one year. As a staff sergeant with the 4th Armored Division responsible for nine soldiers, he found that many young soldiers came to combat straight out of boot camp and were easily distraught. During one such youngster's first firefight, he'd killed an Iraqi civilian. Juan said that afterwards, as the unit headed back to base, "the kid threw his gun down as if it was a snake and refused to touch it. I had to send him back to the States due to stress. But we can't do that too often. We don't have enough guys as it is."

Two of Staff Sgt. Juan's soldiers had been killed in Baghdad: an 18-year-old, direct from boot camp, died when a grenade exploded in his face; his 19-year-old replacement was killed when an RPG destroyed the Humvee he was riding in.

I related Anwar Jeward's story of witnessing her family members murdered at a checkpoint, and he responded, "That's heavy, but I know it happens. Some soldiers are inexperienced and not well trained."

Into the Green Zone

Before passing through the first checkpoint into the Green Zone (green for the surrounding palm groves? or green for the money changing hands within?) I approached two guards with 82nd Airborne patches who, I thought, might know my son.

"How are things for you here?"

One volunteered, "We're pretty bored. We've been guarding this place for weeks now."

"Yeah. We're trained for more than just guarding...."

"We'd rather be fighting and blowing things up!"

I said, "But you can get hurt blowing things up...or hurt other people."

"Nah. We won't get hurt."

"And if we are hurt we'll be sent home. That'd be cool!"

I couldn't argue with their logic, but after Anwar's story I couldn't sympathize.

By then about 530 American troops had died in combat in Iraq. (More may have died, but the U.S. military only releases statistics of those killed in "combat situations.") Since General Tommy Franks had declared, "We don't do body counts," no one knew how many Iraqis had been killed.

After Roseyanna and I passed through the third checkpoint, we wagered on how many more we'd face before entering the compound: I bet nine; she bet ten.

We both believed the eighth checkpoint, manned by Nepalese Gurkas as intimidating as junkyard dogs, was the last. Eventually we passed through eleven, each time signing in, peeling off backpacks or purses, emptying pockets, and wincing when the sonic wand bleeped at a watch, a ring, or a belt buckle.

Inside the compound at last, we met Son Gul Omer Chapook, a Turkmen member of the Iraqi Governing Counsel, who spoke optimistically about the role of women in new Iraq and expressed support for "unification," in which Arabs, Kurds, and Turkmen live together harmoniously. Was her opinion political pragmatism or because she wanted to keep her position as one of the few females on the male-majority council? She must have known of the long-term conflict among these groups.

Jodie, Anne, Kate, and I made the second trip into the Green Zone to replace Anne's stolen travel documents. This time we passed through only five checkpoints: was security getting lax?

The Green Zone (also known as the International Zone, IZ, Emerald City, or "the Bubble") is a four-square-mile area in central Baghdad. Surrounded by 30-foot-high concrete barriers (similar to Israel's Security Wall), miles of razor wire, chain-link fences, and earth berms, the Green Zone is defended by sandbags, watchtowers with heavily armed guards, M1 Abrams tanks, Bradley fighting vehicles, and Humvees mounted with .50 caliber machine guns.

This city within a city houses the U.S. and British civilian ruling authority as well as the offices of major U.S. consulting companies. Many diplomats and contractors visiting Iraq live entirely within "the Bubble" and never see the blood and misery that result from the orders issued here.

For all of the hoopla surrounding it, inside it was as prosaic as any bureaucracy. Employees dressed in skirt suits, pantyhose, and high heels or white button-down shirts with conventional ties and Dockers hustled papers back and forth across the open expanse of the Convention Center where Saddam once celebrated his birthdays.

Jodie, Kate, Anne, and I—looking like orphans on a field trip—carried papers through one short line for the application of a stamp, through another line where that stamp was reviewed and another added, and were told to "come back tomorrow."

Here was bureaucracy at its most clichéd: Anne received her travel documents days later—at Queen Alia International Airport. After these visits to the Green Zone, I was not surprised at the mounting evidence that the Coalition Provisional Authority, the Iraqi Governing Council, and the Bush Administration had fumbled Iraq's reconstruction.

Baghdadis at play

Thursday night, the weeknight before Islam's holy Friday, is party night in Baghdad, and the delegation, drivers, translators, and friends people-watched from the patio above the street at the Blue Sky restaurant (hamburgers and fries were the house specialty).

The crowd jostled and laughed. Music blared from open car windows. As families and friends socialized, teenagers eyed one another. Newlyweds celebrated by driving up and down the crowded street while friends with guns emerged through moon roofs and shot into the sky.

Then a Humvee appeared, and a masked GI mounted behind a gun tower scanned the crowd. The squad automatic weapons (SAWs, or "mini machine guns") used in these vehicles can fire 725 rounds per minute. A second Humvee followed, with a masked gunner who swiveled the weapon so that it menaced people on both sides of the street.

Pedestrians drew together. Passengers shooting through moon roofs slunk inside. The festive music seemed to flatten, as if heralding the end of the party.

I turned to a Swiss videographer in our group. "I loathe this bullying, this show of force when frightened people forget for a moment that their country is shriveling before their eyes, this slap in the face by the strong-arm military!"

He frowned. "You don't know much about the psychology of war, do you?"

He was correct. Somehow, even after growing up in apartheid South Africa, I maintained vague ideas that "people" really didn't know the suffering they inflicted upon others. Surely, if they really knew, they'd simply stop that behavior.

Denial is as powerful as any drug.

I visit my son

I was in a different Internet café, trembling from fever and flu, when I received an email from my son with vague directions to a base somewhere near Balad. Elated, I hurried out of the café...and into a cordoned street. In the half-hour I'd surfed the Internet, the street had transformed: traffic was stopped in both directions, irate drivers honked horns, Iranian pilgrims milled about the sidewalk while soldiers searched their bus, and a bevy of tanks encircled Firdos Square. Staff Sgt. Juan stood in front of one with his M16 cocked.

"What's going on?"

"Ma'am, get off the street, ma,am. A live IED was found in the square and we're cordoning off the area. It's not safe here, ma'am. Go back to your hotel."

"But...."

"Ma'am, get off the street."

At the Aghadeer, Mike Ferner, author of *Inside the Red Zone: A Veteran for Peace Reports from Iraq*,[16] shared his notes about the region around Balad, where a 23-hour-a-day curfew had been imposed on Abu Hishma village. The 82nd Airborne's battalion commander, Lt. Col. Nathan Sassaman, had been forthright about his tactics in the area: "With a heavy dose of fear and violence, and a lot of money for projects, I think we can convince these people that we are here to help them."[17]

I wrote Camp Anaconda's Public Affairs Officer (PAO) that I'd visit the following day. My plan was to hire Issam, the delegation's driver and translator, for the day trip. Issam had been a colonel who deserted Saddam's military during the Iran-Iraq war. For 20 years he'd been on the lam, no small feat in Saddam's Iraq with its prodigious security apparatus.

I felt safe when Issam said, "Perhaps there is no one in this land who knows the country better than I do."

But the night before we were to leave Issam changed his mind and said he couldn't drive. He was convinced the military wouldn't allow me on base.

A few months before my trip, another military mom, Annabel Valencia, had traveled to Iraq to visit her two children in the military: her son, 23, had been deployed to Baghdad with the 82nd Airborne, and her daughter, 24, was in Tikrit with the 4th Infantry Division.

When the military got wind of her trip, they'd sent her son back to the States to convince his mother not to visit. "Mom, you're crazy! What do you want to go there for? It's very dangerous. Don't go there. And don't think about visiting me!"

Annabel told him, "Don't worry. I won't visit you if you don't want to see me. I'll visit your sister."

Issam had driven Annabel and a camera crew to Tikrit—a trip that takes several hours—where they were refused entry to the base. They returned to Baghdad that night. The next day Issam drove Annabel to Tikrit again, this time without a camera crew, and she was permitted onto the base.

Balad is less than an hour's drive from Baghdad, faster for someone who knows the way, but Issam wasn't willing to risk it.

Dahr Jamail's driver and translator, Ahmed, was willing to drive me and at 7:00 a.m. the following morning, we traveled north into the notorious Sunni Triangle.

Camp Anaconda's PAO had not responded to my email. Ahmed and I could have been on a wild goose chase.

Roseyanna lent me her *hijab* and gave me advice on how to drape it. Ordinary scarves are too slippery to remain in place for long, while a *hijab*, with its slight elasticity, clings to the head; a pin under the chin secures it. Although I was wearing trousers and a red winter jacket, to those seeing me through the car's windows, the *hijab* signaled modesty. Ahmed, at least, was reassured.

On the way, he told me he'd married recently, and his young wife was three months pregnant.

"Ahmed, why are you driving me? I could have found someone else to drive who has less to lose if we got into trouble."

"I am doing it because you are a mother."

All I could say was "Thank you."

Ahmed stopped at a bus stop to ask directions, and as several men approached Ahmed muttered, "You are now a French journalist." I was certain we were lost.

"But I haven't spoken French in 20 years!"

He told me I should simply not say anything.

Ahmed spoke with a man in a blue dishdasha who had been a lawyer before the war and worked as a middleman supplying workers to the local U.S. military base. He showed Ahmed a manifest listing Iraqi names over an English signature.

Then he glanced at me and demonstrated someone forced to the ground and held there with a boot placed upon his neck; he mimed a covering placed over his head and his wrists cuffed. Then he gestured angrily to a side road upon which sped dozens of semis loaded with prefab houses and building supplies. Later Ahmed explained that this middleman had quit his job because of the harsh treatment meted out to Iraqis working on the base.

We departed the bus stop and joined the line of trucks, our car so small amongst these that I joked we were like a clown fish among whales.

But now Ahmed wasn't in the mood for jokes. He kept glancing at the marsh and reeds on either side of the road; his face was shiny with sweat.

"What's up, Ahmed?"

"This is the vegetation the insurgents like to hide in to attack the trucks supplying the military base. Today, if they miss their target they will hit us."

The trucks halted near the entrance to the base and we drove around them and took our place in a line of cars being searched by U.S. soldiers. Ahmed told me, "Get out of the car, walk slowly to the soldiers, and introduce us."

Still wearing the *hijab*, I approached a young soldier rummaging through a trunk with an M16 slung over his shoulder.

I said quietly, "I'm coming up behind you. I mean you no harm but I am expected here."

He didn't look at me. "Ma'am, get back in your car!"

"I have business here. I mean you no harm but I do need to speak to your sergeant."

"Ma'am, get back in your car!"

The other soldiers aimed their weapons at me. I pushed the *hijab* off my head and waved my passport. One soldier noticed. "Hey, are you American?"

At that point several soldiers approached as if I were their long-lost mother. "Hey, you're American! What're you doing here? Why're you wearing that thing?"

"I have business here."

A soldier walked to the nearby office, waved me up, and directed Ahmed to a parking lot.

Inside, I stated my name and mission. The GI said, "You're Sgt. G's mom? I know him. We were in Afghanistan together. Gee, I wish my mom would visit me. On second thoughts, maybe not. She'd just cry all the time."

While he called my son on the radio I read the notices on the walls:

Do not engage Iraqi children.
Do not hand out candy to or play with Iraqi children.
Full uniform and helmet must be worn outside always.

I asked the GI what kind of food he ate on base.

"We get all kinds, Domino's Pizza, Round Table, McDonald's, we got it all."

"Do you eat Iraqi food?"

"Nah, we don't see any of that here."

"Do you ever get off the base?"

"Nah. We can't do that. We'd be killed if we stepped off the base without armor and weapons and lots of buddies to back us up."

An Iraqi man sat quietly in the corner of the office and I turned to him. "Too bad there is no Iraqi food served here. Maybe sharing a great meal would foster understanding...."

The man stared.

"What do you think about serving some delicious Iraqi dolma here?"

I'd eaten dolma the previous day in a well-known Baghdad restaurant, with wine. Meats and vegetables are wrapped in cabbage and grape leaves, embedded in grain, then steamed. When the dolma is cooked, the upturned bowl releases the shaped contents onto a serving platter. (After the rise of the Mehdi Army and the crackdown on secular living habits, the restaurant was forced to close because it served wine.)

The Iraqi warmed to the conversation. "Yes, yes, much delicious food in Iraq. Have you eaten fish from the Tigris?"

"Not yet. It is good?"

"It is delicious...the best in the Middle East!"

The GI stared at us. Figuring that including the Iraqi man in a conversation about something other than war or work might humanize the situation I tried engaging the GI in the conversation. "Since you're here, aren't you curious about Baghdad? Wouldn't you like to check it out, maybe learn about its ancient history and culture?"

He ignored that. "How did you get here?"

"I hired a driver who is outside in the parking lot. Is he safe there?"

"Yeah. All the hajjis park there. They come onto the base only with special permission."

Just then my son arrived outside and I stepped out to hug him. I handed over the goodies I'd brought, and he sheepishly carried a box of See's candies (nuts and chews, his favorite) while we talked. For the next hour, he showed me around that section of the 22-square-mile base. We didn't go too far onto the base, but I hadn't come to tour; I was here to see my kid and his situation, and to fumble through my "don't do anything here that you might be ashamed of for the rest of your life" speech.

We climbed a rickety 30-foot wooden ladder to the top of the watchtower, and he pointed out the direction the missiles came from when they entered the camp at night.

Below us Abrams tanks entered and exited "the wire" on their daily patrols.

Later, while counseling troops, I learned how much the soldiers resented these patrols: "Man, it is so stupid. Every day at exactly the same time, we're forced to patrol. All the 'bad guys' had to do was set their watches, line up their RPGs, and with military precision, along we'd come, pigeons in a shooting gallery!"

As my son walked me to the parking lot where Ahmed waited, I asked if he'd been off the base. He said he was due to convoy materiel back to the base from Baghdad Airport the same day I departed Iraq.

I introduced him to Ahmed, they shook hands, and we drove away. Only later did I realize how dangerous it was for Ahmed to shake a U.S. soldier's hand. Military bases often host Iraqi trainees who take off their uniforms at the end of the day and fight against the occupation at night. If one of these Iraqis observed Ahmed shake my son's hand and interpreted it as collaborating with the military, Ahmed could be killed. Months later, I learned that Ahmed, his wife, and their newborn daughter had left for London.

Returning to Baghdad, we ran into a military unit defusing an IED on the same road we'd traveled less than two hours earlier. Traffic was backed up 20 vehicles deep, so Ahmed took a dirt road through a small, dusty village where impoverished children stared with wary faces.

We stopped for falafel in a Baghdad suburb where trash had not been picked up for over a year. The Coalition Provisional Authority had not restored garbage service since the first day of Shock and Awe. It was just a matter of time before disease raced through the country. Indeed, in the fall of 2007 the World Health Organization confirmed more than 3,315 cholera cases in nine of 18 provinces and at least 14 deaths from the disease.[18] By early 2008 roughly 30,000 people had fallen ill with acute diarrhea, and blackwater fever, never before seen in Iraq on such a scale, threatened the lives of thousands. This disease, a severe form of malarial infection that destroys red blood cells and leads to kidney and liver failure, can kill within 24 hours. Iraq lacked the medicines, hospitals, and doctors to fight these diseases.

Back at the Aghadeer by early afternoon, I gave in to a lingering fever, climbed into bed, and slept until the following morning.

Two days later we climbed into the same SUVs to race back along Highway 10 to Amman.

As we departed across a bridge over the Tigris I opened the vehicle's blue velvet curtains and watched a U.S. military convoy heading into Baghdad on the other side of the bridge.

Was my son in there?

Then, simultaneously, with a percussive whoosh something spun across the bridge toward us, a Humvee disappeared over the bridge, and I heard an explosion.

I thought, "If he dies here, please, let me die here too."

Soudoun controlled the SUV and sped on. The hubcap that had rolled toward us—not an explosive as I'd feared—fell into the water below.

My son was not in that convoy.

He left Iraq in June 2004.

On October 16, 2007, my son returned to Baghdad for a tour of duty as a Special Forces medic. In September 2008 he was discharged with Honor from the U.S. military and enrolled in university to complete studies he'd interrupted eight years previously. By then almost 5,000 American troops had died in Iraq and almost 600 had died in Afghanistan. Figures for Iraqis and Afghans remained inaccurate and underplayed by the Bush Administration and the Department of Defense.

ANWAR, Baghdad

"I want the whole world to know…"

Anwar welcomed over a dozen delegates and three translators into her parents' modest Baghdad home, where she lived with her surviving children since the shooting that killed her husband and three other children. The family served Coca-Cola as Anwar spoke. At times she broke down crying but there was no mistaking her rage when she said, "I want the whole world to know what is happening here."

It was about 9:30 p.m. on Thursday, August 7, 2003. The electricity was off and the streets were dark. My family was returning home after visiting my parents in another Baghdad neighborhood. I sat next to my husband who was driving. I was pregnant with Hassan [indicates the 6-month-old playing with Abir, her daughter]. Our children were in the back seat: my 18-year-old son had just taken his exams for medical school; my 16-year-old daughter was in high school and my second and third daughters—10 and 8 years old—were in grade school.

U.S. troops seldom patrolled our neighborhood, but when they did, the neighborhood men chatted with them, gave them water, and shared cigarettes. That night, ours was the only car in the street when two Humvees appeared out of nowhere. Their bright headlights pierced the dark and I couldn't tell how many soldiers were aboard.

Without provocation they began randomly shooting. When my husband shouted, "Stop shooting, my family is in this car," they started shooting at us. They shot for about fifteen minutes. I was wounded in the stomach and the leg. My husband was shot eight times, and as I laid his head on my lap, I was covered in his blood. The soldiers continued shooting randomly into the neighborhood and my husband told me to run and hide. I ran about 150 meters, then stopped to see what had happened to my family. People from my street found me unconscious behind a concrete barrier.

I learned my son was dead, shot through the head. My oldest daughter was dead, shot through the face. My youngest daughter was dead, shot in the head, the arm, and the leg.

This middle daughter, Abir, was alive. She'd lain wounded outside the car for an hour and a half, covered in her siblings' and father's blood.

Apparently it was about three hours after the attack that American soldiers took my husband and Abir to Saddam City Hospital. They were fortunate. In many of these random shooting incidents involving Humvees, victims are simply left in the street.

At the hospital, Abir overheard the doctors saying that my husband's life could have been saved had he received medical treatment sooner.

Later Abir told me that a female American soldier had found her in the street. After tapping Abir with her foot and thinking she was dead, the soldier bent down, removed the gold earrings from Abir's ears, and passed on.

I learned that three people in a car on an adjacent street had been attacked that night, too. The driver of that vehicle died and two passengers were shot, then badly burned after the car caught fire.

Weeks later, an American woman came to my parents' house where we live now. She asked how the "accident" happened and mentioned I might be entitled to compensation.

My lawyer submitted my claim to an American lawyer who said I had no right to submit a claim but must await the new Iraqi government and request compensation from them.

My lawyer asked, "What sort of government? How long will we wait? Why would the new Iraqi government compensate us for something that occurred under U.S. occupation?"

I received a letter stating my application was denied. By this time I'd learned that the bullets that killed my family—fragmentation bullets— are banned by international law. You can see them on the X-rays." [Author's note: I held these X-rays and, indeed, bullet fragments were embedded in the ghostly images of a skull, jaw, arm, and leg belonging to her children.]

Since then we have U.S. military checkpoints in our neighborhood.

My neighbors tell me how sorry they are for my loss. But I've lost my family. This baby on my lap, Hassan, will never know his father or siblings. All he has are photographs of how it used to be in this family. Being "sorry" has nothing to do with me. We—Abir, Hassan, and I—will never recover from this. And who is working for my dead family's rights? I want the whole world to know of this loss. When you return to America, tell Americans there is tragedy in Iraq.

AGLAME, Baghdad

"Now the children have nightmares…"

Aglame hosted me in her modest apartment in a poorer section of Baghdad. A few blocks away the Tigris flows, and on the other bank are the presidential palaces and many government offices bombed during Shock and Awe. Aglame's mother, Ibelene, was recuperating from an illness on a daybed in the living room, and she filled me in on the family while Aglame prepared coffee and Wian, Aglame's 10-year-old son, served it.

Ibelene

I have twelve children, five boys and seven girls, and all are married. Well, Aglame is separated now, but her husband lives in this neighborhood. Besides Aglame, all my children have left Iraq and live in France, Belgium, and the United States: Detroit and San Diego. I visited them once, but I couldn't stay for very long because I got so homesick for Baghdad. Homesickness is very powerful. It made me very sad to go such a long way to visit my children and then have to leave due to homesickness.

Can you stay for lunch? We are Chaldean Christians celebrating the Christian holidays and we cannot eat meat, but we have other food that doesn't include meat.

Aglame

There are eleven of us living in this apartment now: me, my mother, and nine children. The children don't want to go to school, because there have been attacks by U.S. soldiers with grenades on schools. I am concerned for their safety and I do not force them to go to school when they are scared. But I worry about their education.

There are patrols that conduct searches in this neighborhood. In nine months there have been two house searches with U.S. soldiers kicking in the doors in the middle of the night, pulling the family out of their beds, and making them stand in the streets without giving them time to get fully covered. For Muslims this is very bad. For Christians this is bad too, but it is worse for Muslims, who have strict dress codes. Thank God there are no injuries so far in our neighborhood.

Before the war started the young men in this neighborhood said that Saddam wanted them to enlist in the army and fight the Americans. Our neighbor, Issam, told these young men not to do that. Issam was a colonel in the Iraqi army during the time of the war with Iran. Then he said he would no longer fight in that war or for Saddam as there was too much waste and useless death. From 1983 to 2003 Saddam said, "Bring me that man Issam, dead or alive."

But Issam was very clever and avoided Saddam's spies. When Saddam called the young men of our neighborhood to fight in this war, Issam told them about the reality of war and that they would surely die if they try to fight the Americans. Best for them to hide from Saddam and live long lives.

When the war started, my children and I looked into the sky and saw the bombers flying over our home. We saw the bomb bays opening under the airplanes and saw the bombs dropping on the big buildings. We heard so many explosions from so many bombs. Now our children don't want to play outside; if they do go outside, they stay nearby. Everybody in this neighborhood knows everybody else, and the children can duck into any house if there is trouble. But now the children have nightmares.

Ibelene

My husband, Shou-ket, used to work as a waiter in the nightclubs. He made a good living, but after 1986, all the nightclubs were closed. Now, our family outside this country is supporting us. I ask the Christian God to get the U.S. soldiers home soon, back to their country. *Inshallah* (God willing).

Aglame

Life with Saddam was the same as now, except now we do not have jobs and we do not have safety. Nobody in this neighborhood liked the days of Saddam, but now we cannot go out at night like we used to do. I cannot even go to the store alone; I must wait for one of my sons to go with me. Sometimes I think it was better in the days of Saddam, because then at least we had safety and security.

EMAN AHMED KHAMMAS, Baghdad

"The most precious things on this earth…"

Eman Ahmed Khammas is a writer, a translator, and the former director of Occupation Watch. She acted as advisor on Iraqi women's issues for the delegation from January 24 to February 4, 2004. I conducted this interview at Baghdad's Al Mansour luxury hotel during dinner on our last night in Baghdad; the hotel was devoid of other guests.

I have two daughters, and they are the most precious things on this earth to me. My 18-year-old is in her first year of college in English literature and my 17-year-old is in high school. My oldest daughter will be a novelist when she finishes her degree. My youngest daughter is still deciding on her career.

My husband and I have given our girls psychological strength, and they are very independent minded. We have offered them as many choices as we can about who and what they'll be as adults. This is a vulnerable position in Iraq today. It is risky to be independent minded, and it will remain risky as long as we have the authority and power vacuum we now have.

This occupation is making it physically risky for women to go outside their homes—if they are lucky enough to still have homes. Many families have not been able to keep up with inflation, and with unemployment above 60 percent, may lose their homes when the rents become too high. Many women no longer drive or visit friends and family as they did before, and they seldom shop. The streets are dangerous, with theft, attack, and kidnappings common.

This is new in Iraq. Iraqi women were used to many freedoms in this country, the achievement of a century's struggle. Now, Decision 137 passed by the Iraqi Governing Council [an interim body put in place since the occupation] is threatening to replace Iraqi civil and family law with strict Shari'a law. Decision 137 denies earlier freedoms and laws about marriage, divorce, custody of children, and heritage. Iraqis are very worried, and I am very concerned for the future of my children. Passing this law would be a big step backward for Iraqi women, men, and families.

I come from a large family, and our extended family is very large and very mixed. Some of us are religious and some of us are not; this is awkward sometimes. My husband and I, and our girls, are not religious. If my girls want to follow a religious path, that is up to them. At this time neither of them wears the *hijab*, although one daughter tried it for a week and then gave it up, and has not tried it since.

My oldest brother was killed in the war with Iran in the early 1980s, and I took his place as the oldest of my six brothers and three sisters. This experience made me grow strong and determined.

I finished my M.A. in English literature and began working on a women's magazine, where I met my husband. Perhaps the fact that he worked as an editor on a women's magazine tells you that he is not really a traditional Iraqi man—maybe in some things he is—but he'd thought about the issues that women face in this world and that is why he, too, was working for this magazine. Now he has his Ph.D. and teaches film at the University of Baghdad. Let me insert here that education is free in Iraq to anyone who has the capability. It is true that Saddam Hussein discriminated against non-Ba'athists in the universities—especially if a student talked about subversive political topics—but Iraq has one of the highest per capita rates for Ph.D.s in the world, and all studies are free.

About my marriage: I do not pretend that it was always easy, but my husband and I work out our issues and our marriage is strong. He respects my views and I respect his. Our daughters see and learn from this. Sometimes I worry about where my daughters might find partners with this heritage, but I wouldn't change a thing about them.

Another worry for all Iraqi women is that so many Iraqi men have been killed in the wars that Saddam Hussein brought upon us. Many smart, well-educated, loving women in our country will not marry and have families because of the lack of men. It is a tragedy that will affect our country for a long time.

In the 1980s and 1990s men were in the army and women in the workforce. Since this war and subsequent occupation, with the unemployment rate so high and security such a big issue, jobs tend to go to men. Company managers say they want to hire men even though they believe women make better employees, as they are more committed to their work. They hire men because women must leave the office earlier in order to arrive home safely. Generally salaries are the same for both men and women; salary discrimination, if it exists, tends to favor women.

Under Saddam Hussein I had a good job with the General Federation of Iraqi Women. Even though it was a favor from the Ba'athist Party, it was a good place for women to work and it did many good things for Iraqi women.

"WIDJAN," Baghdad

"I hoarded medicine…"

Delegate Victoria Cunningham interviewed "Widjan." I include her story in this collection as it describes the trials of everyday life even for wealthy residents of Baghdad during the early days of the occupation.

During my pregnancy with my son, my family and I hoarded as much medicine and anesthetics as we could lay our hands on. I kept it all in my living room, where I could keep an eye on it. There was a possibility that, when I went into labor, the hospital delivery room wouldn't have any medication.

When labor started, my family and I began the rounds of hospitals. The first was simply too poor in resources and too poorly maintained—filthy really—to risk delivery there. The next hospital was also filthy, but by then I'd realized I needed a caesarean section and I didn't have the time to look for a cleaner hospital.

I want to emphasize that before the imposition of U.N. sanctions, Iraqi medical facilities were the pride of the Middle East, with the cleanest and best-maintained hospitals, up-to-date equipment, the best doctors, and more than enough well-trained and helpful nurses on staff—and medical school was free. Supplies were abundant and care was free or cost very little.

Now, just the opposite is true. To see the filth, lack of resources, overworked and underpaid hospital staff, and the inadequate care for very ill patients is heartbreaking. The mortality rate for children in hospitals is 85 percent. Even the private, expensive hospitals are struggling for medicines, doctors, and nursing staff, and they lack all resources.

The night my son was born, I was on the delivery table in my street clothes; even my shoes were still on my feet.

As labor progressed, the ob-gyn administered the anesthesia from my home supply. Then the electrical power failed and we lost light in the delivery room, and the nurses lit candles so the doctor could see what she was doing.

When I regained consciousness I discovered that my family had taken my newborn son home from the hospital because he required surgery on his stomach. Luckily for us, my aunt is a surgeon [and] performed the surgery at my home.

Osama, my son, is fine now. Well, as fine as a child can be in Baghdad these days. He is healthy and shows no ill effects from his risky entrance into this world.

DR. NADA H, Baghdad

"People are terrified"

Dr. Nada H is a mother and a pediatric dentist in Baghdad. I interviewed her by telephone in May 2004.

The situation in Baghdad gets worse each month. A big mistake the Americans made was allowing people to lose their jobs and not paying salaries. So we see rich people kidnapped and ransom notes delivered to families with apologies, suggesting the kidnappers have no other way to make money, and their families are starving. If older women are kidnapped and released they are welcomed back into their families. But younger women who are kidnapped tend to commit suicide or are killed by their families when they return; this relates to family honor.

Nowadays many militias operate and each needs money, so they kidnap famous and wealthy people for ransoms of US $250,000 or $300,000, although families don't automatically pay ransoms for women. We see famous male doctors or United Nations workers kidnapped and ransomed. We don't know who is behind many of these kidnappings.

Each day brings bombings and killings and terrible looting. We've seen U.S. troops open private and governmental institutes and tell the simple people, "Go inside. Ali Baba, Ali Baba! Go inside and take whatever you want." That happened in the Iraqi National Museum. Iraq doesn't have an effective security force. If a policeman captures someone in a criminal act and hands the thief over to the military, the military releases the captive, saying there's not enough evidence.

I work in a hospital with simple children who've never used a toothbrush or toothpaste before. When aircraft fly over the building the children cower. I give them materials to make drawings, and their images show their trauma. Trauma shows up in children in various ways: some wet their beds; some chew their nails. My brother, for example, became a nail biter after the 1991 Gulf War. Schools are open intermittently; some children refuse to go back to school after their school buildings were bombed and their parents couldn't find them. Their parents are traumatized too. Children are under the authority of their parents, and if their parents are under pressure, their children suffer.

Getting to work is a problem, and people can't just take taxis, because the costs have gone up so much that hardly anyone can afford them. Right now ordinary Iraqi families don't own generators and out-of-work family members stay home in 130-degree heat all day without electricity to run air conditioners. Imagine American families sitting at home with those temperatures and unable to go anywhere. Gas for cars costs more than ordinary people can afford—or [they must] get it on the black market, which can be dangerous. Or people wait for hours in line for gas.

I was one of the people who wanted and waited for this war [hoping] that Saddam would not be around anymore. I thought that if he was gone I'd be the happiest person on earth. I'd be able to pack my bags and travel to any country and not be suspected of terrorism. I'd see justice in my college and not have to belong to a socialist group to get my rights. But nothing has changed. I still can't travel anywhere but Jordan—and that's only if the Jordanian government is kind enough to allow me to visit. Yes, certain people still play their games and get what they want. Yes, Iraq is still classified a terrorist country. I feel ashamed because I'm Iraqi. I feel rejected by the whole world.

Many Iraqis believe that Iraq won't be empowered after the June handover [to an interim Iraqi government]. They don't believe that the Americans will give Iraq power but will keep their hands on the ministries and keep the upper hand. Many believe that Iraqis who take powerful positions in the new government will be American puppets, so already, we don't have faith in Iraqis who take power....

Is what is driving the militias a power grab? Some seem to feel disrespected because they did not get power in the new structure. Some seem to feel rejected because they have nothing left, no jobs, no power, and nothing to lose. Some are from the former Iraqi military...and some are from outside the country.

One of the worst things the Americans did was fail to protect Iraq's borders. Now weapons are available from anywhere, for anyone who has money to buy them, as well as from previous Iraqi forces. Americans permitted the looting of weapons storage facilities. I've seen bombs sold in front of American troops who do nothing to stop it. Why? I believe that many American actions come from naïveté, that Americans don't know what is culturally provocative here.

Iraqis watched the whole episode with Ahmed Chalabi, for example, with great skepticism. Here he's considered a fool, yet Americans were taking him seriously. Even after that relationship soured many Iraqis believed the break was really a setup to ingratiate Chalabi to Iraqis. They said, "The Americans will wash his face and set him up as [a] puppet so we believe he's on our side."

But most Iraqis hate Chalabi's guts; he's considered a clownish, disreputable person. He's been convicted for fraud in Jordan, and no Iraqi would accept him in a place of power. In fact, many people wish the former king and prince would return to rule.

There is talk of reinstituting Shari'a law, but I believe the Americans would never allow another regime like that in the region. Here women can wear T-shirts and jeans in the streets, and not many women wear veils in Baghdad. If Shari'a becomes the law, those women will leave. Many of them say, "We'd rather have Saddam than Shari'a, and we certainly don't want Saddam back!"… Even during Saddam's regime, Najaf and Karbala were different, and women had to wear veils there, but that won't spread.

We are really living a very harsh nightmare; we have no electricity, no gas, and a vague, scary future. We're just growing old with no hope and so much violence everywhere. I wish we could live in a country with democracy and freedom, and that I could wake up in the morning without hearing bomb explosions.

But let me say that I've seen American soldiers helping injured Iraqi people. They have been so polite. And they are so young! It is a shame to see such young soldiers doing the kind of work that they're doing here. I don't blame the simple American soldiers for this disaster. Rather, I believe the soldiers are victims the same way that the Iraqi people are victims.

Political dirty work is responsible for what we are going through: it is the White House and the Saddam regime.

GROUP OF WOMEN—OFFICE OF ORGANIZATION OF WOMEN'S FREEDOM IN IRAQ (OWFI), Baghdad

I interviewed the following women in the Organization of Women's Freedom in Iraq's Baghdad office. OWFI shelters Iraqi women targeted in honor killings and sectarian violence, monitors women in jail, and assists formerly detained women. Founded by Iraqi Yannar Mohammed, who lives in Canada, OWFI opposes Iraq's growing Islamism and calls for secular law and women's legal rights.

Yannar Mohammed (President, OWFI)

Iraq's local currency has devalued to the extent that landlords feel the need to raise rents exorbitantly or to evict current tenants in an effort to make ends meet. This sets off a chain reaction that further destabilizes the social environment.

A typical family—mother working in the home, employed father, and children—cannot afford the increases.

With an unemployment rate somewhere around 50 to 70 percent and the increasingly likely scenario of the man of the house losing his job, whole families lose their homes. Unable to afford new housing, they move in with parents or family members lucky enough to still have work. Then these families are pushed to the point of collapse when their living quarters are crowded to bursting. Where do they go? If intact families are endangered, households without adult males are completely adrift. Some of these gather in camps of more than 500 people. Adding to the complexity, many are Kurds fleeing the war and already in dire economic straits.

Wissam

My landlord raised our rent and we could not afford to pay it every month. We looked around our town for an apartment we could afford but found none. My husband is a shoemaker, and he heard there was more work in the city of Baghdad and that he would make more money. He brought us here, but there is no work here. We live in a building owned by the previous government. It was bombed during this war and has no running water and no functioning toilets, but it is a shelter. We live with many other families. In many cases, widows with children head these families.

Nadia

My husband lost his job; he seeks another one. Meanwhile, we shelter in a bombed building that has only walls and a roof.

Eman

Now the new government tells us we must move because they want to use the building again. We tell them, "Where can we go? How will we live?"

One of my neighbors, a widow with nine children, lives in a bathroom. It is damp, the roof leaks, but it is a shelter from the cold, the rain, and prying eyes. She puts a piece of wood over the squatting hole and she and her children sleep on the floor.

Sureya

The feast holiday is coming up. My family lives in Houda Camp and we do not have water. I tell my husband, "Our children must be clean for this holiday. Where can I clean them? How can I make sure they start the holiday clean and well dressed?"

WHERE ARE THEY NOW?

Dr. Ali Rasheed Hamid

In October 2007 I received an email from Dr. Hamid:

I am living in United Arab Emirates and working in a private clinic. I managed to leave the country and start again from scratch. While I am not very satisfied I do earn a living and support my family. I consider myself lucky in comparison to many colleagues who are stuck in Iraq or who managed to travel to Syria yet remain jobless for a year or more. All of these supported their families from savings.

There are numerous stories of the pain and agony, and these losses are compounded by brain drain. Dr. S, a successful orthopedic surgeon, for example, received many death threats and even assassination attempts, and he fled the country. The only people remaining are those who are unable to support themselves abroad.

My mother and three of my sisters are still in Baghdad, where they suffer a lot. They contact me regularly and convey pictures of unimaginable agony and pain. So far they have managed to pass through many hard times with many scary encounters with gangs, armies, militiamen, and others.

As you know there are many gangs who dominate the field in Iraq and they share one thing in common: the destruction of Iraq's reputation and the devastation of our country.

Now I am very scared that the coalition forces might suddenly leave and the country will be even more chaotic. It seems that rebuilding the infrastructure of this torn country is not on the agenda of the White House policy makers. It will take decades for Iraqis to rebuild the country...and decades more to help us overcome these painful wartime experiences!

It is a very sad and frustrating thing that coalition forces and other invaders can protect neither themselves nor those who worked for them. This is why many of the translators who worked for the coalition forces were either kidnapped and never seen again or were assassinated.

In fact there are not many choices if anyone wants to flee this disaster.... as you probably heard Syria requires visas for Iraqi refugees...and that is a nightmare for the 2 million now living there...and only a fraction of Iraqi refugee children are getting the chance to go to school....

Anwar Jeward

In January 2006, Anwar was one of six Iraqi women delegates invited by a U.S. women's organization to travel to the United States and speak about the situation in Iraq. Of the six delegates invited, four received visas to enter the United States. Anwar's visa was refused. The reason? Since she no longer has family in Iraq, she is considered a flight risk who may not return to Iraq at the conclusion of the trip.

The most recent news is that Anwar, Abir, and Hassan live in Anwar's brother-in-law's house in Baghdad. There is no word on whether the family has become part of the millions of displaced people in the region.

Eman Ahmed Khammas

In March 2005, Eman and five other Iraqi women came to the United States to speak about the effects of the invasion on their country. While walking with Eman near Congressional offices in Washington, D.C., she began crying. As I comforted her I asked why she was upset.

She answered, "Americans have so much. Look at these clean, orderly streets, the wide-open spaces, the quiet, and the obvious wealth of the people. Yet your military is in our country and our land is a living hell. Why? What do you want from our small and comparatively poor country?"

I had no answer.

Eman and her two daughters live in Spain; her husband remains in Baghdad.

2—ISRAEL

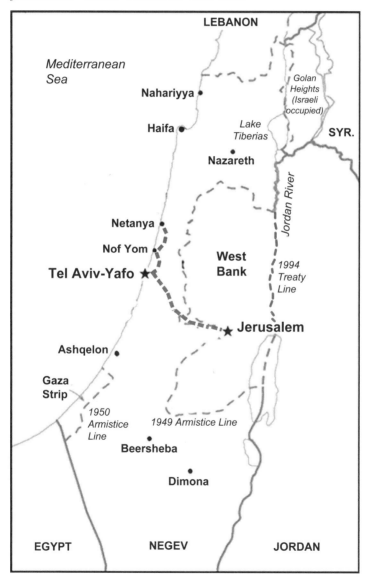

Like a king sitting on the ashes of his throne[1]

THE DUTCH AIRPORT SECURITY GUARD did a double take at the Iraqi visa in my passport. "Why were you in Iraq?" "I went to visit my son, who was a soldier there." He stared at me then walked to an Israeli security agent, who looked me over. The Israeli dismissed me with a flick of his hand: yes, I was permitted to board the plane.

I was apprehensive about my reception at Ben-Gurion Airport, but the graveyard shift clerk offered a cheerful "Welcome to Israel," and after 27 years, I was back. The old cramped airport is long gone, replaced by a vast mall arranged in a circle. A grand, overwhelmingly tall stone wall emulates the Wailing Wall...or prepares visitors for a first view of the Security Wall that snakes through the West Bank.

The good old days

As a 12-year-old I'd been fascinated with the idea of Israel after Habonim groups stayed at my family's rural hotel. Habonim was a youth movement established in the 1940s for young people in Western countries who planned to settle in Israel. Habonim ideology encouraged establishing farms—like kibbutzim—living communal lives, and learning to grow vegetables and to tend animals.

For two weeks, these kids learned Hebrew, followed kosher dietary law, and studied Zionism. I joined them to watch home movies of kibbutz life and footage of the 1967 War. Here was something that appealed to my sense of "doing something useful" with my life, and I traveled to Israel in 1975. I volunteered on Kibbutz Na'an, learned Hebrew in daily classes called Ulpan, and worked in the garden ("making the desert bloom") with Manya—a Polish Holocaust survivor—from 5:00 to 11:00 a.m. six days a week. Later, I lived with a *zera'im* (seed) community of 30 *sabras*—literally "prickly pear," this term refers to a native-born Israeli—on Kibbutz Ramat Rachel, picked persimmons for German Holocaust survivors in Nehariya, packed bell peppers for a *moshav* (a community in which members own their homes and share the land) in the Sinai, stayed in a monastery in Galilee, worked in an institute for disabled Palestinian children, and labeled artifacts at the Rockefeller Museum. I explored the Negev and Sinai deserts; I visited the ultra-orthodox Jewish community of Me'ersharim and hitchhiked to Hebron, Jericho, El Ayrish (then in the Gaza Strip, now in Egypt), Ashqelon, Beersheva, Ein Gedi, Qumran, Rehovot, Ramle, Tel Aviv, Latroun, Haifa, Golan Heights, Nazareth, and Bethlehem. I floated in the Dead Sea and lived on a desert beach in a tent I patched together from windborne plastic. I negotiated the rocky shoals of Catholic marriage, instructed by a radical nun who believed women should conduct Mass and a traditional Franciscan who conducted Mass only in Latin. I was married in a chapel formerly a refuge for lepers and honeymooned in a reef cave at Sharm el-Sheik (then home to one small scuba-diving enterprise and now a bustling Egyptian resort).

Israel educated me about art, architecture, archeology, religion, and a version of history, and stimulated my enduring fascination with intercultural communication and communal life. I learned to be suspicious of unaccompanied packages, to avoid looking into the eyes of Palestinian males, to appreciate the outspoken, direct, energetic, can-do *sabra* disposition, and to ignore young Israeli and Palestinian men who asked, "Hey, d'you want to fuck?"

I departed in 1977, the year Menachem Begin became prime minister.

"A full human being..."

I met Dorothy Naor at the Tel Aviv courthouse, and she translated pertinent aspects of Tali Fahima's trial. The 29-year-old Fahima "had been an apathetic legal secretary who voted for the right-wing Likud Party and carried Israeli prejudices about Palestinians until in 2003 [when] she decided she wanted to understand why the Palestinians were attacking Israel," according to a report in the British *Guardian*.[2] Then she read an interview in which Zakaria Zubeidi, chief of Jenin's Al Aqsa Martyrs Brigades, described his transformation from peace activist to "wanted terrorist" at the top of Israel's assassination list. After talking to Zubeidi, Fahima went to Jenin, a West Bank Area A town[3] off-limits to Israeli civilians, and saw the destruction wrought by the Israeli Defense Force in April 2002. IDF soldiers apprehended her in Jenin and accused her of aiding members of Al Aqsa Martyrs Brigade.

During the 18 months she was held in administrative detention, Tali Fahima was threatened with 30 years in jail, vilified by Israeli media, and—considered the worst of her crimes according to Israeli social mores—accused of a romantic affair with "the Arab terrorist Zubeidi."

Her aunt introduced me to Fahima as she sat in the witness box before the hearing began. She explained, "I needed to know what the word 'occupation' meant, so I went to Jenin. Now there's no going back. I can't be a full human being if I don't speak about what I learned, like Israel's attack on Jenin, how many people died, how many houses were destroyed…and about how I'm being persecuted for speaking the truth. I can't go back to my regular job and my regular life."

Fahima was convicted of contacting a foreign agent, passing information to the enemy, and violating legal instructions. She was sentenced to three years in jail with time off for good behavior.

After the hearing, Dorothy and I crowded into the elevator with three Israelis. One suggested they make an example of Tali Fahima by taking a rope and swinging her from the nearest tree. The others laughed and agreed.

Not like us…

I hadn't noticed the Tel Aviv Internet café attendant reading over my shoulder until he asked, "Are you one of those U.N. political people?"

"What is a U.N. political person?"

"You know, those people who don't know about how those little Palestinian kids look at you with those big eyes so you feel sorry for them, and then, bang, the next thing you know they've blown you up."

"I'm not with the U.N...."

"I see you are writing about Fatah."

"Yes, I just came from the hearing for Tali Fahima. Do you know of her?"

"No. Is she a U.N. person?"

"She is Israeli, like you. You can learn about her on the Internet."

"I come from Russia. Does she?"

"No, she was born here. Her family came from North Africa."

"They're different from us, the North Africans."

"But Israeli, no?"

"But not like us. We're educated, they're not."

"They're not like us" is a common theme in Israel. Nurit Peled-Elhanan bemoaned this mentality as we sat in the cool shade cast by her large, airy home in Beit Moza. Around us, construction workers hammered and sawed on nearby houses, dogs barked, birds twittered. I noticed that we instinctively accommodated the intrusive roars of military jets overhead by remaining silent until the sound faded. (Can accommodating the roars of military jets result in quietism? Does responding with silence encourage silence about ubiquitous militarism?)

Political analyst Phyllis Bennis explains the ranking Nurit was talking about: "Within Israel there are really four levels of citizenship, the first three being various levels of Jewish participation in Israeli society, which are thoroughly racialized.... [In the top class] are the Ashkenazi, the white European Jews. At the level of power, recent Russian immigrants—about 20 percent of Israeli Jews—are being assimilated into the European-Ashkenazi sector; the next level down, probably the largest component of the Jewish population, is the Mizrachi or Sephardic Jews from the Arab countries. At the bottom of the Jewish pyramid are the Ethiopian Jews, who are black."[4]

To contextualize this, Nurit says: "Here we say that it is too bad that the Palestinians are not European or American, for Europeans and Americans are much crueler than Arabs" in securing their interests, yet are not anathemized. "The Arabs are good people, [yet] it is unacceptable to be Arab...because Arabs are not 'us.'"

It was only years after I departed that I understood that I had been as comfortable as I had in Israel because Israel echoes apartheid South Africa's racism. While it is unwise to compare and contrast degrees of oppression (the grand prize for being the most oppressed is, after all, more of the same) the similarities are clear to anyone willing to step back from the fear-mongering rhetoric—including labels of anti-Semitism, self-hating Jew, and critic of Israel—and see what is actually going on there. For starters, Israel repeats apartheid South Africa's discredited activities in that it disrupts indigenous communities; appropriates land; relegates native people to particular areas; categorizes people arbitrarily then mandates identification documents to concretize those categories;[5] imprisons capriciously; offers reprieve from legal and sociopolitical difficulties in return for collaboration; punishes fraternization between "in" and "out" groups;[6] and coerces dissenters.

If anything, Israel, far smaller than South Africa, applies more pressure on densely packed Palestinian communities than apartheid South Africa applied on African communities. An unbiased examination of Israel's network of checkpoints and forbidden roads, its arbitrary application of rules that cannot be referenced because they are not codified into law, its practice of collective punishment and home demolitions, and its overwhelming firepower against civilians in what amounts to free-fire zones, would give any honest, unbiased observer pause.

The similarities don't end there. As apartheid South Africa ground to a halt, it briefly shared an idea similar to Israel's Two State Solution. Those benefiting from apartheid floated the fantasy of a New South Africa as a Swiss-style confederation with a weak central government and 306 local bodies that chose their own economic and social systems. Radical blacks and right-wing Afrikaner—and everyone in between— would conduct their utopian lives in enclaves that obviated the need to acknowledge one another's problematic existence. Never mind that the fastest way to xenophobia—especially in a country with entrenched views of race, religion, ethnicity, class, and social hierarchy—is to enable rather than confront unreasonable fear, distrust, or hatred of strangers or anything perceived as different.

The fig leaf of Israel's Two State Solution disguises the "naughty bits": Israel, propped up by the United States and currently marketed as the "only democracy in the Middle East" (albeit without a constitution) has no intention of relinquishing any Palestinian land. It should more honestly be described as a Two State Holding Pattern, for it will never be a just, permanent solution for the region. But, as author and professor Joel Kovel observes, the United States–Israel axis "has been...the most powerful indirect cause for the rise of political Islam in its theocratic form. [A] Westerner who wishes to undercut the power of Islamic fundamentalism cannot do better than work for the overcoming of Zionism."[7] And there's the rub.

Via Dolorosa

Much has changed in Israel. The kibbutz system that operated on the principle "from each according to his ability, to each according to his need"—wherein kibbutzniks and volunteers pitched in to serve the thriving, human-centered community and received free board, lodging, laundry, and child care services—is a thing of the past. Today, two-thirds of the 268 kibbutzim are privatized, so kibbutzniks pay for most services and own their homes. Kibbutz Ramat Rachel, once a small, bare-bones outpost overlooking Bethlehem, is a flourishing hotel, spa, and Congress Center whose website extols its "winning combination of luxurious accommodations, convenient location, and extensive facilities."[8] When I worked and lived there it had a small dining room, a few shacks for *sabras*, and a communal stone house for volunteers (could it have been the home of a displaced Palestinian family?).

The Tel Aviv–Yafo road to Jerusalem winds up rock-strewn hills and passes rusted military vehicles carefully enshrined on stone pedestals. In my day, these monuments to Israel's 1948 War of Independence, known to Palestinians as Al Naqba (The Catastrophe), were miles outside the city; today Israeli suburbs engulf them.

The first taxi driver I approached at the bus station for a ride to the Old City sneered...then drove away! The next agreed to drive me to Damascus Gate but not into the Christian quarter, where I had a reservation at Ecce Homo Convent. Even that was too much for him; he dropped me a quarter mile from the Gate, then yelled at me when I objected. This behavior rocked my long-held belief—ironically, formed in Israel—that taxi drivers are under-recognized heroes, helpful, informative, and socially astute. Later I learned that a Palestinian had stepped from the crowd near the Damascus Gate and killed an Israeli taxi driver with a shot to the head. Or I may have been the object of a general antipathy toward "volunteers" or "internationals" perceived as critical of Israel, suspected of assisting Palestinians and of analyzing the region with a "jaundiced" human rights perspective.

As I schlepped my luggage over ancient cobblestones in the Old City I noticed an unfamiliar barrenness, fewer people, less street chatter... something about the place that dampened my spirit. Nevertheless, Ecce Homo, located on the Way of the Cross and known for the Roman Lithostrotos associated with Jesus Christ's trial, sits peacefully, as it has for hundreds of years, amid the Dome of the Rock and Al Aqsa mosques, the Wailing Wall, and the Holy Sepulcher. A little farther on is the Muslim Quarter with its 22,000 Muslim inhabitants and the 500 street cameras that keep tabs on them. Eighteen trash collectors are assigned to the Old City's 31,500 Muslims, Christians, Armenians, and others. In contrast, 22 trash collectors pick up the garbage of the pristine Jewish Quarter's 3,000 inhabitants. This means, Kovel observes, "that the average Jewish resident of the Old City gets 13 times as much garbage removal as the others—and much more than that compared to the Muslims of Old Jerusalem, who live amidst piles of refuse like slum dwellers everywhere."

At 4:00 a.m. each morning the muezzin's calls to the faithful echoed around the Old City. He was so close to the microphone that I heard him breathing.

Fast road to nowhere

American psychologist Dr. Jerry Lawler and I departed Jerusalem for Hebron by bus and arrived there by taxi. This is standard procedure for traveling between Israel and the Occupied West Bank. Despite color-coded Israeli and Palestinian vehicle license plates (yellow indicates Israelis or "Israeli Arabs," white and blue indicates Palestinians, and red indicates Israeli police and authorities) the state, under the aegis of Ariel Sharon, also builds roads that restrict—or completely prohibit—Palestinians from using them. No official written prohibition explains the classifications or their restrictions, although B'Tselem, the Israeli Information Center for Human Rights in the Occupied Territories, categorizes three restriction types—totally prohibited, partially prohibited, and restricted use—that affect over 730 kilometers of roadway.[9] (For comparison, Israel's Mediterranean coastline totals 273 kilometers.)

Who checks the checkers?

The 30-foot concrete Security Wall loomed as Jerry and I crossed the dusty, barricaded no-man's land and boarded a taxi with an image of an Apache helicopter etched on the rear window along with a tag line that said—according to Arabic-speaking passengers—something like "Apache go home."

Of the hundreds of checkpoints, roadblocks, and earth berms throughout Israel and the Occupied Territories, some are impromptu affairs that change location throughout the West Bank and can last for several hours or the whole day.[10] In 2004, the West Bank had eleven occasionally staffed and 47 permanently staffed checkpoints. At eight of these, tall concrete lookout towers allow soldiers to observe travelers who, in turn, see only gun barrels pointed at them. Nineteen checkpoints are located at entry points to Israel, some of which are staffed by Border Police and some by the IDF. The Police Department's Samaria-Judea District and the General Security Service share information gathered at checkpoints and apprehend Palestinians listed as "wanted" or "needed for interrogation."

The permanent transit points—like Qalqilya and Kalandia—are soccer-field-size swaths of earth peeled by bulldozers into dismal, dusty lots laced with wire barricades and assorted concrete barriers, narrow turnstiles, and fenced passageways.

Journalist Michael Finkel describes the most famous Christian town, Bethlehem, six miles from Jerusalem: "[It] has a cylindrical guard tower and a sliding steel door, like that on a boxcar, that opens a temporary gap in the wall for vehicles, [then] slides back, squealing on its track, booming shut. You're in Bethlehem.... This is not how Mary and Joseph came into Bethlehem."[11]

Each pass through these human filters further convinced me that they are designed to provoke, frustrate, and humiliate Palestinians...or anyone mistaken for Palestinian.

The camel, a constant

A half-skinned camel carcass hanging outside a Hebron butcher shop with intact head and death grin took me back almost 30 years. Today Hebron is a ghost city whose once vibrant street energy is gone. Elderly merchants hawk plastic umbrellas, flip-flops, and key chains from China, and desultory shoppers riffle through wilted produce. Misery wafts through the alleyways where wire mesh strung overhead prevents religious fundamentalists living above street level from hitting pedestrians with garbage aimed from windows. So much litter collects in the wire netting that pedestrians looking up cannot see the sky through it. In one spot, wire mesh exhausted with the weight of garbage sagged so far down into the alley that Jerry and I had to walk around it.

The closer one comes to the checkpoints guarding this zone, the more deserted are the streets. Adam and Eve, Abraham and Sarah, Isaac and Rebekah, and Jacob and Leah are buried here. If that isn't enough for the People of the Book to contest, Esau's head (according to Midrashic sources) and Joseph's tomb (according to Islamic sources) are here too.

Jerry and I arrived in Hebron on Shabbat, when the Cave of Machpela (the Patriarchs) was closed to the public. The Ibrahimi Mosque was open, so we removed our shoes, I donned the shapeless robe modesty decrees, and we entered.

As the imam displayed the bullet holes that mar the exquisite marble décor, he seemed astonished still by Dr. Baruch Goldstein's shooting spree that had killed more than 30 Ramadan worshippers on Purim, the Jewish holiday, in 1994. "Here, yes, see, yes, the holes from the bullets. Yes?" He raised his eyebrows to ensure that we saw what he saw.

He invited us to peer down the shaft into the subterranean burial chambers below. "Yes, see, look down, yes, look down." The ancient blind man who sat cross-legged next to the opening cupped his hands, muttered a prayer, and nodded his thanks as Jerry placed a coin in his palm.

Following Goldstein's shooting and subsequent riots and deaths, Israel divided the mosque in two parts and established a synagogue in one half. It also closed main roads to Palestinian vehicles, shut down the Palestinian vegetable market, prohibited buses serving Palestinians from entering the city, and established a military base to connect two small Jewish settlements. These security measures remain in place.

Gaza reprise

Jerry had been volunteering at a Gaza City clinic when the IDF bombed then Palestinian Authority president Yasser Arafat's compound in retaliation for the arrest of four Israeli soldiers who took a wrong turn in their vehicle. Two of these were brutally murdered by vigilantes in a Ramallah police station. Jerry described the day's events:

> The area was on high alert as I walked north along El Nasser, shopkeepers closed up their stores, and people on the street talked excitedly or looked into the western sky. I heard two explosions, maybe about two miles away, [then] saw an aircraft hovering off the coast, perhaps 3,000 feet up.
>
> On Omal el Muchtar Street, I saw two Apache helicopters hovering off shore, out of range of anything that the Palestinians could shoot at them. As I watched those warships with such destructive power, suspended in the sky in full view, safe from harm yet able to wreak havoc on a whim, it all seemed so colossally unfair that I found myself raging at the Israelis. Here they are, again, acting on the belief that only weapons, power, and violence can make them secure. They've tried it for the last 60 years. Has it worked? No.
>
> Later, a man told me that rockets hit, "not 100 meters away." He insisted I follow him to the terrace where he used a flashlight to show me the "Palestinian Navy": one inflatable raft and two rowboats moored alongside a crude concrete pier jutting into the water. It seemed so ridiculous yet it highlights how helpless the Israelis must feel. How can it strike such an elusive [and] annoying enemy? Israel is like an old lion trying to digest his kill in the shade but [being] forced, instead, to swat at thousands of stinging, tormenting flies.
>
> The next day I received a deeply troubling email from another volunteer. It implied that, since the two murdered IDF soldiers were "undercover agents (whose organization has a history of violence against, and murder of, Palestinians) intent on infiltrating Palestinian demonstrations" and because the crowd that stormed the police station had just returned from the funeral of a Palestinian boy killed by the IDF the day before…"those Israelis may have had it coming.…"
>
> I am angry that IDF undercover agents infiltrate and murder Palestinians. Nevertheless, I was dismayed that this peace-seeking volunteer suggested the IDF soldiers "had it coming." Does this justify vigilantes breaking into a police station and stomping two men to death? While we might understand why an angry mob did this, as people seeking peaceful solutions to conflict,

we must make it crystal clear that we disapprove of the action. The emailer blurred the crucial distinction.

Ariel bloc

While Ariel settlement bloc encompasses over 29,653 acres, it is laid out like any planned and gated community in the United States—except that it overlooks established, venerable olive and fruit orchards confiscated from the Palestinian villages Marda, Kafl Haris, and Iskaka in Salfit governorate. Established in 1978 following the Camp David Accords between Egypt and Israel, by 2004 Ariel was home to over 18,000[12] including more than 7,000 immigrants from the former Soviet Union. It is the second-largest Israeli settlement (after Ma'ale Adumim) in the West Bank, and along with the 26 other settlements that comprise the Ariel settlement bloc, its total population surpasses 38,000.

Prior to 2001, residents of Palestinian villages north of Ariel—Haris, Kifl Haris, Qira, Marda, Jam'in, Zita-Jam'in, Deir Istiya, and Salfit—had access to a local road that branches off the Trans-Samaria Highway (Route 5) and continues south. This three-kilometer road also served as the main access road to Ariel settlement. Then, in early 2001, the IDF forbade the southern entry point of this road to Palestinian traffic. To reach Salfit, villagers must take the Trans-Samaria Highway—a "restricted use" road—on an alternate route past Yasuf, exit their vehicles at a physical roadblock, cross the road by foot, enter a different vehicle and travel an extra 20 kilometers. A trip that once took five minutes now takes 20 to 30 minutes—if there are no other delays.

In 2003, the Israeli authorities began constructing the 114-kilometer Security Wall around the Ariel settlement bloc, and bulldozers uprooted fruit trees and razed vast areas. The "Ariel finger" veers 22 kilometers east of the Armistice or Green Line into the West Bank. Nevertheless, the then Prime Minister Ariel Sharon declared in September 2005 that constructions in West Bank Settlements would continue despite international condemnation: "There's no need to talk, we need to build, and we're building without talking."[13] Today, British real estate agents advertise these large, airy two-story houses for sale as "good investment vehicles sure to appreciate over time."[14]

Nearly 270,000 Israelis live in settlements in the West Bank. The settlement watchdog group Peace Now found that construction continues in 88 of the 122 settlements.[15] Even U.S. Secretary of State Condoleezza Rice, presiding at the Annapolis spectacle for "permanent peace negotiations" between Israel and Palestine in 2007, condemned Israel's Housing and Construction Ministry budget's proposal for 2008. It included plans to build 500 apartments in Har Homa (Bethlehem) and 240 apartments in Ma'ale Adumim.

In a supreme understatement, Rice said the construction would "not help build confidence" for peace talks.[16]

Ysrael, Adieu

Exiting Israel was tougher than entering. The officious young lieutenant checking passports at Ben-Gurion Airport questioned the very elderly Greek woman and her young companion ahead of me in line: Why did you come? Where did you stay? What did you do? Whom did you visit? How did you travel?

Nervously, I fingered my passport with its Iraqi visa. Just when I was next in line the lieutenant was called away and his replacement motioned me to load my luggage into the X-ray equipment. Alas, something in my bag was suspect. At the inspection table, I followed orders and stood aside as a security agent dug through my clothing and inspected the cassette tapes that held all my interviews. He located my small video camera charger—the suspicious item—and whisked it off to another part of the building.

Another agent asked, "Where were you today?"

"Ariel."

'What were you doing there?"

"Visiting."

"Are you a volunteer?"

"I was a volunteer 30 years ago."

"What kind of volunteer?"

"On Kibbutz Na'an."

"I live on a *moshav* near Rehovot."

"That is a good life?"

"Yes. But now I am finished with the army and I am studying geography at university."

He held up a cassette and pointed to the label: "What is this writing?"

"It is the name of the tape."

"Is it Arabic?"

"No, it is English but my handwriting is poor."

He detained me for over 90 minutes, during which time other security personnel searching other people's bags interrupted his search of my luggage to consult him. When he found two booklets in my bag from the bipartisan Israeli human rights organization B'Tselem, he carried them to the lieutenant, who inspected them then returned to ask me: "Are you a volunteer?"

"No, I was a volunteer many years ago but now I am just visiting friends."

"Where are your friends?"

"Some in Jerusalem, some on Kibbutz Na'an, some in Nof Yom."

"Where is your husband?"

"I'm traveling alone."

"But you are not a volunteer?"

"No, I am not a volunteer."

Incredibly, they had still not seen the Iraqi visa in my passport.

"My plane leaves in 30 minutes. Will you return my charger in time?"

"Yes, yes, no problem."

I made the plane with minutes to spare, the charger in my hand.

DORIT ELDAR, SHUVI, Netanya

"I just don't want my son there"

My trip by minibus to the beach town of Netanya after an exhausting day in the West Bank was fraught with miscommunication. I exited the vehicle prematurely and ended up lost somewhere along the freeway, pulling my luggage along. Dorit picked me up and we returned to her apartment for the interview. The next day, a young Palestinian man wearing an explosive-packed belt killed himself and five others in Netanya's Sharon Mall.

Shuvi (Hebrew for "return") was a women's group formed by a group of nine or ten women—and one man. We appealed to the women settlers of Gaza: "You're women, we're women; you're mothers, we're mothers. As women, we understand the value of life. Return and build your homes within the borders of the State of Israel and start afresh. Let's no longer risk the lives of our children—whether soldiers or civilians. Come home."

While the thousands involved in Shuvi believe that the Occupied Territories are a major issue, the group was formed with a specific agenda: soldiers and civilians were being killed in Gaza for a worthless cause, and we must withdraw. The timing was good and we sensed we could reach that goal. Politically, this is not the case with the West Bank in general. Personally, I think Israel should withdraw from the whole West Bank, for there is no political, moral, or historic reason for us to be there. Since 1967 I've belonged to the community who believe this should happen, and at that time very few believed it. Today everybody knows that there will be two states. But it is a very slow, complicated process, made more so by the settlements, historical notions, religious beliefs, and so on.

As a social worker I take advantage of opportunities when they're offered; if I get one foot in the door, I try another step. If that succeeds, I take the opportunity to do more. So it was with Gaza, where the human cost had become so heavy that Shuvi saw an opening to accomplish a withdrawal. For example, during the 1980s war in Lebanon the Four Mothers group raised a very clear public voice about getting our soldiers out. Indeed, some in Shuvi who'd been active then shared those experiences. I'm not saying that Israel left Lebanon because of the Four Mothers or left Gaza because of Shuvi, but every voice that influences public opinion increases public awareness.

We pointed to Gaza's impossible demographics: 8,000 Jews and 1.5 million Palestinians. The financial discrepancy was impossible: Palestinians were starving and Jews were thriving. Our soldiers were dying in large numbers. When soldiers' parents looked at the map of Gaza they saw a sliver of land and wondered if it was worth their child's life. There were fewer settlers living there than there were soldiers guarding them 24/7. It was wrong morally, and politically and it was ridiculous. Every time a girl had a ballet class, a whole army troop escorted her to class. It was awful when a soldier, a child, a woman, whomever, was killed doing that. Between 1967 and the withdrawal, about 255 Israeli civilians were killed there—and that excludes the numbers of Palestinian killed. In the last year, more than 60 were killed. It was out of all proportion, and there came a time—much like in Lebanon—when the dread of who would die today overcame us as a society. It couldn't continue that way.

We emphasized these facts by putting up a sign on the road from Tel Aviv stating we had to get out of Gaza. At the top of the sign we put the number of Israelis killed since 1967 and we changed it every time someone was killed. In the last year we couldn't keep up with the deaths. The time was ripe for huge changes in our society.

None in Shuvi supported Ariel Sharon. We hadn't supported him in Lebanon and we didn't support him in general, but we did support him for his stance on Gaza. In the public mind we were able to differentiate supporting his actions and supporting the person. We found tens of thousands of people ready to join, sign petitions, write letters, and so on.

We prepared and were ready to go public with a letter to the women of Gaza as Sharon planned to get support for a pullout at a Likud Party convention. Then a pregnant settler mother and her four daughters, heading to that convention to speak against a pullout, were shot and killed at a checkpoint. The news arrived just as Likud was about to vote, and they all voted against Sharon. You can imagine the anger, fear, shock, and sadness throughout the country.

We prepared a letter telling Sharon that although he lost the support of 60,000 Likud members he gained the support of more than 60,000 Israeli citizens, and to remember that he was the Prime Minister of Israel, not just the Likud Party. Before sending him the letter, we went public with a big demonstration in Tel Aviv with T-shirts and banners and asked people to sign our letter. The response was amazing: people signed via our website, by fax, and by email. The over-80-year-old grandmother of one family—her grandson was preparing to deploy to Gaza—said, "My husband has been dead a long time and he'd not believe that I'd be at this demonstration. But my grandson is going to the army and I don't want him in Gaza. That is not what my husband and I came to Israel for as young immigrants. I came today to raise my voice." She was among tens of thousands.

We got more than 60,000 signatures; the Prime Minister's email and fax machines collapsed from the volume; Shuvi received cartons of letters. It was so empowering to be on the popular side of politics for a change!

We went to the government offices on Sundays when government meets and we stood near the Prime Minister's office. In June they decided to withdraw from Gaza the following March. The media gave Shuvi the right attention with the right message at the right time.

Shuvi registered as a one-time organization, accomplished what it set out to do, and closed down after the pull out. But the Gaza settlers who worked with us paid a heavy price in abuse and discrimination. The main reason mothers joined Shuvi was because they wanted their sons out of there and not because they wanted to work with settlers.

Many mothers said, "I don't care about the settlers. I don't know why you're putting energy into the settlers. I just don't want my son there."

NURIT PELED-ELHANAN, Beit Moza, Jerusalem

"Saving the children from politicians"

Nurit is very active in Parents Circle–Family Forum, an organization of about 500 families seeking to solve the conflict between Israelis and Palestinians through dialogue and mutual understanding. Nurit shared the 2001 Sakharov Prize for Freedom of Thought with Palestinian father Izzat Gharzawi. Both lost children to the conflict in their homeland: Nurit's 13-year-old daughter, Smadar, died in a suicide bombing on a street in Jerusalem; Izzat's 16-year-old son, Ramy, was shot to death in his schoolyard by an Israeli soldier. Nurit's two oldest sons actively resist militarism.

Nurit's father, General Matti Peled, was renowned for his courage—he commanded a battalion in the 1948 war—for his intellect—he taught Arabic literature at the Hebrew University—and for withstanding accusations that he was a traitor for suggesting Israel forge a comprehensive peace with Palestinians.

Mine is really a personal message, and I say things that people never admit or don't dare to say, "Our children are murderers."

It is also a message about saving the children from politicians. We have to redefine the camps, because the camps are not what the politicians make us believe they are: Israelis against Arabs, Americans against Afghans, and so forth. Rather, we should look at it as the people against politicians and armies who do whatever they want with us and our children.

Bush, Saddam, Milosevic, Sharon, and so on, they're all the same. That one judges the other is inconsequential, for they share a Mafia logic: They take over a place, they slash, they burn, and they move on. They don't really care for anything…. These politicians use our kids like chips in a gambling game, and when our children get killed they say, "Oops, sorry."

Essentially, this is a failure of democracy. Every four years we, the people, give license to somebody else, another politician, to kill us, to manipulate us, and to rob us of our children, our money, everything.

Once this so-called War on Terror is over there'll be another one… because the politicians will need more money, or more oil, or more funds from drug trafficking.

Mothers are beyond such games. Most don't serve in armies or participate in high-level politics, so they have a clearer view of life and of what is important. Mothers are able to dialogue—and carry on dialogues with many children—they deal with real things and real people, and they're capable of judging cleanly. This is more than most men can do, especially here in Israel, where men are so oriented toward the army, what it is, and what it does.

But most Israeli mothers cannot think cleanly about Israel's situation because they are in it. Education here is so heavily biased toward the military that most mothers cannot say to themselves, "My husband is a murderer, my son is a murderer, and I have to do something about that."

Very few mothers can go against their husband, their society, their friends, their family, everybody…it is very hard to do. Nevertheless, mothers should be encouraged to do this, not on a movement basis, but privately.

In America people are so brainwashed and so ignorant that they don't know anything except the fascist propaganda they have from their government. They don't know where Iraq is…and they don't want to know…they don't know and they don't care, because it is not America and it is not American. For example, the gesture of the one thousand shoes that were displayed around that country, I asked myself, where are the Iraqi shoes? Then I thought, well, maybe it is because Iraqis don't wear shoes when they kill them that their shoes aren't included.

It is shocking that the organizers didn't consider that…even the peace seekers didn't consider that.

I've heard that people in the United States—including military family organizations—believe that the war in Afghanistan is a "righteous war" but the war in Iraq is not "righteous." But this is faulty thinking, even the terminology is faulty. It is not war. It is genocide, it is slaughter, it is robbing those countries—and we should call it that. But people don't think that way because they don't know…and they're not interested.

In Israel people don't know what happens 20 meters from their house. It is very easy to not know. [We] used to ask about the Nazis in Germany: how come the Germans didn't know what was going on? But nowadays, many of us don't know what is going on.

People no longer have the excuse "But I didn't know." All the information is on the Internet and anybody can have any information about what politicians are doing to us. But it is easier—and more comfortable—not to know.

Mothers have always been rebellious. In the Bible, in Greek mythology, there is always a mother who defies authority. The Talmud described mothers as prophets, because they looked ahead and understood what would happen to the children, then they defied—or lied to—their king or husband.

Mothers' voices should be heard. But mothers, women in general, are not used to saying, "No! No, I am nobody's property. No! My children are nobody's property. No, my uterus is not a national asset."

In Israel mothers are afraid to have their children turn 18. That is a tragedy. But mothers are panicked. I have a friend whose two sons served in Lebanon as guards. Palestinian fighters learned of these positions and each night one or two Israelis were picked off and killed.

My friend called me up and said, "I cannot function with the Prozac the doctor prescribed."

I asked, "Why do you need Prozac?"

"Because without it I am panicked."

I told her, "Well, you should be panicked. This is natural under the circumstances. We are taught that we shouldn't panic, we shouldn't cry, we shouldn't scream. We should! Nobody can take your child away from you."

I don't know how to teach this message. It is all education from a tender age. This is why I say it is a private decision: I'm not going to let this thing happen...even if my child hates me for five years.

My son went to a very elite military unit in which they tell the soldiers that they are the best of the best, then they train them criminally...they break their backs, all in the name of being the best. My son called me one day and said, "I've given everything I've got. I don't know that I can give anymore."

I told him, "Desert. Come home. What do you want me to say?"

He said sarcastically, "I'll always remember your motherly support."

Some time later I was invited to speak at a conference about military refusal. So I asked both my sons about their experiences being refusers [Israeli troops who refuse to serve in the Occupied Territories]. My other son, by the way, was kicked out of his commando unit when I refused to sign permission for him to fight in Lebanon. If there is tragedy in a family [in this case the death of Nurit's daughter in a suicide bombing] both parents must sign a statement declaring the remaining family members may participate in dangerous activities. I would not sign, and my son was kicked out of his elite unit and sent to work in a garage. Being a jobnik with the Russians, who were often drunk, was a terrible humiliation for him, and we had some very bad months with him because of it. He was a victim of the military's revenge on me; normally they let bereaved brothers stay with their unit as counselors, teachers, or monitors. They don't try to break them, but they broke him. It was terrible, and they did it to get back at me.

Nevertheless, he went to this garage and it was a wonderful experience for him. He met people that he'd normally not meet—because he'd been in an elite unit—and he got to know them and to love them and to be interested in them. It was a good experience for all of them.

He said, "By refusing me, my mother not only saved my life but saved my humanity. I realized that I can contribute much more to my country doing civilian work with people who come from all over the world, who are thrown into the army for what they don't know, and who hate every minute of it."

This son didn't hate me. He was just miserable, and it was very hard on him. Because if you are a refuser after having been a murderer, you are more appreciated than if you are a refuser without having been a murderer.

My other son—the one who told me he'd remember my motherly support—recently said in a lecture that the person who taught him to refuse was his mother, when she refused him.

When I had asked him earlier about the realities of being a refuser, he had explained "A soldier is a soldier is a soldier. His only context is the square meter around him, his friends, and the thought of going back home."

This is why we cannot blame the soldiers. We have to blame those who send them to war and the war-supporting mothers.

The message came through to both my sons, but it took a few years. Meanwhile, we parents pay the price.

A friend asked, "How did you do that?"

I told her, "You have to kill the Father inside him...or whatever the Father represents. In Israel the Father represents the army. The army is everything and all that friends talk about, 'Oh, the army is so much fun, and so funny, and so lovely, and so manly.'"

This is what our children grow up on.

It is very difficult. Parents must show their children something different. We must save our children, because if we don't save them we betray them, and we betray our jobs as mothers.

Even if you say to children that something is dangerous, they don't believe you. They think that parents wouldn't stay somewhere if it was dangerous. They cannot grasp this fact, so they don't take it seriously. So we even betray them by living here....

One way to keep them from harm is to keep them away from society's atmosphere, from the President, from all the symbols that they like so much. This is even truer in fascist America than it is here, but it is becoming that way here.

It is very hard to educate children about other people being just as good, because for children, it is always "us" and "them." This thinking includes the racist educations people receive—here and in United States—that whoever is brown, or black, or barefoot is inferior and should be cleansed.

The Arabs are good people, they're gentle, they're peace loving, they're not quarrelsome at all...and they love children, no matter whose children. Yet it is unacceptable to be Arab...because Arabs are not "us."

MIRIAM, Jerusalem

"The lords of the land, the air, and the water"

I interviewed Miriam in her small backyard garden that looks over an open valley to the hill upon which the Yad Vashem Holocaust Museum sits. We ate Miriam's freshly baked cake and listened to the intermittent jackal calls. This is the perfect spot for Miriam, who finds herself seeking solitude more and more as her disappointment with her people grows. She makes time, however, to participate in actions with the women's peace group Bat Shalom.[17]

I was born in America and was one and a half years old when my parents brought me to Israel. They also established Habonim in America. [The organization founded in the 1940s for Western youth who planned to settle in Israel and establish farms.]

In 1946, my parents immigrated here. My father was still serving in the U.S. Navy, and he went to Nazi camps and brought Holocaust survivors to Israel and Europe. While he and the other fathers were finding camp survivors, my mother and I arrived in Israel with other Habonim mothers and settled on Kibbutz K'far Blum with a group of Americans, English, South Africans, Eastern Europeans, and other affluent ideologists to build a new state for Jews and those for whom sheer survival was a slender hope.

My father was at sea for the first six months after we arrived. Then he was killed in the 1948 War of Independence.

Despite Jews believing that this was a barren land, there were Palestinian villages all over, including Galzia, across the Jordan River. Jews took the land of a people who had been living here for centuries. A few days after my father was killed the Israeli army went to Galzia and annihilated it and chased thousands of people to the mountains, to Syria, to Lebanon, to Jordan. Then they built a kibbutz on that land.

I was the only child on K'far Blum who grew up without a father and the only one who'd lost her father to war. I only understood years later how formative this was for me. I was 12 years old when my mother met and married another man, who didn't want to stay on the kibbutz. She left, and I stayed for a few more months; then I told the kibbutz leadership I wanted to leave. Back then, if anyone left the kibbutz—especially someone as influential as my mother—he or she was considered a traitor. Nevertheless, I left and joined my mother and her new husband in Ashquelon.

The collective message on the kibbutz was that Arabs were not human beings but something to fear; they were dangerous monsters who ate children; all the same legends one group still hears about the other. Knowing that my father was killed by "one of them," Arabs were a big threat, and I was terribly frightened of them, even Arab music scared me. I avoided anything Arab. All of us on the kibbutz carried such fear that we weren't able to see Arabs as human beings.

In my school there were kids from Iraq, Iran, Morocco, Tunisia, Yemen, and other Near East countries who'd come on a big *aliyah* [immigration to Israel] in the mid-1950s. More than a million people left everything in these countries and came to Israel with nothing. Israeli authorities dispersed them all over the country, but mainly in the Negev Desert where they threw them into the sand to fend for themselves. Somehow a group got to Ashquelon. I'd never met such people before. They were very poor and they were treated badly in this country and considered only one step above the Arabs. Their descendants are the Misrachi—those born in this country—and still discriminated against. So there I was, with my prejudices, seeing these people every day. But instead of fear and resentment, I felt the opposite. We took an immediate liking to one another and found commonalities. They lived in the old city of Ashquelon in the former homes of Palestinians as if they were still in their Arab countries. We became good friends and visited one another's homes.

Something started to build up in me, and by the time I was due to enter the army, I didn't like the idea of an army. I'd realized there were two sides to every story, and I thought that we, the Israelis, must be doing something wrong to make the Arabs hate us at least as much as we hated them.

I got into a left-wing group, even though I never considered myself a political person but tried to look more at human beings and their behaviors. Anyway this group was [far] left—and persecuted by Shin Bet [Israel's internal security service]—and believed in living peacefully with Arabs. Their message reflected my feelings—perhaps because my father had been killed by something man-made and unnatural, that is, hatred between people. I didn't want anyone to grow up without a father, or a mother, or without their siblings. I felt that we were all human beings sharing a common humanity.

My mother and her husband created an intellectual group that included Palestinians, but I was interested in looking at things from a less intellectual perspective. I was swept up in looking at the stupid and awful things going on in this country.

I married a South African from Port Elizabeth, and we lived there for two years; then we returned to Israel. My husband was involved in university issues and was chairman of the U.N. group that was fighting apartheid. Israel wasn't a big issue then, although, from my studies, I could see the similarities between the two countries. There were only a few left-wing activists who shared my view, although I wasn't an activist—that is, I wasn't brave enough for activities with dangerous consequences or going to jail. My husband, as a young Zionist, was very active and believed he had a solution to South Africa's problems, although he didn't want to stay there but wanted to live and do positive things in Israel.

Later, he became part of the center while I became more left-wing, so we couldn't live together. We are very good friends; he is a very nice person and I am less so. When he starts to talk to me about issues we disagree upon I get even less nice. He's still in the same political and intellectual place that he has always been in. He cannot seem to change or see other possibilities.

Yet I was still naïve. For example, I believed that when my oldest son turned 18 years old he wouldn't have to go into the army. But of course, he went. This was very much against my will—and he knew it—and he also knew that he had my blessing for living his own life. After all, if he refused to serve, he was the one who'd go to jail. But he had my full support if he decided against serving. Back then it was a huge deal to refuse: the cases were all over the media and the refuser was jailed and ostracized and so on.

My second son knew he had my support if he didn't go. But he went and he did his best. Recently, after he went to a one-week annual reserve training in the south, he returned saying the military has no budget to keep them in reserves for longer than a week. I responded, "Hooray, we've arrived at good times."

All war is man-made, and we need real will and real desire from both sides to end it and see the benefits of peace.

I don't see why we Israelis cannot free most of the Palestinian prisoners, which is a huge issue.

I don't see why we can't be more lenient and behave better at the checkpoints.... I have gone there and I've seen the behavior.

I don't understand why we can't accept Arabs as human beings rather than the monsters we were taught they were as children.

Many Palestinians are Israeli citizens who pay taxes yet don't get health care, or sewage systems, or road-cleaning services.

Take a place like Hebron, where the settlers living above the souk throw their garbage onto the people in the streets below. This is government supported, in that the government won't deal with those Jews who are criminals. Some Israelis cut down Palestinian olive trees and other Israelis from kibbutzim come to protect the trees and help during olive picking and pressing season. But at night the terrorists—an overused word that, in this case, fits; I believe those settler Jews are terrorists because they terrorize Palestinians—destroy the trees. They do everything in their power to damage Palestinian property and do it in their god's name. They get his blessing to do what they do and they see no harm in it. The fact that they kill people and damage property is not important—to them, Palestinians are just animals while they are following religious beliefs.

Here and there settlers are arrested for a short time, but not one has ever received a life sentence for killing innocent children.

Recently an officer in charge of killing a 14-year-old girl had his charges dropped.

Palestinians have no rights and no say in what happens to them. Some ask, "Why doesn't the Palestinian Authority do anything?"

Well, it has no power. It is a puppet organization. The Israelis are the lords of the land, the air, and the water.

Even when good-hearted and well-meaning people on both sides get together to try to understand one another, they are discouraged when an event happens—an attack or an assault at a checkpoint that ends in another Palestinian carried off in a military vehicle. Then all dialogue and good feelings disappear and hope is crushed.... We've learned that there is no point in beginning dialogue, because something always comes and destroys it. Sharon used to say, "IF the Palestinians do not cross the border, and IF there are no Qassems [lightweight rockets]...." But we know that they will cross the border and we know that they will use Qassems. Both sides feel that they have done their part, but look, nothing good came of it. In truth, neither side trusts the other.

I cut back on my regular support of Bat Shalom after Rabin was assassinated. I have become so sad at my own people.

For so many years I told myself, "No, it can't be true. There must be more to it than what I am seeing." Now I see that there isn't. People don't change. The way this country was built with all different ethnic groups within the Jews—Polish, Americans, Moroccans, the original immigrants and the newcomers, the fundamentalist and other religious—it is one big puzzle of non-fitting parts. Each group tries to keep to itself and doesn't want to make real change. If one's own life is good why bother?

Generally, I don't talk this way with other Israelis, but with those with a similar understanding I don't have to explain my views.

I am very disillusioned now, and I'll say something that may sound terrible. I believe that Israelis hate each other and the different factions of our society so much that the Palestinians are the best thing that could have happened to this country.... They are our scapegoat. We put the fattest generals on top—and this militaristic society is run by fat generals who need to grow more innocent kids to fight for them—and the generals keep things in order.

"JOY," Jezreel Valley

"I feel I have no other possibilities"

"Joy" contacted me when she heard about the project from Bat Shalom after I invited Israeli mothers to share their stories. She requested anonymity, partly because she is apprehensive about how fellow kibbutzniks would view her story. I interviewed her by telephone.

I was born in Detroit and finished college in the United States. Before moving permanently from the United States to Israel I thought about it a lot, then moved in 1973 and later married an Israeli kibbutznik, the grandson of the second *aliyah* [wave of migration to Israel]. We have four children, two girls and two boys.

We live on one of the oldest kibbutzim in the eastern part of the Jezreel Valley with about another 300 families—a total of about 500 to 600 members—about ten kilometers northeast of Jenin. This kibbutz makes a living in high tech—night-vision equipment—and agriculture.

Since Israel has compulsory military service all our children served in the army—my youngest is still in the army. She rides buses everywhere and witnesses lots of dangerous things. I feel she is vulnerable and insecure on buses and I've offered to get her a car, but she likes riding buses.

One son served during the height of the violence from this second Intifada and got out of the army in March 2004. Another son served in Lebanon with the Golani Brigade. My third son was a medic and went on to teach a medic course.

When my son was in Lebanon I didn't sleep well. I think any mother with a child in an active military area virtually stops breathing until that child comes home again. Three of his friends and army buddies were killed in Lebanon. A terrible waste. Nothing good comes out of it.

The past four years have been the hardest. I feel we're in a psychologically untenable position, but it seems we have no choice. The extremists in this country are developing policy, and there's a sense that the rest of us can't do anything about it. I have a terrible sense of heaviness and sadness. When there are fewer attacks on Israelis I can block out those feelings, but dissociation only goes so far.

An overwhelming majority of people in Israel want peace, but when great violence occurs, as in the suicide bombing of the Park Hotel in Netanya on Pesach in March 2002, people get frightened and they vote toward the right; even leftists do so when fear overtakes them.

I think everybody is living with psychological trauma now. There are days when I don't want to go out of my house. In our area we don't have the concrete wall separating Israel from the West Bank, but we do have a wire fence that follows the Green Line. We had a lot of suicide bombers out of Jenin, and the fence cut down on the trouble, so things are quieter here.

Our kibbutz has a night guard from 7:00 p.m. to 4:00 a.m. During the worst part of the Intifada, April 2002, we had a security guard 24/7.

We have an area citizens' patrol coordinated with the border police that existed before this Intifada, when there was a lot of agricultural theft. My husband volunteers for this once a month from 6:00 p.m. to midnight when he patrols in a jeep.

I feel bad for the Palestinians—it's hard not to. I don't understand how anyone could become a suicide bomber. Most Israelis don't have any contact with Palestinians as there is too much hatred and distrust.

If I didn't live in this land and I was reading about it from a distance I'd wonder why people chose to live here. But as someone living here, I feel I have no other possibilities. I've thought about going back to the States, but my husband won't hear of it. He's very much part of this land. He's a war hero and his politics are the same as mine, but he has a much higher tolerance for uncertainty than I do.

I've joined various groups, including Bat Shalom. For a while I was going to Jenin to work with a women's peace group, but the second Intifada made that harder to do. Also, I feel some of these groups don't deal with specific concerns and needs. Other groups see things in very black-and-white terms and don't deal with the complexity of the situation. I'm uncomfortable with that.

At one group I said, "I like the fence. It has cut down a lot on violence. Does this mean I can't be part of this group?"

While I hold conflicting feelings about the usefulness of my political activity, I feel I must do something. But sometimes I feel as impotent as many political parties have become.

During the latest wave of violence I felt very alone and isolated. The worst thing is feeling the loss of hope.

I grew up during the height of belief about the American values of integration, pluralistic education, and people of all backgrounds mixing. During the 1960s I was anti-military and anti-war, and I really believed we could change things. Now, I feel pessimistic and it affects my everyday functioning. After one terrible incident, I couldn't do anything and felt almost paralyzed. It affected my work performance and being with my family.

In Israel, there is very much a war hero mentality, especially on kibbutzim, where so many kibbutzniks succeed in the military and so many are killed. In other countries parents boast about their children becoming doctors or lawyers but in Israel parents praise their children as fighter pilots and [for their] military exploits. This mentality doesn't allow criticism. Refusers, for example, have a right to do what they believe is right, but our society has a real problem with those refusing to participate in military service.

A while ago, 13 Israeli Arabs were shot dead by the military. I believe that was very wrong; we can't just shoot people like that. When I said that, people acted like I was a traitor. I felt vindicated when, three years later, an independent commission said the same thing.

When I was in college in 1968 I attended a speech about apartheid by Desmond Tutu of South Africa. I liked what he said, and over the years I watched South Africa go through their violent period, then turn things around in 1994. Desmond Tutu, now an archbishop, talks about the long journey his country made. If South Africa can do it, Israel can too.

BEATE ZILVERSMIDT, Tel Aviv

"One cannot do less than protest"

Beate works with Gush Shalom ("Peace Bloc" in Hebrew, a leftist peace activism group), and I interviewed her by telephone.

I am in my 60s with children and grandchildren in Holland. I was born Jewish under Nazi occupation, and survived by being hidden by different families who took part in the Dutch Resistance. I think that this strange beginning definitely had an effect on the rest of my life. For example, I cannot think of war as something patriotic, or romantic. I always consider war to be a disaster, not a solution, and I have a need, like the people who saved me, to do what I can to act peacefully against the injustices of military systems.

As a matter of fact, in the 1970s my little son was one of the reasons why I didn't make *aliyah*, as my then-husband wanted to do. Mothers have an important role educating their children, and I wasn't willing to prepare my son for being a soldier in a war zone. The refuser movement moves me deeply, as do parents who support their sons who prefer military prison to military action. This sort of support didn't exist in the 1970s.

In 1987, after my children were grown, I made *aliyah* alone—and joined the Israeli peace movement. Now, I travel to Holland to visit my family, but I live in a suburb of Tel Aviv and work out of my home for Gush Shalom. We do many activities for peace, some more successful than others.

While Sharon succeeded in delegitimizing Arafat, Gush Shalom proclaimed that Arafat was the partner with whom the government of Israel must sign a peace agreement. This proclamation does not always make us popular. Nevertheless we have been to the Ramallah Compound (Muqata) as human shields several times. According to Sharon, our presence was a factor in the considerations that led to the decision not to send lethal missiles to the Muqata.

Gush Shalom was also the first group in the peace movement to break the silence on Jerusalem and speak out for sharing Jerusalem: West Jerusalem should be the capital of Israel and East Jerusalem the capital of Palestine.

One of our most successful and popular actions is informing people which items are created or grown by Jewish settlers on illegally acquired land. We publish a Boycott List of settler products to alert people about which products to avoid buying to avoid supporting settlers.

We also raised the alarm to Israeli soldiers about their possibly committing war crimes; some soldiers may have been encouraged by our words and refused to participate in such activities.

Gush Shalom repeatedly demonstrates against the so-called Separation Wall and the destruction of Palestinian farmland and orchards. So far, unfortunately, we've been unsuccessful in changing the fence's route so that it does not take big chunks out of the West Bank. Nevertheless, one cannot do less than protest.

WHERE ARE THEY NOW?

Each of these women continues her work for justice in Israel.

3—WEST BANK/ PALESTINE

NOVEMBER AND DECEMBER 2004—JERUSALEM—
BEIT HANINA—WEST BANK VILLAGES—NABLUS—
HEBRON

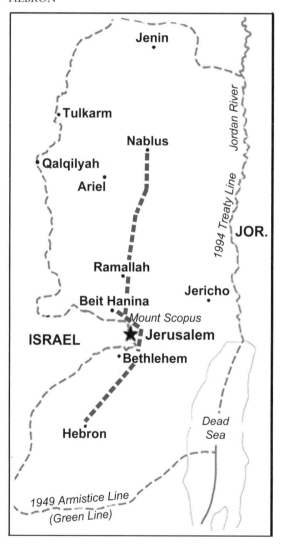

Promises of a relief...gifts and parcels[1]

AFTER SETTLING INTO ECCE HOMO CONVENT and admiring the view, where the serene turquoise and gold Dome of the Rock dominates the skyline, I walked to the dilapidated bus station where decrepit buses puffing diesel fumes depart to transport Palestinians around East Jerusalem and the Occupied Territories. It's a sharp contrast to the new, clean Israeli bus station with armed guards, security gates, and luxury buses. Palestinian Counseling Center's Sihan Rashid had directed me to disembark at the Garden of Eden in Beit Hanina, and as I played with images of a biblical garden with fecund apple trees and garrulous serpents, I queried the female passengers about this location by repeating the name in my best phonetic Arabic. Nevertheless, they were puzzled and thoughtfully tongued the phrase. Then one woman's face lit up as she realized I sought the corner fruit and vegetable store. Lost in my fantasy, I'd almost missed seeing the shop's canopy emblazoned with large bright yellow lettering. Sihan met me and we walked up the hill to the counseling center's office. (Her story begins on page 91.)

Later, I arranged a trip to Nablus, enjoyed dinner at the Jerusalem Hotel, and walked back to the Old City through the Lion's Gate. It was a clear, crisp Thursday evening, but the streets were empty. Just inside the Gate, Israeli police milled around barricades and about 300 people, mostly men, sang and danced at the foot of the Temple Mount (Haram al-Sharif, or Noble Sanctuary). I joined them, then departed when I noticed that the few women present were dressed alike in narrow-brimmed hats, loose long-sleeved blouses, and ankle-length skirts: I didn't want my bare head and arms or my knee-length skirt to offend.

Back at Ecce Homo I learned the group was the Temple Mount Faithful, who believe that the modern state of Israel is the beginning of the redemption of the world, which will be complete when the Jewish Temple is rebuilt and the ancient rites and rituals reinstituted. This means tearing down, removing, or tampering with at least one of the two mosques on the Temple Mount, something likely to provoke Muslims around the world. (Destroying the Dome of the Rock has been a topic of conversation since the 1967 War. Indeed, the state jailed Jewish extremists in 1985 for planning to blow up this third most holy Muslim site.) I'd crashed a small weekly gathering of the faithful. During the larger monthly gatherings, thousands converge on the Old City from settlements throughout the Occupied Territories. According to Old City residents, the group marches, shouts, and sings its way through the ancient streets carrying flags and banners. Sometimes the members jeer at and spit upon pedestrians; often they ram their flagpoles and staffs against the doorways of homes.

Tallying change

In my good old days here, East Jerusalem was predominantly Palestinian. Now, Israeli settlements, denoted by clusters of houses with orange terra-cotta tile roofs, pave former open space, farms, and orchards. This zone represents a physical and psychological sore spot between Israelis and Palestinians. The 30-foot concrete Security Wall—an omnipresent testimonial of intolerance and refusal to communicate—polishes the brittle veneer of Israeli settlers' security while implicitly questioning the stereotype of the can-do, fearless *sabra* (native-born Israeli).

My first experience of the Security Wall occurred inside Eyad's car on a trip to Nablus. Eyad acted as my interpreter and driver and is an "Israeli Arab," that is, a non-Jewish, Arabic-speaking (and in Eyad's case also Hebrew-speaking) Palestinian with Israeli citizenship. One second I mulled East Jerusalem's sprawling urban panorama and its accompanying historical narrative that "Palestine wasn't a *real* country," that "the land was empty," and that only Jewish hard work "makes the desert bloom." The next second, confronted by the Wall, I fell into a universe of light-absorbing gray concrete. As Eyad described how the Wall disrupts every aspect of Palestinian life, I caught his blend of businessman's practicality overlaid with profound sadness: having to work around this inert slab demands so much from Palestinians that there is little time to mourn a rich culture's passing or to assimilate its psychological disruption.

Déjà vu all over again?

The Security Wall makes getting to and from places of employment so difficult that many Palestinians lose their jobs. Ironically, financial necessity forces them to accept work building the very structure that strangles their communities. The decimation of Sheikh Sa'ad village exemplifies the Wall's impact. Though it was once contiguous with East Jerusalem's Jabal Mukaber neighborhood, Israel's Political and Security Cabinet designated certain sections of Sheikh Sa'ad village Area C (Israel has complete control) and others Area B (Palestinian Authority controls civilian affairs), while some sections remain within the Jerusalem Municipality and others border the city and the West Bank.

Israel annexed parts of the West Bank in 1967 and recognized some Palestinians as permanent residents of Israel with the right to hold Israeli identity cards; the rest have Palestinian identity cards. After Israel imposed a general closure of the Occupied Territories in 1993, Sheikh Sa'ad villagers who were not Israeli residents could enter East Jerusalem only with special permission from the Civil Administration. Villagers who had worked, attended school, visited doctors, hospitals, friends, and the local cemetery, or who shopped in East and West Jerusalem faced Kafkaesque scenarios that only worsened with time. Today the Security Wall chops up the area and leads to absurdities that entangle Palestinians in red tape, roadblocks, barriers, and trips on foot up and down hills and valleys that are onerous for the athletic and impossible for the ill or elderly; failure to obey leads directly to jail or to fines that further burden families.[2]

Here is a regurgitation of apartheid's Influx Control laws that regulated the inflow of blacks with passbooks into urban areas to serve white labor needs. Since October 2000 the number of Palestinians with permits allowing them to work in Israel has decreased by the tens of thousands while numbers of foreign workers imported from Eastern

Europe and Asia have increased. Moreover, Palestinian workers who lost their jobs were prevented from asserting their rights in Israeli courts, as they could not obtain permits to go there; in particular, complaints concerned unpaid wages, severance pay, various social benefits (such as paid leave), and non-observance of the minimum wage.[3]

Nablus

The day before Eyad and I arrived in Nablus, the Israeli Defense Force flattened a house in which, they said, "terrorists" were hiding. According to locals, it was simply a family house, but because Nablus's population resists Israeli authority, "these things happen." This house, with its collapsed roof, was on our way to the Khalili household, and the equanimity with which the family referred to the demolition told me that, in Nablus, one conserves one's anger.

Both Khalili sons—in their early 20s—are in Israeli prisons. Years previously, the boys' father had been jailed in the Negev. He explained, "It was a tent prison, and 40 men were packed into each tent. We were not permitted outside—it was very hot inside—but we'd run from one tent to another so that we could talk, teach one another, and so on."

Israeli guards counted the entire prison population each day. Mr. Khalili demonstrated how he was forced to sit one way—legs crossed, head down, hands behind his head, elbows forward—then, after Israeli guards counted him, he was forced to swivel around while holding his position. As he dredged up his and his friends' humiliation, he cried. Then he apologized for crying.

Eyad and I drove to the edge of Balata Refugee Camp and peeked in: A young man with a rifle slung over his shoulder stood in a tight alley and watched us watch him. Watery sewerage puddled at his feet.

Eyad said, "I wish I could do more for these people, at least help educate the children, but where do you begin...and where do you end?"

Balata started in Nablus in 1950 on a patch of ground about two and a half kilometers square. Today, it has a registered refugee population of more than 21,903 and is the largest camp in the West Bank.[4] In 2002, the total registered Palestinian refugee population was approximately 3.9 million; over a million live in camps administered by the United Nations Relief and Works Agency since 1949, with 1,047,940 in

Jordan; 328,360 in Lebanon; 308,410 in Syria; 477,190 in the West Bank; and 586,540 in the Gaza Strip.[5]

Huwarra checkpoint

The young Ethiopian guard at Huwarra checkpoint frowned with testiness as I walked down the tight wire passageway, through the turnstile, and toward her impatient hand. Her fellow guard caught her eye then glanced at my U.S. passport. Her demeanor instantly changed. She smiled, looked through the document, and handed it back to me with a cheerful, "Thank you."

Eyad passed through as easily, and as we walked to the parking lot, he said, "You look a little bit like an Arab, which is why she was angry with you at first. If you had a Palestinian ID you'd have experienced what so many other women go through every day at this checkpoint." (Amina and Sihan share some of these experiences in this chapter.)

Temporary checkpoint

Dorothy Naor and I picked up Clara, an "international," near an orchard where she'd interrupted settlers bent on tearing down olive trees. We'd just learned that there had been a suicide bombing in Netanya's Sharon Mall, and as we drove to Umm Munria's home we stopped at a hastily erected checkpoint.

An Israeli Defense Force vehicle partially blocked the road. One of three soldiers smoked nearby, another checked the papers of a long line of Palestinians, including bus passengers who stood, resigned, on the grass median strip. A third watched several men near a minibus.

Dorothy and Clara approached the minibus. I leaned against the trunk and observed.

The driver reported the soldiers had confiscated their IDs and refused to return them. The men had to get to work. They couldn't wait. How long would they be detained?

Dorothy approached the nearest soldier, "Why are you detaining these men?"

"There has been a bombing...."

"Yes, I know and I'm sorry. But why won't you return their papers?"

He shrugged. "Because...."

"Because? Why?"

As Dorothy mediated between the Palestinians and the soldier, Israeli settlers, usually one to each late-model economy car, drove swiftly around the growing cluster of halted vehicles and agitated people. After an hour of Dorothy's dogged persistence, the soldier returned the IDs and the minibus departed with all its passengers.

I remembered Dorothy's story of the transplanted American Jewish fundamentalist settler who birthed a male child and said, "Thanks to God: another soldier for Eretz Israel."

Suicide bombers: Are they crazy?

The stereotype of a suicide bomber is that of a crazed, underprivileged, undereducated, over-religious, sexually frustrated male. There is no definitive evidence that upholds this stereotype. Young Palestinian men between the ages of 14 and 25 are most commonly the perpetrators of suicide bombings in Israel, but not always. Additionally, the number of female bombers is increasing.[6] Many Palestinians who carry out these deeds, including the women, are well educated and come from middle-class families; some have families themselves. For their time and place and circumstances, they are, apparently, quite ordinary people.

Similarly, the psychological profiles of the team members that pulled off the violence of September 11, 2001, indicate that the majority had decent childhoods with protective, caring, even doting parents.

Psychologists, criminologists, scholars, and pundits offer diagnoses from "personality disorder," "paranoia personality disorder," "brain chemical imbalance," anticipation of 72 virgins in Paradise, to no pathology to explain this violence. Professor and former CIA case officer Marc Sageman states, "The personality pathology thesis suffers from the fundamental problem of specificity.... Conspiracy theories are a ubiquitous feature of human life, not particularly indicative of mental pathology and definitely not specific to terrorists. Experts on terrorism have tried in vain for three decades to identify a common predisposition for [such acts].... These studies concluded that there was no psychological profile for terrorism."[7]

Perhaps this is the most frightening aspect of suicide attacks for those of us brought up to believe in the efficacy of a statistical approach to human behavior: *we* can't quantify why *they* do it.

Moreover, judging by the lack of effective political will in response to what suicide bombers and their families state as the reasons for these actions, it appears that, to those in power, the reasons simply are not worth bothering to change.

Wounded narcissism most closely explains this situation. An analogy may help understand it: Americans, for example, are proud of their reputation as exceptional, generous, open-handed, innovative, and "can do." Yet our national response to the September 11 attacks was to bomb Afghanistan, a country even then suffering from decades of war and literally unable to deny safe haven to Al Qaeda operatives. American pride—and narcissism—was wounded by the effrontery of the attacks. In the name of the United States and its citizens, the Bush Administration exacted knee-jerk revenge, an eye for an eye, clothed in the language of righteousness.

Could Palestinian suicide bombers, deriving from a proud people who, under normal conditions, value education, hard work, ambition, community, and family, be enacting a similar scenario? Unlike America and Americans, however, Palestinians have no resources, no effective political representation, and no well-supplied military—there is no longer even an internationally recognized sovereign state called Palestine. Instead, they have pride, stones, and a powerful will for autonomy. Are they freedom fighters, resisters, terrorists...or "just crazy"?

A word about history

Anyone may be forgiven for accepting that the history taught in school is accurate. After all, events "happened," and proof exists in the form of dates, names of participants, artifacts, and so on. I was certainly shocked when I discovered that history—British, Dutch, African, even my own family's history—was as mutable as any fairy tale.

Versions of Palestine's history include these assertions:

- Palestine was "empty"...except for a few impoverished Palestinians and nomads scattered here and there.

•

• "Arab leaders" urged Palestinians to depart their homes in preparation for an overwhelming Arab victory against the Jews. Ergo, Palestinians "deserve" what happened after the Arab military was defeated. (This was the first version I learned, bolstered by films shown to the Habonim groups at my parents' hotel. This footage from the 1967 War showed shoes and clothing scattered on battlefields with commentary that cowardly Arabs, confronted by Jewish military prowess, bolted so precipitously that they literally ran right out of their clothes.)

• Haganah, Palmach, and Irgun militias defended the Jews who, after Palestinians willingly departed en masse, moved into abandoned Palestinian homes as a practical matter.

• Jewish militias murdered villagers, aggressively forced Palestinians from their homes, and deliberately obliterated villages from the historical narrative by building over and renaming them.

After I broadened my view of history to include congruence with what I saw and heard around me I was shocked at how friends and acquaintances reacted. Even the suggestion that, together, we research—and hold open the possibility of reevaluating—Israel's activities in the Occupied Territories rankled these people.

They said, "You just don't understand" or "You're anti-Semitic."

Jews who concur with my experience say they're labeled "self-hating Jews."

People far more erudite than I take on—and lose—this battle of the "truest truth." Besides, merely disseminating an updated version of the region's history will not solve the region's crises. Impediments include the psychological wounds carried by Jews today for the massacre of millions of their number in World War II; billions of dollars in military equipment and aid annually flooding to Israeli coffers (much of it flowing back to U.S. weapons suppliers); a lack of independent political courage and leadership; and widespread denial of—or comfort with—garden-variety neocolonialism, racism, and xenophobia.

Barbara Lubin, cofounder of the Middle East Children's Alliance, whose Jewish family staunchly supported Zionism and the Irgun (a Zionist paramilitary group in the 1930s and '40s, by today's standards a "terrorist" organization) reevaluated the version of history she had been taught after visiting the region and concluded, "Forget all the bullshit about 'the heart' and so on. This is simple: what happens to Palestinians is, by any reasonable standard, unjust."[8]

According to every Arab I've talked to, the disposition of Palestine and Palestinians is the root of the troubles in the Middle East today. Author Joel Kovel recommends that those of us concerned with the way injustice affects our world, our communities and families, and our own psyches, "should turn on its head the insulting offer that coercively tells oppressed people to abjure violence in advance before negotiating what is rightfully theirs: Open for them the hope of self-determination, and violence will wither away of itself."[9]

Empty?

Theodore Herzl, founder of the Zionist Movement, wrote:

> We [Zionists] must expropriate gently the private property on the state assigned to us. We shall try to spirit the penniless population across the border by procuring employment for it in the transit countries while denying it employment in our country. The property owners will come over to our side. Both the process of expropriation and the removal of the poor must be carried out discreetly and circumspectly. Let the owners of the immovable property believe that they are cheating us, selling us things for more than they are worth. But we are not going to sell them anything back.[10]

Plans to expropriate property gently didn't translate to gentle actions. Israeli historian and self-proclaimed left-wing liberal Benny Morris—"I always voted for Labor, Meretz, or Sheli...I refused to serve in the territories and was jailed for it"—in a 2004 interview with *Ha'aretz*, addressed the occurrence of "about a dozen" cases of rape in 1948:

> In Acre four soldiers raped a girl and murdered her and her father. In Jaffa, soldiers of the Kiryati Brigade raped one girl and tried to rape several more. At Hunin, two girls were raped and murdered. There were one or two cases of rape at Tantura; one case of rape at Qula; at Abu Shusha, there were four female prisoners, one of whom was raped a number of times.... Usually more than one soldier was involved [and the] event ended with murder. [W]e have to assume that the dozen cases of rape that were reported...are just the tip of the iceberg.

Additionally, there were at least 24 massacres perpetrated by Israelis. Morris continues:

In some cases four or five people were executed, in others the numbers were 70, 80, 100. There was also arbitrary killing in the village of Dawayima [near Hebron when] a column entered the village with all guns blazing and killed anything that moved. The worst cases were Saliha (70–80 killed), Deir Yassin (100–110), Lod (250) [and] there was a unusually high concentration of executions of people against a wall or next to a well in an orderly fashion.[N]o one was punished for these acts. Ben-Gurion covered up for the officers who did the massacres. Under Ben-Gurion, a consensus of transfer [a euphemism for expelling Palestinians from their land] is created.[11]

Mohammed's family was removed—although not discreetly or circumspectly. Today, he lives near Lebanon's Ein el-Halweh refugee camp where he grew up. His apartment is not registered in his name because Palestinians cannot own property in Lebanon; legally the Lebanese government can take away this home. This is what he told me:

I was conceived in Palestine, but I was born in Lebanon after my parents were kicked out of Palestine in 1948. Our village was Mayroun[12] and my parents' dream, until they died, was that they'd return there. One day I traveled to southern Lebanon and looked through binoculars to see what used to be Mayroun.

I have two daughters and two sons who are highly politicized and believe that one day they will be back to Palestine. This is our culture and part of our lives: to teach our children that they are Palestinian, that they have rights in and to Palestine. As long as there is history, I am Palestinian. While I love Lebanon I am not Lebanese. The Lebanese are my brothers, they are myself, but if I am Lebanese it means I will forget my land is Palestine.

I don't mind living with Jews. When I visited southern Lebanon I talked to an Israeli soldier of perhaps 20 years old. I told him that this is my land.

He said, "No, I was born here."

I told him, "I was born here, too."

He said, "You are not Palestinian. You live in Lebanon so you are Lebanese."

I answered, "I live in Lebanon but I am a Palestinian refugee and I will be back one day. Let us share our land."

He said, "Go away or I will kill you."

I told him, "This is the way you deal with people. You only know the language of the weapon. I'm not armed. I'm talking to you as a countryman yet you threaten to kill me."

It seems to have been discreetly forgotten that eminent philosopher Martin Buber lived his golden years in Edward Said's family home. The Buber family paid rent for their house in Jerusalem to Edward Said's father. Around 1948, a tenant–landlord dispute erupted between the senior Mr. Said and Professor Buber. The latter lost the case and had to leave the premises. As he returned the keys to Mr. Said, Buber said: "Mr. Said, you just wait. I will be back."

After the expulsion of approximately 75 percent of the indigenous Palestinian Arab populations and the partition of Jerusalem, the Said family was classified as "absentee"; their rights to their properties in Jerusalem and elsewhere in Israel were nullified and reverted to the Israeli Custodian for Absentees' Property. Buber returned to the Saids' house as a tenant of the Custodian and lived there for the rest of his life.[13]

The other side...

To be sure, Israeli civilians in the Occupied Territories are killed with frightening frequency. B'Tselem's website lists Israelis from infants to over-80-year-olds killed by knife, gunshot, explosive belt, bomb, bullet, beating, and Qassem rocket.[14] Palestinians are killed with frightening frequency too—with what seems like a total lack of concern or public outrage. If the story were simply about which "side" lost the most people it would be horrifying. B'Tselem's figures for the death toll from September 2000 to February 2008 are more than 1,033 Israelis and more than 4,604 Palestinians.[15] (Other data may vary. I select B'Tselem's as it is a respected Israeli organization renowned for conducting its own fieldwork and research, thoroughly cross-checking relevant documents, official government sources, and information from other sources, among them Israeli, Palestinian, and other human rights organizations.)

But the killing has gone on for over six decades, and there is no indication that it will end anytime soon.

SIHAN RASHID, Beit Hanina (East Jerusalem)

"It exists in Israeli and American societies too..."

Sihan Rashid was born in the United States and attended school there. She now lives in East Jerusalem and works as a counselor at the Palestinian Counseling Center (PCC). Sihan challenged my assumption about the power of media—the belief that showing images of war and presenting accurate accounts of its devastation would enrage Americans to the extent that we'd force our politicians to end *all* war and militarism.

A group of psychologists, social workers, sociologists, and activists established the Palestinian Counseling Center in 1983. We conduct research and share information and offer long- and short-term therapeutic care based on assessment. In the north—Nablus, Jenin, Qalqiliya, for example—we find people working in groups respond better than they do with individual counseling. Since the second Intifada we've been treating about an equal number of men and women: about 50/50 in the Jerusalem and Ramallah clinics and mostly women in the Jenin clinic. For many years we fought the paradigm of mental illness that says you're either sick/crazy or you're healthy/sane.

Our financial support used to come from local individuals, but with our lack of economic independence, funding now comes from Swiss, Swedish, Norwegian, Dutch, and some Arab donors. We don't accept USAID funds, as we see the contradiction in their providing humanitarian assistance to Palestinians *and* military assistance to Israel. For example, the United States provides Israel with Apache helicopters, yet when they're used to attack Palestinians and Palestinian infrastructure, America turns a blind eye.

The recent Regarding Terrorist Financing addendum attached two years ago requires any organization receiving USAID funds to sign a document stating that the funded organization does not support individuals, groups, or entities that supports terrorism. Within the addendum, however, is the 55-page Executive Order 1432,[16] which appears to deem *all* Palestinian political parties, religious parties, members of the PLO, and individual private businesses as suspected of being "terrorist." This seems to mean that *all* Palestinian political parties and organizations are terrorist and that ours is a terrorist struggle. Further, it appears to mean that a Palestinian doesn't have a right to an opinion, or the right to a political party, or the right of self-determination. Yet, every group of people has different political parties, the Democrats, the Republicans, the Greens, Israel's Likud, and so on…. Why are Palestinian political parties declared terrorist entities?

We met with a donor agent who told us, "You know, you have to own democracy, you have to fight."

I am not very diplomatic but say what I feel: "You stress 'owning' democracy, working on democracy, but how can we own democracy when we don't own freedom, when someone else controls every aspect of our lives?"

He turned red. He didn't expect anyone to address a high government diplomat like this. No one in the room said a word. I didn't say what I was thinking: you visit here for a day or two yet have the nerve tell us, who live here day in, day out, to own democracy.

In Iraq and Afghanistan the Americans and British trumpet, "We liberated the people!" while they actually occupy and control every aspect of those countries, imprisoning and killing tens of thousands, ruining homes and families, and never looking back to see what's destroyed. The Israelis do this too. So when representatives of donor countries on diplomatic missions talk to us about "owning democracy," about "controlling our lives" and "democratic elections," I say, "Hold on a second. Where are you living? I agree we *should* have democracy. But we don't. How can we, when we live in a big prison?"

Within the traditional Palestinian family, usually there is a support system. But with everyone under the same kind of trauma, those support systems are weak. People expect psychologists to take away the pain and make things better.

Palestinians have been under occupation for over 60 years, and we see many signs of psychological conflict, much of it related to the inability to control one's life. Human beings tend to seek "the other" upon whom to vent their own anger and frustration. Even though I never justify domestic violence, physical abuse, or sexual abuse I must consider why they occur: what is the trigger for this behavior manifesting now? One doesn't need to dig deep to find triggers. For example, ours is a patriarchal society and men are judged by their skills as breadwinners and family providers. Recently, 100,000 Palestinian male adults working inside Israel lost their jobs overnight. Suddenly, these men were denied a fundamental organizing principle of their lives. Isn't anger and frustration a predictable response?

PCC had one of the first teams in Jenin after the massacre. The place smelled of death, bodies were strewn everywhere, and more were buried under their homes, destroyed by Israeli bulldozers.

We brought different forms of expressive arts therapy. It was especially beneficial for widows and mothers who'd lost husbands and sons. People did a collective burial to say good-bye to their relatives, and the PCC team conducted therapy techniques with the women—movement, writing, modeling clay, and drawing. It was very difficult in the beginning. Women said, "What are you doing? We just lost someone we love. Why bring us clay and paint?" Weeks later we saw the benefit.

We work with children as young as 4 to adults well over 60. Since the Intifadas, we're seeing symptoms we've never seen before. We believe it has to do with Israel's use of weaponry—dropping bombs, shelling and so forth—that hadn't happened before. Within one year, we diagnosed three children with selective mutism, and all were survivors of home demolitions. Their parents thought their children were in shock and therefore not talking. We explained that home is not just bricks stuck together, it is an identity and a place of safety and security that a child relates to: everything there is mine, my books, my toys, my pictures, my albums, my birth certificate, and so on.

Israel, with no accountability, purposely demolishes Palestinian homes left and right. In Nablus, people live in partially destroyed homes because they have no other place to go.

Other symptoms children manifest include depression, withdrawal, low self-esteem, and academic regression. Parents say, "This was an A student who is now a C student" or who is failing classes. But children are fearful, because classmates have been shot to death in classrooms—or coming to and leaving school. They don't want to go to school, or to stay in class, without their parents or some assurance that someone can protect them.

Whenever there's an increase in Israeli violence, there's an increase in people reporting flashbacks of intrusive images. This may also relate to Palestinian TV, which shows, at any time of day, footage of people's heads blown open, or gunshot victims lying on the ground, or ambulances trying to reach the injured. Some children, seeing the images of Muhammad al-Dura, the little Gaza boy who was shot to death in his father's arms, perceived the father as protecting his son and they got closer to their fathers. Others perceived the father as protecting himself and they began hating their fathers.

Meanwhile, the international media's attitude seems to be, "Oh, just another child killed in Ramallah." No one ever asks: Who is that child? What was her or his life like? What grade was she in? Who are that child's parents? How do they cope with the death of their beloved child? There is a parallel in the attitude toward Iraqis killed in Operation Iraqi Freedom. How many dead? Half a million? A million? How many refugee families? From 2 to 4 million? But, who cares?

We're seeing mental disorders such as mania, depression, and unstable behavior, with high incidences of long-term depression. We see secondary trauma from TV but also from volunteering at hospitals, seeing injured people, and hearing stories. Adults who were tortured as political prisoners but received no medical care on release have [panic attacks] triggered by, for example, footage of Israelis entering Palestinian houses, blindfolding, handcuffing, and throwing people into jeeps and driving them away. We see footage of people injured passing by—not even participating in—demonstrations. Israel uses live ammunition, even those rubber-coated bullets kill, and we see tens of thousands of injuries in the upper body and increases in paralysis and spinal cord injuries. Affected men isolate themselves, students drop out of college, workers can't work, married couples can't have sexual relations.

As an organization, we don't believe in prescribing medication.... This might be the fastest way to feel better, but it's a temporary fix that doesn't deal with the underlying causes. Another concern we have is that there is no accountability or accreditation for those prescribing medication. Much of the medications we receive has passed its expiration date...it is as if whatever was left over in other countries was tossed our way as backhanded support for Palestine and the Occupied Territories.

We are a resilient society, but there are two aspects to this. Positive resiliency allows someone to get on with life, ensures that he or she gets to work or school, finds ways to accomplish tasks, even if forced to use alternative roads. Negative resiliency shows up, for example, at checkpoints with in-fighting between people because someone cut in front of someone else and each has been waiting for hours. I've seen people raise sticks against one another or punch one another. I've tried breaking up such fights. Normally, I would not jump in between two men threatening one another, but isn't my reaction normal? What gets to me, besides people hitting one another, is that the people watching are so passive. Some of these men are so shocked that a woman dares get between them that they stop fighting. But after seeing people dying or severely injured and being helpless, I changed too. I became so angry and frustrated at the world's silence over these horrors that I had a nervous breakdown. I grappled with questions of worth: is Palestinian or Arab life not worth [the creation of] just policies, not worth the world's outrage? Then I understood Edward Said's concept of Orientalism: *we* are the "other," the "people of color" who dress differently, who have a "different" language, and darker skin.

I was stopped at a checkpoint after a suicide bombing on a very cold winter day. There was a long line of stopped vehicles and we all sat in our car for two and a half hours while not a single car moved. Not everyone has heaters in their car, or some cars ran out of gas so drivers took their children and abandoned their cars.

I was scared but I left my car, approached an Israeli soldier, and said, "What are we waiting for?"

He shouted, "Don't you know about yesterday's suicide bombing?"

"Yes, but I didn't do it. You cannot blame me or these hundreds waiting here."

Angrily he repeated that there'd been a suicide bombing the day before.

"Why are you yelling at me? I'm a human being, just like you. Why are you using this approach with me?"

He didn't know what to say. I returned to my car, but it was almost out of gas—I'd been running the engine for heat. I was so angry I started to cry, "Why are you doing this to us?"

"What am I doing to you?"

"Look around you at these cars. Don't you see children? Don't you see people? We're human beings. What're you doing? Why are you doing it?"

He started to cry. "It's not my choice. I don't want to do this, but I have orders."

"But please, can't you tell them what's happening here? Can't you tell them that it is freezing…and that this whole thing is not right?"

He finished crying and talked to another soldier who looked at him as if he was crazy. That guy came over.

"I'm the captain. What do you want?"

"Let us go. We've been here for hours. Why are you doing this to us?"

"I'm sorry, ma'am, but we have orders."

Yes, something wrong had happened the day before. But does that wrong equal this wrong of collective punishment in the middle of winter? Fifteen minutes later, the cars started moving.

Everybody loses in this thing. There are no winners. Everyone's humanity is degraded. That is part of the tragedy.

My response to the theory that Palestinian children innately hate Israelis is that one can't teach hate, but one can teach fear. Hate comes as a result of fear. Palestinians grow up knowing Israelis only as soldiers. We fear them. They hurt us. We begin hating them. The average Israeli is a human being like any other human being. Their government, however, is expert at making Israelis feel threatened by Palestinians, and they live with paranoia.

Now refusers [Israeli troops who refuse to serve in the Occupied Territories] are admitting their actions...and that their sergeants and captains order these acts and that they are pushed to comply, even if they don't want to...but they don't want to be the only one in a unit who won't comply. Consider the checkpoints and the humiliation our people endure with soldiers screaming at and controlling them: "Turn around!" "Spread your legs!" "Open your arms!" "Let me check your bag!" Something stronger than just the individual is behind this behavior.

The 1982 Sabra and Shatila massacre in Lebanon highlighted the carnage on both sides and renewed the debate on Israel's participation. Israel was forced to withdraw because Israelis took to the streets saying, "We will not see any more body bags coming home!" Tens of thousands of people, beginning with mothers, began asking, "Why? What for?"

Where are all those people now? Surely, with so much alternative media, they don't have to listen only to the official government line?

I say, "Come and see how we live." No one has a right to say, "I didn't know," because anyone can come and see our refugee camps, our villages, our way of life. Anyone can count our dead and our injured, our 8,000 prisoners, and our bulldozer-demolished homes. Where are voices raised about this? There are groups such as Women in Black, Yesh Gvul, and Ta'ayush calling for one state for two peoples, and I agree. Because we're here and Israelis are here. Whether we like it or not, we have to find a way to live together. Neither the Israelis nor the Palestinians are going away.

Putting up walls and living in a big prison is not a solution. If the international community is interested in the two peoples here, they have to help ensure that no walls separate us. This so-called Security Barrier has not stopped suicide bombings. But Israeli women's organizations report an increase in domestic violence in Israeli society. Perhaps it has to do with Israel's military service. Perhaps the anger and frustration, and yes, the lack of control, that soldiers feel at checkpoints translates into lack of patience and empathy at home. Are they taking out their anger and frustration on wives or partners?

An increase in domestic violence on both sides worries me, as a woman and as a feminist. The Israeli government has been looking at soldiers' loss of humanity. But they're taught that, they're taught to see me as an enemy at the checkpoints, or walking home, or at the airport.

Americans see this in their country too. While some women protest war, others say, "I am proud of what my son did. I support him all the way. We shouldn't leave [Iraq] until we finish what we meant to do."

The same paradox is expressed in Israeli society.

"JAMILA," West Bank Village

"This cannot continue!"

"Jamila" is married to a man who works for the Palestinian Authority (PA), and she requested anonymity for herself and her family. While she told her story, "Jamila" received word that a young Palestinian man had detonated a belt bomb near the entrance to Sharon Mall in Netanya. He and five others died; some 50 were injured.

I was very young when the Israelis imprisoned my father—for "resistance"—and our family went to live with my father's brother. We did not have a real family life, and growing up, I told myself the only way to ensure that same thing doesn't happen to my own family is by not marrying.

But I married. We had one son, Rabia, before the Israelis arrested and imprisoned my husband—also for "resistance." He was in jail for ten years, and Rabia was a teenager when his father was released. Our second son, Sadjit, is 5 years old. Sadjit adores his older brother. But when he was 16 years old, Rabia was arrested for throwing a stone at an Israeli tank—this is "resistance"—and sentenced to five years. He has been in jail since July 26, 2004.

After Rabia went to prison, Sadjit asked about him all the time and wanted to see him. At first, I didn't want Sadjit to suffer the pain of knowing Rabia was in jail, so I told him that Rabia was in France and that we couldn't reach him by phone. Nevertheless, after a few months he understood what had happened and we took him to see his brother in prison.

Prison visits traumatize all of us; there are no places to sit, for example, and we wait a very long time before authorities allow us to see our family member. Sadjit's first visit was dramatic. He screamed the whole time and insisted that he wanted to take his brother away from there and bring him back home. Since that time, the visits are especially difficult for Sadjit. Sometimes he just screams, sometimes he tries to hurt himself. For a while I felt it was better not to take him with us. But that doesn't work, because he knows when we plan to visit. Besides, it doesn't seem right that he not visit his brother: what if he forgets he has a brother? I can't find a way to make it easier for my son.

The reason for this trauma is the occupation.

For the mothers the occupation means total insecurity and a constant state of fear for our children, our husbands, and our families about what might happen. Will our children be killed? Will our husbands be killed? What will happen to my children when they grow up? Will the future be worse than this horrible present? I have no way of protecting them now, but how bad *could* it get if the situation deteriorates?

I know this is the same for Israeli mothers—in fact, mothers all over the world, including Iraqi mothers. What is it like for the mothers of the foreign soldiers in danger in Iraq right now? If I never have a peaceful moment and always have fear and uncertainty, it must be similar for them.

There is a double standard as the world looks at the Palestinians' situation. For example, with another suicide bombing today, everyone, even Abu Mazen [the Palestinian Authority prime minister, Mahmoud Abbas] and other Palestinian politicians and Bush and the Americans will condemn it. I, too, am against suicide bombing. But where is the international outcry when the Israeli army kills, injures, and harasses Palestinians? Where is the international indignation when Israelis confiscate our land and demolish our homes? Not a day goes by without the Israeli army doing these things. Where is the outrage? I don't understand this. We hope for international understanding and support. We are desperate, yet there is no outrage about these things. Instead, there is always a reason to accept the killing of another Palestinian. When we are driven crazy with stress, frustration, and humiliation, and my people react in this horribly negative way, suddenly everyone takes notice and condemns it.

My son is locked up in Alpha Prison, and two weeks ago the Israelis were beating up Palestinian prisoners. The jaw of a Palestinian political prisoner was broken; another man lost an eye. The Israelis used tear gas and shot rubber bullets. I talked to my son on the phone while he was choking on the gas. Remember, prisoners are unarmed and have no way to defend themselves or fight back, yet this is their treatment. Sadjit knew what was going on from the news. He talked to Rabia on the phone and said he was coming to the prison to beat up the Israelis.

Rabia said, "No, things are okay, nothing is happening," but Sadjit didn't believe that because he already knew the truth.

The other day two young Palestinians were killed, and I wondered how their mothers felt.

When my son went to prison, I felt like my life had ended. I barely cared about the rest of the family for a while. He was my first son, and because his father had been imprisoned so long, I was sort of a single mother. We'd shared a very special relationship, because for so long he was all I had of my marriage and my husband. When he went, I thought my life had ended, and I couldn't think of anything else. I really had to struggle with myself to take care of my family.

AMINA and LENA, West Bank Village

"You are Palestinian. That is the problem."

Amina and her husband, Fahrid, have two small children, one of whom was born with kidney disease. This disease is exacerbated by the politics of water rights, including Israel siphoning off water for settlements and the lethal pollution of rivers. During the interview Fahrid returned home from working on the upcoming elections, ultimately won by Hamas. He had also participated in negotiations to release four Christian Peacemaker team members kidnapped in Iraq. (The negotiations were only partially successful. Eventually, three hostages were released; Tom Fox, the only American in the group, was executed.)

When Lena was a baby she needed dialysis several times a week at local hospitals, usually in Nablus but sometimes in Jerusalem. Since Fahrid doesn't have a permit to enter Israel, I, as Lena's mother, took her to Jerusalem's Hadassah Hospital alone. This meant traveling through Ramallah, passing through Kalandia checkpoint, and paying for a private car to Hadassah. Under normal conditions, these trips from our village to the hospital are short, but now, because of the political situation, they can take a very long time.

All Palestinians going into Israel must pass through the military checkpoints. Sometimes there are very long waits while the army checks each person going or coming. Whether there are many people passing through or just one person who appears more suspicious than everybody else, the rest of us wait while the Israeli military focuses on that one person. Of course, Lena and I arrive late for treatment, and then we have to wait at the hospital too.

If there is a different sort of medical emergency with Lena—when fluid enters her system, for example—and we cannot delay her dialysis, the time spent at a checkpoint can mean life or death for her. During one emergency, we had to go to the Jerusalem hospital but the ambulance did not have a permit to travel into Jerusalem, so I waited in line at the checkpoint with Lena in my arms. Once on the other side of the checkpoint, I would travel by bus to Hadassah. I was frightened because my very sick child required emergency medical attention and I was stuck at a checkpoint with no control over the situation.

The development of settlements such as Ariel brought another set of restrictions: only Israelis are permitted to travel on certain roads, and Palestinians may not enter or drive on them at all. In some cases, we must use agricultural roads, really just tracks through fields and orchards, or travel many miles out of our way to arrive a place only a short distance away. For example, Salfit was a 15-minute trip. Now that road is forbidden, and on the new route it takes more than an hour to reach Salfit—four times longer than before.

Overnight, a road may become forbidden to Palestinians, yet we're never officially informed, nor is a sign ever posted. Instead, we learn about it through trial and error.... This increases our travel time and aggravation, and sometimes means we have to find money to pay fines.

In summer 2003, Lena received a kidney donated by a South African woman. Fahrid's application to travel to Jerusalem for the surgery had not resulted in a travel permit by the time the surgery was scheduled. An Israeli journalist was documenting the story, and when the authorities saw the camera and realized it meant publicity of one sort or another, they wanted to appear humanitarian: Fahrid quickly received a permit. He arrived at the hospital and noticed that people entering the hospital were just getting a cursory pat-down and were not required to show IDs. He was almost through the security zone when someone noticed that the shopping bag he was carrying had Arabic script. The security agents called him back and asked for his paperwork. He showed it and they said he should be in a jail and not in a hospital.

He said, "I have the permit. I have ID. I have a daughter receiving care here. What is the problem?"

They told him, "You are Palestinian. That is the problem."

The security guy told him that because he was Israeli and Fahrid was Palestinian, Fahrid was suspect.

Fahrid said, "Come to Palestine as an Israeli and I will welcome you."

He responded, "You will kill me if I come to Palestine." A woman at the hospital intervened and persuaded the security people that Fahrid was not a threat. After another half hour, they let him pass. Had that woman not intervened on his behalf, he would have been jailed.

Before Fahrid obtained his permit, he used to accompany me as far as he could to the hospital. After passing through the checkpoints, he'd detour and find a vehicle that allowed him to catch up with me in Israel. But he was taking a big risk: had he been stopped by an Israeli and not been able to produce a permit, he might have been beaten, fined, or jailed. Palestinians are jailed for less than that.

While the surgeon who performed Lena's transplant was an Arab doctor, hospital security was harsh toward Palestinians or people who look Palestinian. If I wanted a cup of tea or a short break in the garden while Lena was on dialysis, I had to carry my passport. I was checked entering and leaving the security areas no matter how many times the security people had seen me.

Sometimes the checkpoint guards are quite arbitrary. On one trip, Fahrid and I took Lena to the hospital in Nablus. We don't need permits for Nablus, and I was carrying her medical paperwork and her medical supplies. The soldier looked over these things and let me and Lena pass but refused Fahrid permission to accompany us. Fahrid insisted that he be allowed to pass and the soldiers beat him. I called the soldier's superior officer to intervene and he checked the papers too. Eventually, they permitted Fahrid to leave with us...but we were two hours late for the appointment, and Fahrid had been physically beaten.

Nowadays the checkpoint at Hurawiya is better than it was in 2002 and 2003. Then, soldiers sealed Nablus off altogether to control the resistance. I had no choice but to get Lena to the hospital, however, and I begged the soldiers at the checkpoint to let me through.

They'd say, "No, there is a complete closure and a curfew, and you cannot go in." Then they'd ignore my pleas.

I knew that if I didn't get her to hospital she might die. One winter I climbed over the mountains in the cold and the pouring rain carrying Lena and all her medical equipment. It took over an hour, but I got her to the hospital.

Life under occupation is not easy. No matter what we have to do, we suffer doing it. I suffer taking my daughter to the hospital. I suffer going shopping. Fahrid suffers going to work. Fahrid works in Salfit, about three kilometers from here. Since the main road to Salfit is closed to Palestinians, he must take three different transportation vehicles and spend 30 to 40 minutes for a trip that used to take five minutes. When the soldiers put up a checkpoint, he must wait while they inspect cars one at a time. If he tells them that he has to get to work, they say, "I don't care."

In emergency situations, there are catastrophes. My uncle had a heart attack and died before he could get through the checkpoint. Another local man required emergency dialysis. His family called an ambulance, but it was stopped at a checkpoint and the man died waiting for it.

Today there was a suicide bombing in Netanya. No matter which city or village that young suicide bomber came from, we will all suffer collective punishment for that horrible deed. When I hear about suicide bombers now, I think to myself, there are many Palestinians killed every day by Israelis, by settlers, by soldiers, and their deaths don't make the news. Or, if they are mentioned at all, they appear in the inside pages with little fanfare. Yet when Israelis die by suicide bomb, it is huge news that goes all around the world and shocks everybody. I am not for suicide bombers. I utterly refuse that activity. But they do highlight the fact that Israeli deaths are news while Palestinian deaths—unless spectacular such as suicide bombings—are not news.

Lena's story is not representative, because it is a success. The usual Palestinian story is one that doesn't include donated organs or medical care at Israeli hospitals. If, by some miracle, a Palestinian is permitted care at an Israeli hospital or clinic, his or her permit provides one day of care only—from 5 a.m. to 7 p.m.—during which time she or he is, basically, imprisoned in the facility and cannot go anywhere in the hospital but must stay in the room where care is provided. The usual story is that Palestinians do not even get to the hospital, because they do not get the permits. In our case, our many international and Israeli friends advocate for our child's care. For Palestinians who do not have such friends, there is no hope at all.

UMM MUNRIA AAMER, West Bank—in a house isolated from the village by the security wall

"He sells water now"

Umm Munria and her family live in a house that is completely fenced in: on one side is the Security Wall and on the opposite side is a wire mesh fence erected to protect a Jewish settlement. Gates on the other two sides allow Israeli Defense Force security patrols to pass through the area that used to house the family's greenhouses and chicken farm. The IDF locks all the gates at night, including the only one that allows the family to enter and leave their property.

I live with my husband and six children—the oldest is 22 and the youngest is in kindergarten—in a house that has been totally enclosed: a 30-foot concrete barrier separates us from the village we once were part of; on the other three sides we have 15-foot wire fences separating us from an Israeli settlement built on land that belonged to our village. There are three gates: two vehicle-size gates used only by IDF vehicles patrolling the fence, and one—the size of a doorway—for our family to use.

When we first married, my husband and I ran a thriving business growing garden vegetables in two large greenhouses, we had chickens that provided meat and eggs for sale, and a small restaurant. A little over three years ago the IDF erected this concrete Security Wall, and in the process they demolished our greenhouses. Last year they demolished our chicken farm.

When the army erected the wall, people from peace movements around the world arrived to support our family. An artist from International Women's Peace Service painted a mural of a phoenix rising from the ashes along with a lovely scene that reminds my family of the landscape we used to see from our house.

The Israeli government offered us money for our land, but we refused. This was our home, and our livelihood, years before the Israeli settlers arrived, and we refuse to sell our heritage for a few shekels. We have a right to remain. No Israeli offered compensation for our loss of income or for destroying our business.

After they destroyed our enterprise, the Israeli army installed the doorway-size gate that they would open every morning and lock every evening. The army held the only key; if no one showed up to open the gate, it stayed closed all day. My family could leave the house only when the army opened the gate. This situation was intolerable. The children, for example, could not exit the yard to go to school. Eventually, various NGOs and peace movements worked with the IDF to improve things. Now there are two locks on the gate: the army holds a duplicate of my key. But I am obliged to lock the gate each time it is opened. The army checks that I'm doing this whenever they pass by in their vehicles. There is a third key for a larger second lock on the same gate that the army uses to lock the gate at any time it deems it necessary. I do not have a duplicate of this key. When it is locked my family is locked in—or out—of our home until the army unlocks it.

At first, when the children came home from school unexpectedly and I was in the shower or in another part of the house, I couldn't hear them calling from the gate. There was one occasion when I didn't hear my young daughter calling, and she was outside in the summer sun for two hours. She fell asleep out there and got sunstroke.

For a short time, there was a wide enough space under the gate that the smaller children could scrape under it. The army saw this through the camera they erected to keep an eye on the situation and they added wire under the gate to close that space.

I have not left this yard since the army enclosed it. I am afraid of leaving: What if I am not home and the army finds the place empty—or with only children here? Might they take the opportunity to refuse us reentry to our home? If I leave the house with the smaller children inside, might the soldiers come in and harass them?

On the occasions when friends or family members come to visit, the army often tries to prevent them from entering the yard. If visitors are already inside the house, the army has entered the house uninvited and searched our guests. The army comes any time they want, opens the gates, and drives through our yard. They also honk their horns, rev their engines, or yell from their vehicle as they pass.

The settler neighbors throw stones at our house, sometimes during the day and sometimes during the night. They've broken windows as well as the solar heating system. This scares the children, and they are very afraid of going outside when the settlers are about. The two smallest children often sleep with me, because they are afraid in their own beds.

Sometimes my 22-year-old son comes home late in the evening after visiting friends and the army prevents him from entering his home. Then he goes to stay with nearby relatives or friends. It is very difficult for him as his freedom is so restricted. When the artist came and painted the mural, she had three days to finish the work. Each day she came to the house the army tried to prevent her from entering and finishing her creative work, and this outraged my son.

My husband sells water to farmers two or three days a week. He earns just about enough to live on. My grandfather has some land that we cultivate. Keeping to a schedule is difficult because the gate is inconsistently opened or closed. One must work the land regularly to keep it growing crops, and there are times when we cannot get to it for days and our crops are affected.

Once, the children were happily playing in the yard with a small pot of water and some toy boats and the army soldiers told them they were forbidden to play in that spot. I don't understand why adults do that sort of thing to small kids having fun.

Many people have asked how we continue this way, that it must be so bad. But we are determined to stay here and not be displaced. I've even become used to it. It also means a lot to us that people from outside Israel have been so kind to us and so supportive of our right to stay here. It means a lot to me that people come, care about how we are, and tell the story of our home and the lives of the Palestinians.

WHERE ARE THEY NOW?

Sihan Rashid

Sihan continues to work at the Palestinian Counseling Center headquartered in Beit Hanina. While Sihan presents information on Palestinians in the West Bank, Gaza's residents are not spared psychological trauma. In his article "Terror and Starvation in Gaza," published in the *New Statesman*, renowned investigative journalist and documentary filmmaker John Pilger writes, "A genocide is engulfing the people of Gaza while a silence engulfs its bystanders." Pilger was invited by Dr. Khalid Dahlan, a Gaza psychiatrist, to observe a clinic of 30 traumatized children. After receiving a pencil and paper and being asked to draw, each child produced pictures of "grotesque acts of terror and of women streaming tears." Dr. Dahlan told Pilger, "Once you look at the rates of exposure to trauma you see why: 99.2 percent of their homes were bombarded; 97.5 percent were exposed to tear gas; 96.6 percent witnessed shootings; 95.8 percent witnessed bombardment and funerals; almost a quarter saw family members injured or killed." Pilger goes on to quote an article in *Le Figaro* by former senior U.N. relief official Jan Egeland and Jan Eliasson, then foreign minister of Sweden, describing a people "living in a cage," cut off from travel by land, sea, or air, with no reliable electrical power and little water, and tortured by hunger, disease, and incessant attacks by Israeli troops and planes. "Some 1.4 million people, mostly children, are piled up in one of the most densely populated regions of the world, with no freedom of movement, no place to run and no space to hide."

"Jamila"

Rabia remains in prison while his family awaits his return in their West Bank village. When he is finally released, he may not recognize the village he grew up in. The wire mesh fence that was being erected through the village's olive orchards when I visited is complete. Indeed, it continues into the distance, with a wide scar of bare earth on either side of the barrier, and there is now only one way to enter or exit the village.

Amina

Amina and Fahrid are doing well under the circumstances and recently had a third child, a daughter. Lena is thriving and recently started school. As Fahrid pointed out, Lena was unusually fortunate to receive a kidney transplant. Kidney disease, not uncommon in Palestinians, is exacerbated by the region's water politics. The United Nations reported in late 2007 that 460 out of 720 Palestinian water wells had been destroyed, were expropriated, or had dried up due to Israel's over-exploitation of resources, which has resulted in the salination of West Bank aquifers. While Israelis consumed 13,425 cubic feet of water per person annually, Palestinians' annual per capita consumption was 3,775 to 5,510 cubic feet. Moreover, many existing wells have been absorbed by Israel. While illegal Israeli settlers have no restrictions on water use, rationing is imposed on Palestinian farmers and they are penalized for exceeding their allotment. The levels of salinity are considerably higher than the safety bar set by the World Health Organization, rendering water unsuitable for irrigation or human consumption, which could lead to kidney failure, congestive heart failure, and other serious health problems. Finally, with the 2006 election, aid from the West decreased, depriving Palestinians with chronic renal failure of new dialysis machines and leaving them with a severe shortage of tubes and filters for existing equipment.

Umm Munria

The family remains in the house surrounded by walls and fences, although Umm Munria risked leaving her house for the first time to make the hajj to Mecca in 2007. As they continue to struggle financially, they have a new aspiration: to arrange for an artistically gifted daughter to enter college to study art—influenced, perhaps, by the mural painted on the Security Wall surrounding her home.

4—LEBANON

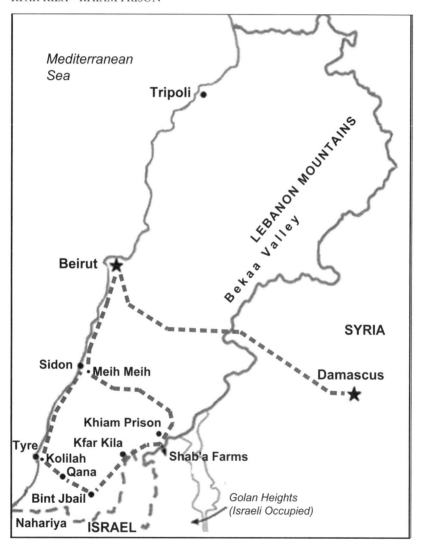

They would
caress their
children's hair
in the dusk¹

ISRAELI SOLDIERS CAREFULLY RAKE the beaches near the Lebanese border to track footprints of infiltrators who may have breached the border overnight. In 1979, they missed signs that Fatah had entered Nahariya in a motor-powered dinghy until the group invaded a four-story apartment house. *Time* framed the story of what followed with the headline, "Here is Israel's history in a single incident: the nation continually at war; the nation as mother protecting her children; the nation unwittingly suffocating her young for the wars in which it is caught."² The article went on to describe how terrified Israeli resident Semadar Haran hid with her 2-year-old daughter Yael in a utility closet. When Yael began to cry, Semadar described clamping her hand over her child's mouth to keep her quiet, and inadvertently suffocated her. Semadar's husband, Danny, was shot to death on the beach allegedly by 16-year-old Fatah member Sumir Kuntar who was further described as cracking open the head of the older Haran child on a rock.

There is no "single incident" describing Lebanon's history, although Israel's founding made that history more complex. For one thing, a large majority of the fleeing Palestinians sought refuge there. Today, the twelve official refugee camps scattered throughout Lebanon house more than 215,890 registered and 10,200 unregistered refugees.³

Another incident on July 12, 2006 resulted in the Israeli Air Force bombarding Lebanon for thirty-four days. Nevertheless, it is never entirely clear what actually happens in the region. In this case, Israel claimed that the Israeli Defense Force was "forced" to respond when "Hezbollah terrorists" fired rockets at an Israeli border patrol and kidnapped two soldiers. Hezbollah's military arm claimed that the Israeli patrol was beyond the border and inside Lebanese territory...and that Israel could swap the two Israeli soldiers for Lebanese political prisoners anytime. Instead, Israel attacked with warplanes and Israeli prime minister Ehud Olmert threatened to bomb *Lebanon* (not "Hezbollah terrorists") "back twenty years," stating that Hezbollah was guilty of "an act of war."[4]

Two years later, in July 2008, the remains of the kidnapped IDF soldiers, Eldad Regev and Ehud Goldwasser, were swapped for five Lebanese and Palestinian prisoners along with the remains of nearly 200 others. After 28 years in an Israeli prison for the Nahariya killings, Samir Kuntar—now in this mid-forties—was among those turned over to Lebanon. Judging by newspaper accounts of the swap, it is likely that the ongoing cycle of incident compounded by further incident will continue. Israeli President Shimon Peres pardoned Kuntar, saying, "In this decision there is no forgiveness or absolution for the murderer's heinous actions. I will not forget, and I won't forgive." Sumir Kuntar arrived in Lebanon to a welcoming crowd and stated, "I return today from Palestine but believe me I will not return until I go back to Palestine." And rather than returning them to Lebanon the Syria-based Popular Front for the Liberation of Palestine-General Command said that it wants its members' bodies to remain on Palestinian land, "as the fighters would have wished." Thirty-one year old Goldwasser had been born in Nahariya and likely grew up influenced by the events of 1979.

After the bombardment of Lebanon began in July, delegates from the U.N., Canada, Cyprus, Egypt, France, Germany, Greece, Jordan, Russia, Saudi Arabia, Spain, Turkey, the European Union, the World Bank, and Lebanon attending a conference in Rome's foreign ministry called for an Israeli ceasefire. The United States and Britain refused to support the call. On July 30, Israel promised to suspend air strikes for forty-eight hours after more than sixty civilians were killed in Qana. Prime Minister Olmert expressed "deep sorrow" over the deaths and said that the area around the village had been used by Hezbollah to launch rockets into Israel. He told Secretary of State Condoleezza Rice that the war would go on for another "ten to fourteen days" until Israel's military's objectives were met.

Sheikh Hassan Nasrallah, the Hezbollah Party leader, warned of new long-range missile attacks on Israeli cities "if the barbaric aggression against us continues." About 115 Hezbollah rockets hit Israel.

Fatalities included 159 Israelis, of which thirty-nine were civilians killed in rocket attacks. Lebanon's Higher Relief Council said the majority of the more than 1,000 Lebanese killed were civilians. UNICEF said that about a third of those were children. Israel claims 600 Hezbollah fighters were killed, but that figure has not been substantiated. Hezbollah claims only 250 losses among its fighters. And on it goes: political recriminations, dissembling, and finger-pointing while civilians take the brunt of the killings and the pain.

The United Nations brokered a ceasefire on August 14, 2006, although the bombing actually ended when Israel lifted its naval blockade of Lebanon on September 8th.

Around 200,000 to 300,000 Israelis and about 974,184 Lebanese were internally displaced; about 200,000 Lebanese remain displaced[5]; more than 30,000 Lebanese homes were destroyed.

Anyone following events in the region may find that statements from politicians, journalists, and academicians contradict one another in facts and in the subtleties that sway the gullible toward a particular worldview. Lara Marlowe, former *Time* Beirut bureau chief, said she quit her post partly through frustration with the fact that the reports she filed were distorted with inaccuracies before publication. "I'd write that, say, 200 people were killed and the story would publish with the number reduced to, say, twenty," she writes. "Under the guise of objectivity, there is no attempt to determine who tells the truth, who is lying."[6] Pacifica Radio journalist Dennis Bernstein concurs: "Self-censorship has sunk deep into the bones. U.S. journalists have lost their understanding of what it means to seek the truth."[7] Moreover, anyone criticizing Israel runs the risk of being accused of anti-Semitism. Not only does this negate the loss and terror of the region's people, it muddies definitions of anti-Semitism.

Six months after the Qana "incident" I traveled to Lebanon to seek the truth for myself.

Each fragment deeming itself a nation[8]

The day I departed the United States, three gunmen assassinated 34-year-old cabinet minister Pierre Gemayel, the son of former president Amin Gemayel and grandson of Pierre Gemayel, founder of the Christian Phalange Party. I arrived very early in January, when the months-old "tent city" erected in downtown Beirut was still the center for peaceful protests against Lebanese prime minister Fouad Siniora, who was accused of corruption, graft, and being a Western puppet.[9]

My luggage was lost in transit, it rained my first four days there, and I trudged the Hamra district in stale, soggy clothes purchasing boots, socks, and an umbrella. As taxi driver Maurice schlepped me to the airport each day for another elusive bag, we passed the new Cité Sportif and I remembered the 1982 massacre of Palestinians in Sabra and Shatila. Journalist and author Robert Fisk, who was in the camps that day, writes that the "brand-new marble stadium was built to replace the old arena torn down after the war...but the testimony of what may lie beneath its foundations—and its frightful implications" may one day be excavated. Maybe then we'll learn why the Palestinian husbands and sons the Israelis turned over to Phalange militiamen were never seen again: Fisk suspects they were likely buried in mass graves.[10]

Judith Palmer Harik, author of *Hezbollah: The Changing Face of Terrorism*, and I threaded through the ropes and wire barricades of "tent city" and appreciated billboards depicting Condoleezza Rice as a schoolmarm lecturing Siniora with the caption: "Lecture as much as you want, it won't do any good." Judith explained that, far from the image of Hezbollah sold to Americans in the United States—that it is a major terrorist organization and irregular mercenary force—the group is well respected in Lebanon. Indeed, Hezbollah's Reconstruction Campaign, Jihad al-Binaa, has evolved a successful social services delivery system that funds hospitals, schools, water works, garbage and sewage facilities, agrotechnical programs, free or low-cost housing, credit, and medical, social, and technical assistance.

Judith says, "I make it a habit to mention these programs to the Lebanese to gauge their reactions. They invariably express amazement at the extensive work Hezbollah is doing and regret at the government's failure to display the same initiative and commitment. One Lebanese Christian told me, 'Everyone knows the work is politically motivated, but it also shows what faith can do.'"[11]

South Lebanon

Old Sidon dates back 6,000 years as a Phoenician trading city where Persians, Greeks, Romans, Byzantines, Arabs, Crusaders, and Mamluks left their mark. The Bible tells of Jesus of Nazareth passing through.

Ein el-Halweh refugee camp, on the outskirts of Sidon near the village of Mieh Mieh, has more than 394,500 registered Palestinian refugees—about 10 percent of Lebanon's total refugee population. Palestinians are prohibited by Lebanese law from working in more than 70 trades and professions, and unemployment is widespread. Despite six decades in Lebanon, Palestinians are still considered foreigners and have no social or civil rights, limited access to the government's public health and educational facilities, and no access to public social services. Most rely entirely on the United Nations relief agency for education, health, and social services.

Ra'fat, a Palestinian, acted as my driver and translator in south Lebanon. His story is common to displaced Palestinians throughout the Greater Middle East. His family lives in Saudi Arabia. He was an engineering student at Baghdad University when the U.S. invasion terminated his studies and he left for Jordan. He came to Lebanon to scope out opportunities to finish his engineering degree—and found them limited by high tuition fees and his Palestinian heritage.

We set off from Sidon for Kfar Kila on the Lebanon–Israel border via Marjayoun, a predominantly Christian town of about 3,000 that was headquarters for the Israel-affiliated South Lebanon army during Israel's occupation of Lebanon from 1982 to 2000.

Every bridge of any significance south of Beirut was bombed during the 34-Day War, and a total of 91 were hit throughout the country. The United Nations and human rights organizations state that Israel dropped more than 4 million cluster bombs—most in the south—in a country with a total population of less than 4 million. Billboards throughout Lebanon illustrate at least six varieties of cluster bomb— some look like exotic fruit, some like children's toys, and some look like rocks.

At a checkpoint outside Marjayoun, a Lebanese army officer refused us access without written permission. We turned around whispering about driving out of sight of the checkpoint then cutting over fields... then remembered the cluster bombs. Instead, we returned to Sidon to the offices of the Grand Sérail. Our first visit was disappointing: "Come back in two days." I was leaving the country in five days, so that wasn't an option. I called someone who talked to someone who talked to someone else, and we were invited to return for our papers the next day.

That night we traveled to Kolilah where, at the Internet café, Ra'fat ran into an old friend, Ali, who introduced us to his family. Their house was festooned with colorful ribbons announcing a family member's recent return from making the hajj (pilgrimage) to Mecca.

Ali's mother, Elham, served tea and described how they'd evacuated their house and fled to the mountains during the war. (Her story begins on page 134.)

Next morning at the Grand Sérail's offices, a young man ahead of us in line learned that he had been refused permission to travel in the south.

He slammed his hand on the desk, "This is ridiculous! I'm *American*. I'm *from* America! I'm here to *help* you! You *can't* turn me away!"

This aid worker, having come all the way from the United States to help, hadn't learned rule number one: never impugn a bureaucracy to the bureaucrats running it. He clattered down the stairs banging his hands against the wall. The bureaucrats glanced at one another and shook their heads. Then they handed Ra'fat a small slip of paper with Arabic script: "If you have questions about these travelers, call this phone number."

We modified our travel plans and set off for Qana, known in the Holy Bible as Cana, where Jesus of Nazareth changed water into wine. These days, villagers sell DVDs of Qana's massacres.

Qana is Cana...and close to carnage

Sixty people died while hiding in a basement in 2006. I wanted to recognize Qana's suffering. I also wanted to understand whether I was missing any nuance that may explain why perpetrators are never called to account. Were the people of Qana particularly violent and thus, perhaps by some Biblical eye-for-an-eye philosophy, deserving of massive violence? Were they overtly militant? Did Qana have modern fortifications that might protect vicious terrorists?

Robert Fisk's account of Israel's April 1996 "Operation Grapes of Wrath" massacre in Qana had touched me deeply:

> There were heaps of blood-soaked blankets, many containing body parts; some of the Fijian U.N. soldiers were walking through this slaughterhouse with black plastic bin-liners, picking up here a finger, there a baby's arm. A U.N. soldier stood amid a sea of bodies and, without saying a word, held aloft a decapitated child.
>
> Another said, "The Israelis have just told us that they'll stop shelling the area. Are we supposed to thank them?"
>
> Behind him, in the wreckage of the U.N. battalion's conference room, a pile of corpses was burning. The roof had crashed in flames onto their bodies before my eyes. When I walked toward them, I slipped on a human hand.
>
> "The Hezbollah fired six Katyusha rockets from near our position. The shells came two minutes later. But the Israelis know this has been a U.N. battalion headquarters for eighteen years. They knew we had 600 refugees here," [the Fijian soldier continued].
>
> Indeed they did. The Israelis knew that 5,200 civilians too poor to flee to Beirut were crowded into the compounds of the 4,500-strong U.N. force. The U.N. had told them...battalion headquarters were clearly marked on Israel's maps. The U.N. buildings were plastered with white and black U.N. signs. They were lit up at night. Not a soul in southern Lebanon was ignorant of their location.[12]

On May 10, 1996, an Israeli army sergeant whose artillery battery shelled the refugees was quoted in the Israeli weekly *Kol Ha'ir*: "It's a war, in a war things happen. It's just a bunch of Arabs. Why are you taking it so hard?"

General Moshe Ya'alon was indicted as a war criminal and mass murderer for his role in this massacre. But no one took that so hard either: he became Chief of Staff for the IDF from 2002 to 2005.

Ra'fat and I walked around what had been the U.N. compound and looked into the charred remains of the U.N. headquarters where so many died. A rusty shell casing lies amid the debris. There are two memorials: a shiny black marble pyramid with chiseled names of the dead, close to the main road, and a series of coffins with a large photo collage backdrop depicting scenes from the disaster, laid out on the plaza and site of the massacre.

We drove to the village outskirts, found Maryam and her family by sheer chance, and listened to their stories. (Their account begins on page 139.) We returned, deeply shaken, to one of the few new constructions: the memorial built over the ruined concrete basement foundation whose coffin-shaped marble headstones bear victims' names and ages—the youngest 10 months old. The yellow flags of Hezbollah and green flags of the Lebanese militia Amal fluttered alongside a red sun-faded banner expressing Korea's condolences. There were no signs of condolence sent from the good people of the United States.

A vendor honked his horn as he drove over the battered road. Two women appeared, picked at and purchased vegetables, and the vendor departed. Life went on in Qana. People got on with their lives. Perhaps this "bunch of Arabs" is too patient.

Bint Jbail

In Bint Jbail at dusk, the smell of char lingered in the air. Fluttering flags—yellow for Hezbollah, green for Amal, and black for the dead—lent a festive air to the bomb-shattered town. The ambulance that had been carrying wounded civilians when missiles struck it remained parked on a main street. At least one missile entered the front window right below one of the bright red crosses marking the white vehicle as a medical conveyance; the back windows are blown out. Pilots *might* have missed the red crosses on the back and side of this ambulance, but they could not have missed the large red crosses on the vehicle's roof and hood, which must have been visible from the altitude at which these aircraft attack.

A resident of Sidon told me, "I was here just before the Israelis departed. There were bodies—including the bodies of many Israeli soldiers—scattered all around. One devout Muslim gently gathered them so that they could be retrieved by family or the IDF for burial. The Israelis collecting their fallen were very angry and forced him away at gunpoint."[13]

Bint Jbail grew up around a valley. The main road curves along the valley's edge, and on the bomb-cratered valley floor stands a three-story school—rebar twisting out of concrete slabs—that is beyond repair. Residences dotting the area are typical of those found throughout Lebanon: large enough that some resemble American apartment buildings and house several generations. While many young Lebanese emigrate—throughout the world they're known for their business acumen—those who remain marry and raise their own children in apartments constructed above the last addition to the family home. Many of Bint Jbail's multigeneration homes were shattered in the summer bombardment. Blasted exterior walls expose dull gray or burnt-black interiors. Nothing remains to indicate that people loved, laughed, studied, cried, and expressed hope and desire here. Where do the knickknacks of family life—photos, tea tables, toasters—go when a home is bombed? Are rugs, coffeepots, kitchen utensils, windows, doors, gardens, and fruit trees simply obliterated? Do they lie forlorn under the piles of rubble?

It felt unseemly to photograph a red velvet sofa poking through debris…yet my fury was greater than my shame. How dare sanctimonious politicians and their media mouthpieces spout claptrap about "terror," "terrorism," and "terrorists" when all around me was a testament to organized and systematic terror perpetrated by the same people and masquerading as self-righteous self-defense. This devastation is what Secretary of State Condoleezza Rice sold as "the birth pangs of a new democratic Middle East."[14] And the American people swallowed it.

A real war on terror would outlaw the arms industry, stop pushing weapons as free or low-cost components of foreign aid, valorize people over capital, insist upon open discussion of Arab grievances regarding Western powers invading and supporting the colonization of their lands, and promote alternatives to the West's geostrategic self-interest and fossil fuel addiction.

Kfar Kila

The bright lights of an Israeli border patrol shone in the shallow valley below the road near Kfar Kila. I was already outside the car readying my camera when Ra'fat and I looked at one another and simultaneously said, "No. No picture. The flash might set off the soldiers and they could shoot us."

The head of the family, Ali, and his wife, Fatima, two daughters and three sons (one of whom is also named Ali) were living on the same floor of their large house. The upper story, charred and bullet-pocked, was uninhabitable. Their kitchen, however, was warm and their generosity evident as we tucked into dinner: tabouli, oven-warm bread, hummus, and lamb kebabs.

After dinner, sitting on cushions around the hot stove, we watched Al-Zahora, the "reality" TV channel depicting footage of American troops blown up by IEDs in Iraq. As a military mom and GI Rights counselor, I displayed my agitation by compulsively feeding the stove with dregs from the olive harvest—pressed, dried olive pits and skins are cheap fuel in Kfar Kila.

Perhaps sensing my horror, Fatima asked, "Do you know anyone in Iraq?"

Ra'fat translated my story, and for a while we watched the grainy footage in silence: distance shots of kaffiya-masked men loading ordnance into outmoded rocket launchers and chanting *Allah-u Akbar, Allah-u Akbar*; close-ups of hasty hands hiding bombs inside animal carcasses on dusty roads; the camera crew waiting. Then, the inevitable U.S. Humvee full of well-trained but woefully unprepared young American flesh arrived. A flash and a bang...and another unit was sacrificed.

Fatima said, "It is very hard for us, too, to see young people die like this. Yet you Americans send more soldiers to a war that you will never win. The Iraqi people will never give up their struggle against this occupation. Nevertheless, our hearts are sore to see the killing."

Ali senior mused, "I did same thing when we were fighting the Israelis during the occupation. Fatima nursed our wounded with a gun over her shoulder. Nothing much has changed, except now the Americans themselves are fighting instead of only supporting Israel to fight us."

The younger Ali and his friend, Ahmed, talked about their war experiences. Just the way things happen in small-town America, Kfar Kila's poverty and lack of options recruited these young men. Ali junior drove a truck for the IDF. Ahmed was a combatant for the South Lebanon army. One year after Ahmed's induction the IDF left Lebanon and he considered accepting the second-class status of non-Jews in

Israel. He realized he was deeply Lebanese and wanted to remain in Lebanon, so he instead surrendered to the new security forces. He was sentenced to five years in jail and was tortured by Hezbollah members incensed that he'd fought for the SLA. He displayed the deep scars from knife wounds on his chest and calves.

Ali spent six months washing dishes in a Tel Aviv restaurant before returning home. Both men were harassed by Hezbollah after they returned to Kfar Kila. Hezbollah later relented after it became clear that the prey of the poverty draft were doubly victimized when their own people harassed them.

Ali says, "Hezbollah helps our village now. There are no more problems from them."

Meanwhile, the IDF patrols less than half a mile away. I asked, "Do you think the Israelis will come again?"

"Certainly. Perhaps they will come next summer. Even now they drive their tanks past [United Nations Interim Forces in Lebanon] posts whenever they feel like it, and UNIFIL does nothing."

I told him, "Every day in Lebanon I hear of people, young and old, dying from cluster bombs. Surely they will not come so soon?"

He nodded. "*Inshallah.*" The family smiled and repeated, "*Inshallah*" (God willing).

At dawn, Fatima and I stood on the patio and watched the sun rise behind the Israeli outpost whose high-power lights had pierced the previous night's peaceful darkness; Kibbutz Ma'alot sprawled below it.

Fatima gave me a bottle of olive oil made from their olive harvest and Ali showed me his collection of missile shells. Then Ra'fat and I departed for Khiam Prison.

At the Fatimah Gate Israeli soldiers and Lebanese villagers come within touching distance of one another. Enlarged photographs hanging here display the youth and earnestness of Lebanon's martyrs.

Khiam Prison overlooks the glorious panorama of Sheba'a Farms, approximately eight square miles richly endowed with fresh water, currently occupied by Israel but disputed by Lebanon, Israel, and to some extent, Syria. Depopulated since 1967, this land of stunning beauty belies the history of misery in the region. The prison facility was bombed during the summer, but the Lebanese refuse to remove the debris, saying it contains evidence of the torture carried out by both IDF and SLA during Israel's occupation. They've turned it into another memorial, and throughout the pulverized compound, enlarged photographs map the original cells: here is the female prisoners' block; there is the chamber where guards used electric shock on prisoners. Photographs of still-missing Lebanese resistance fighters hang from abandoned Israeli military vehicles. If the people depicted here are not already dead, they're in Israeli prisons. Among them are the political prisoners that Hezbollah wants Israel to release, some of whose remains may have been swapped in July 2008.

Four hours after I departed Beirut, protesters closed the airport, burned tires in the streets, and blocked main roads. Stone throwing escalated into street fighting, then shooting; four people died and more than 150 were wounded.

AFIFA DIRANI ARSANIOS, Beirut

"Something terrible happened in America…"

Afifa Dirani Arsanios is president of the Lebanese Association of SOS Children's Villages[15] and a member of the International Senate of SOS Kinderdorf International in Innsbruck, Austria. During our interview, Afifa served tea in her Beirut apartment, which is decorated with gorgeous antique furniture inherited from her parents and in-laws. She reports that none of her own children find the furniture interesting. "Then again," she says, "how can one live with such things and have to consider moving them when life appears so temporary in this troubled region?" This is a common refrain in Lebanon.

Something terrible happened in America on September 11, 2001, and many young people wanted to do something about it. But war is war, and terrible and unexpected things happen in war. Look at Iraq…. I hope that it is moving toward something better, but it is taking so many unexpected directions and creating so much fragmentation and trauma in the population. The population of Iraq, in a way, is eating itself...there are too many levels of complexity...and if this goes on much longer it will really ruin the Iraqi people.

On the other hand, the story of extremism is something terrible. Any extremism, even the kind that means to be "doing good," becomes toxic! It takes the spirit of, say, religion, and interprets it in a way that was not meant. Anyone who knows anything about Islam or Christianity knows that taking it to extremes is not the intrinsic message. Some Muslims have taken what is in the Qur'an and abused it by twisting the spirit of it.

Take women in Islam, for example: the 1,500-year-old message of Islam was one of the first holy messages to promote women's rights. Before Islam, many baby girls were killed as soon as they were born... this still happens in some countries outside the Muslim world, but Islam forbids it. There are very clear statements in the Qur'an that this is forbidden and that females are human beings with all the rights of human beings. So with the new Islamist direction—those who want to kill the intrinsic messages—Islam has been distorted. It is sad, because this is causing a counterreaction from the Christian West. We witnessed a small example of this in Lebanon during the civil war when each group was thinking that their religion was the best and the other was "bad."

There is a growing gap now between the East and the West. I'm not sure who is mobilizing this, or for what reason. Our generation was so open-minded when I attended the American University in Beirut. I am a Muslim married to a Christian, and that was a huge jump into open-mindedness on both our parts. Back then, we thought of learning Esperanto, an international language that everybody would understand. That was an atmosphere that symbolized our openness and true globalization. Now every small group cocoons itself in a small mental and physical ghetto and defends itself against the "other" in the name of culture or religion or whatever. It is terrible.

I work for a worldwide organization, SOS Children's Villages, funded by private people and groups, and the funds are nonconditional. Donors are usually people who are committed to the cause of children and are friends of SOS Children. Anyone giving money cannot dictate an agenda. We need the money but we will not take it with conditions attached. We received a donation locally, and because we did not play their propaganda game during our inauguration they wanted it back. We returned it and felt liberated by that act of independence.

There are about ten or 15 houses in each village, and each house is headed by a woman recruited and trained by SOS as a mother. She stays with a maximum of nine or ten children. We take the whole family and keep all the brothers and sisters in the same home. They go to school with other children in the community. Normally we do not build schools within the village unless the quality of the school or education requires it. If we have a school in a village, then children from the surrounding areas can attend. This is a way to mix and socialize children within their communities. The idea is to reintegrate the children afterwards with their own community; we also keep them in touch with whoever remains of their biological family. Often the mother is dead or both parents are dead...sometimes each parent has gone off and started another family, and the SOS children are left to fend for themselves.

The percentage of success is remarkable, because we somehow succeed in protecting the kids from the major irreversible mistakes like getting involved with drugs and alcohol. Remember, many of these children come from difficult backgrounds that they never really get over.

We try to take mothers at the age of about 30. Some mothers are about 27, but that is risky. We don't want a mother to set up relationships with children and then leave to get married herself. We find mothers by announcing through the media or word of mouth, and the women stay in training for about two years—first as aunts, then as mothers if they succeed.

During the civil war—1975 to 1990—many women lost their husbands and were left to take care of their families alone. So we started the Family Strengthening Program in 1986 to prevent the abandonment or institutionalization of children and to keep the family where they are, rather than admit the children to the SOS village. These families are selected according to several criteria: they have to have no other options, they have to be really poor, and the children have to be small— although if there are older children in the family that is fine, as we train them to support the family eventually. We try to rehabilitate the family economically so that they can stand on their own feet. SOS is for all religions and backgrounds. We look at the victim and not his or her religion or color or anything like that, although in Lebanon SOS mothers are usually the same religious background as their SOS children, so that the children aren't forced to adjust to a new religion too.

The Family Strengthening Program serves the children in their own home. If the house is not good enough, we renovate the house. We try to help according to skills already in place and the ones that are needed, and we also give a small loan with a contract that the family will pay it back...no interest. We're not too worried about the repayment, but more that the family has a sense of responsibility to the spirit of the contract.

This program has a pilot project to go to the families in the community and serve there. The first project was in the Bekaa Valley. This small eight-house village has a big social center with many programs including women's empowerment programs within the community and youth programs that are owned by the young people of the community.

The Bekaa Valley has very fertile land, but it is the poorest region of Lebanon, with few, if any, affordable governmental services. The poverty in the region allowed a few private groups with political and ideological orientations—from all religions—to offer services and gain ground. SOS has this distinction that it couldn't care less about politics: it is nonpolitical, nonreligious, it is human! We strive to build human dignity and improve lives and that is our mission.

Hezbollah has been doing a lot of systematic, excellent services reaching out to Christians and Muslims. This is their strong point. They work strategically and very intelligently. When there was a big snowstorm a few years ago, they supplied fuel and food to all those in need.On the Christian side, the militias and so on are doing similar work in their own constituencies. In fact, they are doing what the government is supposed to do.

Let me give an example of one of our children.

During the latest war the Bekaa Valley was a target because the majority there is Shi'a and because Hezbollah is there. We had just inaugurated our village there and had about 30 children. The day the war stopped, a little baby boy about one or two days old was placed in front of SOS's door. Later someone called and said there was a baby in a small box and to please pick him up because there are many stray dogs around. We picked him up and registered his abandonment with the police and government, and the baby was handed to SOS.

We decided to call him Salam [Peace], as he came to us on the 14th of August, the first day of the ceasefire.

Salam is now 5 months old. He had a growth in his head with water inside. We had scheduled an MRI and I asked the village director to call me as soon as we had results. I was intensely concerned about him, because I didn't want Peace to die; it would be a very bad omen if our little Peace died. I just learned today that Peace's growth is benign and will disappear with diuretics; it doesn't require [drainage] tubes.

Salam will stay at SOS, if he lives, until he is about 19 years old and we will prepare him for his own independence, help him with housing later on, with jobs, and if he is ready to go to university, SOS will support him.

One of our first university graduates has a Ph.D. in urbanization from France. He belongs to the first family that came to the first SOS village. Any children that have the ability to attend university will be supported by SOS or by a sponsor willing to support him or her.

Most of our children are not abandoned like Salam. Most of our children have parents or family who come to SOS villages and visit their children. Circumstances in their lives were such that they couldn't keep their children. Usually we know the parents, talk to them, have an understanding with them, and the children regularly go on vacation to visit their families, and so on. We encourage and nurture continued relationships with families, but at the same time, the children come first and their routines and schedules are honored. The families cannot just drop in on the children any time they feel like it.

But we do have a few cases of abandonment like Salam. And these cases seem to be increasing—especially now, and I'm not sure why. Is it poverty? Is it the system of honor killings? Is it both? I think it is both, but nevertheless they are increasing. To describe the system of honor killings: a girl who is unmarried and becomes pregnant might go into hiding somewhere. Then when she gives birth to the child she abandons the baby immediately and goes back to normal life or she risks being killed. This exists in Lebanon, although not as much as it exists in Jordan or other places…but here it exists especially in the Bekaa Valley and other areas where tribal honor is paramount. A young girl may not blemish the honor of the family.

Salam must be one of these children.

Children do ask about their origins when they are older, and we try to tell them as honestly as possible—with the help of a psychologist—what we know. The private life of each child is kept very confidential.

No one singles out a child like Salam and says, "Hey, you have no parents...."

We have many social workers who study each case—sometimes, cases are referred by a clergyman, another NGO, or individuals—and we take their recommendations seriously and proceed with our investigation. There are times when a parent is abusive toward the children, and we'll try to upgrade the parenting skills. We recognize that some biological families are hopeless cases and dangerous to the children: drug addiction, incest, whatever. We do have success stories of healing these families.

We also work with psychological trauma. After the recent war the trauma seems to be greater than ever; it is, frankly, almost unbelievable. It has had the most impact on children of all the wars....perhaps an accumulation of years of trauma on families is now showing up in this huge increase. Many teachers and people working with children are saying the same thing.

The bottom line is, for 34 days there was a war in Lebanon. Who started it, how it started, whose fault it is, what it was about, is not my concern. My concern is the result on the children—and on the parents too, of course, but mainly the children. At SOS the children may be more protected because we are trained and set up to deal with adversity. But within families, kids are reacting in a traumatized manner to doors slamming and other normal sounds.

One kid heard a civilian airplane overhead and said, "Let's hide the toys, because Israel is going to strike now." So kids nowadays know that airplanes—any airplanes as far as they are concerned—can hit their homes and kill.

There is a generation from the 15-year war—my kids and other kids who are now in their late 20s and early 30s—born and brought up during war. These, I hope, are healing from that trauma, but we're not sure. Now there is a new generation from this war, and they are more traumatized because they don't know when another catastrophe will happen...and it is generalized as coming from above, from the air.

The issue is that people traumatized by war and not fully healed are themselves parenting children traumatized by war. This is becoming the normal state of affairs in families; people have distorted feelings and distorted concepts of life and death. They lack hope and they lack a sense of certainty. Something as simple as knowing that a loved one will come home at the end of the day, or even that there will be home to come home to. There is a prevalent sense of "Why bother trying?" and "What's the use?"

Lebanon has a huge brain-drain problem. Our best and brightest are leaving the country in droves because they do not see a future here. Those staying behind are the older people, people who have less to offer or less ability to pick up and go, people with less hope, less ability to pull off a "miracle future" for the country. I have two children who live elsewhere, one in London and one in Paris. Across the board, all religions, all persuasions, I can list hundreds of families whose children are living elsewhere. All of our children are learning English so they can get away.

Mrs. FADIAH JOBEILY, Sidon

"We've been in this situation for over 25 years"

Mrs. Jobeily, principal of Sidon Secondary Public School for Girls, generously made time in her busy schedule to grant an interview, serve coffee and delicious Lebanese confections, and show me around the school.

We have around 800 students most of whom are Lebanese, although we also have students of different nationalities, religions, and sects as well as from different parts of this city and from different cities. You'll find a complete microcosm of Lebanese society here.

After the civil war [1975–90] we had a lot of clashes about ideas among people. Each person or community followed a particular leader. From that we realized that we had to create a new way of thinking, and that this starts in childhood.

At this school, we work on socializing the children to get along with one another and creating a world as if nothing bad is happening, where everyone is working for the benefit of the nation. We want our country to be united, and we believe that what we're doing here is a reflection of what we want in the greater society around us. The school's mission statement is that we want our school to be the way the nation should be.

During the summer war, the school was home to about 600 people who sought refuge from the bombs in the south. It was horrible to take care of so many people with disrupted lives: old people, young children, women, and men.

We had two births in the school, and it was a very bad situation for those women and their new babies. We didn't have any supplies here, so we asked our neighbors and friends to help: if you have extra clothes, underwear, anything and everything, please bring it.

One of my neighbors—a 7-year-old girl—took her doll and some of her clothes and gave them to the school. I gave them to a 5-year-old girl who had nothing, and nothing to do to keep herself busy. She'd been asking her mother for her things from home, her clothes, her toys, but her mother had brought nothing at all, since her first concern was getting her children away from the bombing safely. She'd had to leave everything behind; she didn't even know if her house had survived the bombing. The 7-year-old wanted to do something for her countrypeople, and on her own, she figured out what she could contribute that might help.

During and after the war we had representatives from many institutes visiting and there was lots of press and so on, but mostly we had local people helping local people. Many who sought refuge here returned to their villages, although they're living in tents because their homes were destroyed and they can't afford to rebuild.

This war, besides destroying infrastructure, is also destroying personalities. I have a teacher here who has always engaged in civic and school activities. Now, when I ask her to do things that she has always been ready to do in the past, she says, "No, that is not my job. I'm sick."

Since the war she has had many aches and pains. She feels depressed and has no energy for things she participated in before. She tells me that she thinks she needs help from a psychiatrist, and I agree. Then she'll say that she is fine, that she just has a few aches and that she is very tired. It is alarming to see this very qualified teacher, a supervisor in school, refuse to take any responsibility.

She said, "I simply can't do it. I feel like everything is bad."

This is a recurring theme throughout the country. I see a lot of people who are losing their will to live...or their desire to stay in Lebanon and contribute to this society. My brother, for example, left the country. We are losing our country to war.

I must say that I experience these feelings myself, but I struggle to overcome them by working a lot and then forcing myself to relax. I even started knitting late at night when I'm at home...just to relax my brain and turn off my thoughts...and I turned off the TV. So far, this is working for me.

The school year started, but construction that was unfinished due to the war is still going on and the students have to work around it. Worse yet is a disastrous sense that even as we fix things around us another war can begin any time and destroy our lives again. This is the situation we've been in for over 25 years.

Our students are not growing normally. The girls that attend our schools appear more aggressive, and we're working on that. From eight in the morning each day I meet with students' parents to discuss issues ranging from aggression to an inability to see a future worth struggling for. Why study when another war will start and everything will be lost again?

Recently two young women from an organization similar to Junior Achievement came to our school and brought various reports. One of them, "How to Be a Leader," will be a workshop for students. These women will create programs geared toward social work and community service, and we'll create an award for the best social worker—serving wounded people, finding food for those made homeless by war. We'll create good social workers in our school trained to do more in community service. I think this will help our children to react to war. I think that if you are in the problem and it surrounds you, you don't find it a big deal anymore. But we need our children to realize that it *is* a big deal, and it's abnormal, to live under war so much.

I began my administration as principal the year [former Lebanese prime minister] Rafik Hariri was assassinated. We had so many plans and goals about what we wanted to do. Then, on our second day of a series of school examinations, he was killed and everything came to a standstill. Now, when we plan exams, anything actually, we also say, "Well, god knows if we will be able to do this. Who knows what might happen and put an end to our plans?" We just don't know. We need to make plans. We need to reach good results. We always have a Plan B, because every day, we feel that something is going to happen to alter our plans.

And this is besides the actual warfare we experience. Not to mention the cluster bombs that even now are killing or maiming two or three people every day. Yes, here in Beirut we are far from that, but in the south it is a big problem. Imagine. If you have children they can't go and play outside. That is disastrous, because small children grow and learn by jumping in the fields, watching the ants, learning about nature. I myself spent my childhood climbing trees and following butterflies, and even now I have this need to look at and enjoy nature. This is normal. This is growing. And children are now prevented from doing this. This is one of the tragedies beyond war itself. Children can't play outside, because they can't distinguish a cluster bomblet from a stone or a toy. And there are many different types of cluster bombs, so it is not as if they can learn to recognize one bomb and avoid it. No, there are many designs. All over Lebanon now are billboards warning people about the bombs and how to identify them.

Then there are the adults who collect different kinds of bombs as souvenirs. Just as you or I collect stamps or butterflies, they collect bombs. Apparently, they defuse them. But how dangerous is that? Yet people are used to living like this, and it is not normal.

VIOLET, Beirut

"I see that I have a deep grudge"

Violet was born in Beir Zeit (Palestine) to a well-to-do family. She and her husband, Gamel, have lived in Beirut since 1956. I met them at their church during the time my luggage was still missing, and I'm grateful that they recognized that, despite my undignified rain-soaked sandals and tired traveling attire, it was worthwhile to share their story with me. They invited me to their apartment in the Hamra district that still displays the original serene Arab architecture.

In much of the world, the going history about Palestine is that before the Jews came—before World War II—the land was empty, no one was living there, it was desert, and that the Jews made the desert bloom, built nice homes, and so on. In fact, it was a beautiful and bountiful country filled with Palestinians working their orchards and fields, living peacefully in villages and towns. Palestinians were, in reality, evicted from their homes, especially after the 1948 war.

Many of the best-educated Palestinians have left the country. Of those who stayed, the occupation has limited their lives' potential and their opportunities. With all that the people deal with every day—roads closed to their vehicles, checkpoints, constant surveillance, limited access to water and medical care—even those with exceptional talent have been frustrated in their ambitions and ability to express their intellectual gifts.

Before 1967 my children and I visited my family in Beir Zeit. The children were very young then. Now, of course, they cannot go back. Most of them have different passports: three have Canadian passports, and one has a British passport—he was born in Britain and now lives in East Yorkshire. My daughter lives in Bahrain after getting her doctorate there, where she also teaches. One of her kids lives there with her.

We lived in this home throughout the civil war, often hunkering down in the kitchen while militias fought in the streets below us. We lived here during the Israeli occupation too. People we know were amazed and told us, "What are you still doing there? You, of all people, as Palestinians, have to leave. If the Israelis come...."

I responded, "No, we're not leaving. Not again. Let them come into my house and try to force me out, but even then I will not leave. This is my home and I will stay here."

My daughter was staying in this apartment block too. She was divorcing her husband, who was Palestinian, and she had a small place with two little sons. The Israelis and Lebanese came looking for her husband and she said, "I don't know where he is. I think he is out of the country. At any rate, he does not live here as we are separated."

It was rough and tough for us because my daughter was married to this particular Palestinian man. Everybody we knew was scared for us; we were scared for ourselves.

This summer [2006] we left Lebanon for Jordan on July 7 and the war started on July 12. Thank God we were spared another round of bombing. My friends who were here said that Israeli planes were flying right over Beirut and the noise of bombing and falling buildings was terrifying. They use the most advanced bombs, and even now the little bombs [cluster bombs] are killing people in south Lebanon.

This home is close to where Rafik Hariri was assassinated. We heard the tremendous explosion that morning, although we didn't know what had happened. Now the investigation! There is something wrong when ten countries don't want to investigate. One cannot just say that Syria did it without any solid proof. One thing I feel sure of is that the West doesn't care too much about what happens in Lebanon. They have their own interests and don't care about us. And we in Lebanon don't know what is good for us. Our politicians are against one another and don't seem to care about the Lebanese people either. Never in my life did I imagine that politicians—in England, the United States, and Israel—can reach this point of inhumanity. A whole people [Palestinians] have had their lives, their freedom taken away; they're at the point where they're talking about splitting that country. Nobody wants that, and yet it continues. Those people could live together. The Palestinians are very emotional people, and with real emotion and real talking people can change their thinking. They are honest and straightforward people who have made many concessions, but nobody cares.

This trend started with the British.

If I told you about my childhood, what I saw in my father's house, you wouldn't believe it. We were still under the British mandate at that time—I think it was 1937, I was a child. There was an uprising against the British government—by the *athuwar*, the resisters—for giving away our land. We, the Palestinians were against that, of course, and in our village the villagers treated the resisters very well as they were considered freedom fighters.

My father was the mayor, so the British would come to our house. I was very curious about what was going on so I'd watch through the door. I've never forgotten what I saw. I remember clearly how cruelly people were treated by the British Army. They'd suddenly show up at the house, bringing people from the street with the idea of jailing them, walk right in, and demand, "Where is such-and-such a man?"

If my father didn't know, the British would beat the men they had with them or someone they'd just apprehended, throw them to the ground, and step on their necks with big boots.

One day they came to the house for the same sort of business and found a pistol that somebody had left behind. So they put my father and my uncles in a makeshift jail that was an unused underground well. My father had heart problems, yet he spent about two months in that dry well. My uncle, who was a commissioner, complained enough about my father's detention that the British finally removed him and placed him in a hospital prison for another six months.

I see that I have a deep grudge against the governments of Britain— even though my son lives there—and the United States. The Palestinians have struggled for so long just to hold on to their land and the behavior of those governments seems so...inhuman.

The American government talks about democracy, and being fair and just—yet it does the opposite. You are worse than everybody!

Remember that my family has been very lucky in our lives here in Lebanon. Go into the Palestinian refugee camps in Lebanon and you'll see a very different way of life. Those Palestinians are not permitted to own property or even to work easily in this country. They have very limited access to education, no freedom of movement, and restrictions on almost every facet of their lives. The Lebanese say this is because, "We don't want them to stay here forever." And the people in the camps have been living as if they are in ghettos or reservations for 50 years! Isn't that a crime?

ELHAM, Kolilah

"The peace they're searching for is for their benefit and not ours"

Under normal circumstances I would consider 9:00 p.m. too late to interview anyone, but Elham assured me this wasn't the case. It was sheer luck that we met. Her son Ali had been a college friend of my translator, Ra'fat, and they ran into one another outside the village Internet café. Elham welcomed us into her house, served us tea, and with her family around her interjecting details, told her story.

I got married in 1978. Nine months later I was pregnant with Ali and the Israelis had invaded our country. Since the Palestinians were here in Lebanon and the Israelis wanted to bomb them, we Lebanese were bombed too. The area around our village was within the firing zone, so we were in the middle of it. So just after Ali was born, I went to Sidon to keep him safe.

In 1982 I gave birth to my second son. The Israelis were still here and we had many disasters due to their presence.

My third son was born in 1984, and until 1990 we lived in terror of the war. In fact, most of our lives, certainly during my children's lives, we've been suffering from war and bombing: in the '80s, in '93, and in '96; then we had a little peace after 2000 with the liberation of south Lebanon from Israel.

For a while Israel seemed far away, and we began to feel more secure. We even dared to hope that we could rebuild our country and live better lives. But last summer we were back to war.

Concerning the kidnapping of two Israeli soldiers [by Hezbollah militia, precipitating Israel's retribution bombing]: that is just not a strong enough reason for Israel to have done all that was done. We feel that Israel has a bad reputation around here since the 1970s—they bomb and kill us if they feel like it.

This summer we wanted to stay in our house and stay on our land during the bombing, but it was just too intense and we had to escape. My family went to a place in the mountains where it was safer. There were massacres around here and in villages in the south.

When the bombing stopped, we returned. There was a lot of destruction in this village, including this house. Over 30 percent of the buildings, including more than 300 houses, were completely destroyed, and more than 350 houses were partially destroyed. Many members of the families living in those places were killed or badly wounded. Many farm animals were killed or wounded so badly that they died later; the losses to farmers have been severe, and it continues with the daily explosions of unrecognized cluster bombs.

Our house was hit and all the windows were broken, but we were lucky, because our neighbor's house was even worse off. All the houses still standing have structural damage with large cracks in the walls, broken windows, and so on. There are about 900 houses in this village, and when officials came to tally the destruction they recorded that more than 850 houses were damaged in some way, including by fire. Only 50 houses here had no damage at all.

Hezbollah helps to repair the damaged buildings here. They've donated the initial payments—up to $10,000—for people to rebuild as well as financial help for people's rent to share space in houses. Sometimes five or six families share one house. Those who rent space in their houses received loans to buy furniture, as so much was ruined, and they have a year or more to repay. There are about 25 apartment blocks that still await the government's help to rebuild. Some in Sidon also share their houses, but rents there are high and have risen as well, depending on the part of town, to anything from a low of $50 up to $250 to $300.

We have received *nothing* from the Lebanese government.

Our house wasn't as badly damaged as some, because it was already quite new and made with modern building materials. We paid for repairs ourselves: fixing the torn-up roof, replacing broken windows, and sealing lots of cracks in the walls.

It is difficult not to think badly of the Israelis. We've had so many bad experiences with them in the past that it is difficult not to expect the same sort of evil from them in the future. They don't even respect the U.N. Interim Force or United Nations. For example, in 1982, the U.N. was in Lebanon, but the Israeli army reached Beirut anyway.

We hope Israel learns from this war that resistance is strong and that they'll not invade again. Yesterday Halutz [Israeli Air Force Lt. Gen. Dan Halutz, who oversaw the air war] was fired. But so what? There'll be another Halutz. All of Israel's political parties are Zionist, so they will not learn. Maybe Israel will consider the two losses—in 2000 and now in 2006—before attacking again. But who knows?

We thought with Israel losing here and the United States losing in Iraq they might finally search for peace in the Middle East, but since the peace they're searching for is for their benefit and not ours, it will be temporary.

We've requested the Americans to give us our rights. As Arabs we believe that America gives Israel—an illegal government—rights to and assistance in taking land that belongs to Palestinians. Israel wants to expand its territory despite our sovereign rights. Why are new immigrants to Israel simply able to move onto our land? We, who have been here for many generations and many centuries, lose our land to those who are not even born here and who know nothing about the history, the people, the language, and the different cultures. Nothing! But they get land and our people live in refugee camps.

We hope the Americans give rights to those who suffer. People around the world have access to the same television news and views, and we all see how much the people suffer. We hope that Americans, who have the wealth and the power, can do something about this suffering.

My message to Americans, especially American women, is, Please try to feel how Arab women feel. Feel how Palestinian mothers feel, and how Lebanese mothers feel when they see their sons martyred for freedom. Lebanese martyrs die daring to fight for their rights and defending their land.

Why do American mothers send their sons to die in Iraq? Is it for democracy? Shouldn't democracy be built by the people? Shouldn't it come from within and not be imposed from outside? If it is imposed by those outside, isn't that occupation? We certainly see them as occupiers...and the people of that land should resist occupation.

When Americans talk about terrorists, I look around and I see people bombing our people, our land, and I wonder, just who are the terrorists? The United States doesn't call the Israeli attacks against us in our land "terrorism," yet calls our defense of our land and our people "terrorism."

America is learning now, in Iraq, what the Israelis have learned, what the British should have learned, what the French have learned, and what the Ottomans learned about Arab resistance. History will not change. Those who don't have a history and who will not learn the lessons of history will not have a future. Americans haven't yet understood that it is not only technology that wins in the long run. The spirit of the people to own their own land and their own culture will always win in the end. We have heroes and martyrs for our cause and their young people are killed just for the material benefit of a few.

The first revolution from the Prophet Mohammed taught all about the revolutions of this world. Ali, the son of the Prophet Mohammed, called revolution the victory of the blood against the sword. This taught us that we can present our blood for victory over any weapon. This is why we have martyrs.

ZUHRE and her FAMILY, Kolilah

"Don't send your sons..."

It was already past 10:00 p.m. when I arrived at Zuhre house in Kolilah. At my knock on her front door, a side door cracked open and a woman peered out, then quickly shut the door. It was the widow of one of Zuhre's sons,

Mohammed. Zuhre, her daughter—both women dressed in the all-black fashion of strict Shi'a women—and her youngest son welcomed us inside and served coffee. At first, Zuhre seemed shy and sad, but she beamed when she held up a photo of Mohammed with Hezbollah leader Sayyed Hassan Nasrallah. She said, "I am proud that my son is a martyr for our freedom."

Zuhre

Mohammed, my son, is a martyr who chose to die fighting this way. We hold up our heads with pride because of him. While we feel sadness that we lost our son and brother, we also feel that that is a small price in the face of reclaiming our rights as a people. I still have three sons, and I will present them to be martyrs to fight for our land, for our lives, for our rights. We will also follow Hassan Nasrallah when he fights against Israel, because we feel that unless we fight back, Israel will continue to attack us.

The mothers in America must understand that we believe they are stupid to send their sons to fight us, because we will not give up. We will fight as long as we have to, even if we all die, but their sons will die here too. I don't know all the reasons for the war—did Israel really inflict so much damage for two soldiers? I don't think so—but we will fight them.

When this war began, we stayed in our house for three days. After it was destroyed—my father was injured in that bombing—most of us left for shelter in Tyre. My son, the martyr, had started resisting the Israeli occupation of Lebanon when he was 15 years old, and he stayed here to fight. He was wounded twice before being killed by an aerial bomb targeting our house.

Zuhre's son

Next time you come here my mother will be holding a photo of me as a martyr. What else can I do about the situation? I know that if we sacrifice now, future generations can be free. I saw my best friend badly burned in a bomb attack during the summer and I took him away from the fighting on my motorcycle.

[I ask if his friend survived.] Actually he was mostly dead when I took him away. His skin was black from burns and it was falling off his body in strips. I took him so that the dogs wouldn't eat his body.

MARYAM and ZENA, Qana

"Don't let my mother see…"

As Maryam told her story, one of her surviving daughters brought me newspaper clippings about the massacre and whispered, "Don't let my mother see it, because there are pictures of my father's body and the broken, dust-covered bodies of her grandchildren." But Maryam did see the clippings. For the first time since that summer, she held evidence in her hands that someone—if only a reporter—had shown an interest in what had happened here.

Maryam

For 18 days, 53 people sheltered in the basement of a large house while the Israelis bombed south Lebanon. It was after midnight and many people were asleep on the floor—children in one corner for added safety—when the missiles came, first from one direction and then right into the corner where the children slept. It was very dark in that basement—we believed that even brief candlelight would invite more bombs—and terrified survivors shouted out names to learn who was all right, who was wounded, and who didn't answer. My daughter Hallah was bleeding from a head wound and her left arm was pinned by debris. Hallah mourns her husband and daughter. [Maryam points to the collage on the wall.] There are my family members who were killed: Maryam Mehsin, Hussain, Ibrahim, Ali, Jaafer, Mahdi, Abbas, Fatemah, and Ruqayya. Ibrahim Ahmed was my husband for over 40 years.

There has been almost no money from the Lebanese government to rebuild, although Qatar, Hezbollah, and Iran donate funds. The memorial to the dead outside is one of the few new constructions in Qana.

Zena

Immediately after the bombing, I don't know where I got the strength, I lifted the rocket shell from my neighbor's body, felt for her pulse, and found none. Since no one else was close by I shifted the rocks, and kept digging for survivors.

I heard the voice of a woman calling for her children: "Are you still alive?"

"Yes, we're still alive," they answered, and she started asking about others. This is how I learned that my sister Hallah was still alive.

You know quickly who is dead, because they do not answer. Many who were too injured to move or help themselves smothered under the debris. My mother died like that. You can see a photo of her in Al Jazeera: the woman wearing green, covered by rubble, with her legs sticking out is my mom.

I tried to rescue a mother and Ahmed, her 10-month-old child. I lifted him up, but when I removed the rocks from his body he died.

A man nearby called and I told him, "We will rescue you so you can help us."

He said, "No, I can't help for I am wounded."

We rescued him. His head, his eyes, most of his body was injured.

An old woman named Habib called, "Hello, someone is still alive."

It was too dark to see her so I followed her voice, "Is it someone under the debris who is still alive?"

She said, "I don't know exactly where...."

I tried to remove the rocks and find that person. It was my sister, Hallah. She cleared dust from her own mouth and said, "I can't talk much but my daughter is under me. Can you rescue her? Or just help me free my arm and hand so I can help her."

Hallah was bleeding from her arm and her head. When our cousin reached Hallah's small daughter we found the child was already dead. I kissed her and hugged her. She was still warm even though she was dead. My cousin took her body away.

My cousin shouted, "Whoever is still alive should escape, quickly, because maybe the airplanes will bomb us again."

I told my sister, "It is not just your daughter but all our family. We don't know what's happened to them. We don't know where they are."

Hallah tried to leave the basement but she was still bleeding and couldn't keep her balance very well, so she tripped and fell as she walked. She found a child on the ground that she believed was her daughter and she picked her up and carried her.

My cousin was shouting, "Please, everybody, go out quickly."

I took the dead child from my sister because she couldn't walk well and I found that it was not her daughter but another woman's daughter, a 6-year-old named Zainab. When they'd pulled her out earlier she was alive, but she had died of her wounds.

Everything was so confusing because of the dark, and the shock of so many dead. All of this had taken less than ten or fifteen minutes.

I heard my cousin say, "Come…follow my voice to get out."

Just as I was leaving the basement—you could only get out through the hole made by the rocket—I heard the voice of someone in pain.

I put the small child outside and told my cousin, "I will go inside again because I hear the voice of someone in pain. I want to rescue him."

That person shouted out to me, "Never mind me. Just you go out quickly. Maybe the airplanes will bomb here again. They're really close and they may come back. Don't worry about us; the Red Cross will come soon and rescue us."

I was tired and I was really scared to go inside the basement again in case I found people in many pieces and lots of blood.

I asked my cousin where I should go and he said, "The father of this child, Zainab, cannot walk. He is paralyzed. I will stay with him but you go and sit with your sister over there near the tree. Too many people are dead here."

So my sister and I sat under a tree about ten meters from this death site; the bombing of the village continued all around us.

We sat and waited under the tree for someone to rescue us while the bombing continued. Hallah was still bleeding, and she kept saying, "I'm feeling sleepy." But I knew she was sleepy because she was losing blood.

We sat suffering under that tree until morning, some of us still bleeding, and the young kids dead under the debris inside the basement.

There was a woman shouting for someone to help her, but she didn't know exactly what had happened. Almost everybody in the basement had been sleeping when the missiles came. In the dark and the dead quiet, no one could tell who was dead and who was still alive. This woman was in shock and didn't know if someone she loved was alive or dead.

My cousin had been awake and he said two rockets struck the house. But while we were sitting under the tree, an airplane hit the basement twice again, this time from the other side of the basement.

We were afraid to leave the place because we didn't want the airplanes to spot us. At one time we heard my father's voice, and we were so happy that he was still alive, that even if we had lost some family members our father was still alive. But by morning he was dead.

At dawn, villagers and some TV journalists came to see what had happened. But we were frightened, and even bleeding and barefoot, we ran away, because we thought maybe it was Israelis coming to kill us if they found people still alive who could tell rescuers what had happened.

Later, these people asked, "Why are you still here?" meaning why haven't any rescue teams come to help?

It was after 3 p.m. when we saw people driving toward us, but the Israeli airplanes bombed the main road in front of them and forced them to turn around.

Later, after rescuers were finally able to open the road, they slowly moved the injured to different hospitals. Civilians were afraid to drive their cars and carry the injured, because they'd seen the airplanes bomb the roads. The U.N. didn't evacuate us but a few ambulances and a few cars arrived to pick us up. Those not too wounded were taken to a local restaurant for shelter and rest.

My sister and I stayed in the hospital for three days. At first, we asked God why this happened. Later, we just prayed for God to bury the martyrs from our family. We believe that our dead martyrs are in paradise now. We feel sad about them, but we also know that they are happy because of this. Look at the pictures of the dead and you'll see how many of them are children who will go to paradise.

Imagine. This is just our one family. Yet this happened all over Lebanon. You can see pictures if you look for them.

WHERE ARE THEY NOW?

Afifa Dirani Arsanios

Baby Salam is doing very well, his health is much improved, and, Afifa says, "He is the spoiled baby of [his] SOS Village."

Mrs. Jobeily

Under Mrs. Jobeily's leadership Sidon Secondary Public School continues to educate girls and heal the war trauma expressed by its girls and faculty.

…and

With the overall political situation in Lebanon very tense, communication with the small villages of Qana, Kolilah, and Kfar Kila is difficult. As this book goes to print, I have received no direct word from Elham, Zuhre, or Maryam.

A member of a group gathered in Qana late February 2008—after the destroyer USS *Cole* was deployed off Lebanon's shore to "preserve political stability"—said, "Everyone feels there is a war coming… especially after the killing of [senior Hezbollah commander] Imad Mughniyeh."

The USS *Cole*'s presence reminds Lebanese of the two-month period starting in September 1983 when U.S. warships shelled the Chouf mountains in support of the Lebanese army. The Lebanese called these huge shells, "flying Volkswagens," and they convinced those opposed to the U.S.-backed Lebanese government that the United States was not a neutral peacekeeper in Lebanon. In October 1983, the U.S. Marine barracks in Beirut was destroyed by a suicide bomber, killing 241 U.S. service members.

5—SYRIA

JANUARY 2006—BEIRUT, LEBANON—JDEIDEH—DAMASCUS

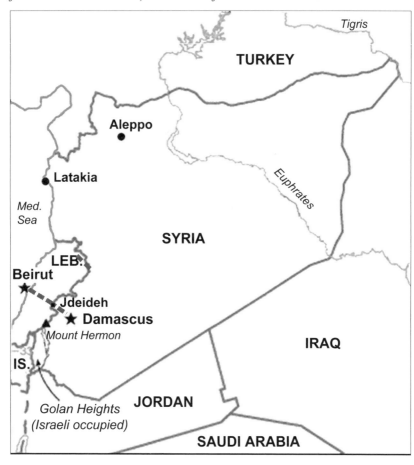

Walled in from mankind's cause and voice[1]

THE DAY I LEFT BEIRUT for Damascus, an impromptu demonstration against Fouad Siniora's cabinet was in full swing outside the Finance Ministry at the Palace of Justice. I asked Maurice, my taxi driver, "Just drive past so I can see how many people show up."

He replied, "We'll get stuck in traffic."

Beirutis have a nose for hot spots, so I didn't press. These peaceful rolling demonstrations were common during this period, and I figured I'd probably have another shot at attending one before I left the country.

Instead, we drove to Charles Hélou station, where Maurice bartered with Syrian drivers for a reasonable fare to Damascus. He settled on Carlos, who—after he learned I didn't have a Syrian visa—agreed that, if necessary, he'd wait up to five hours with me at the border before returning me to Beirut. Actually christened Kariken, Armenian Christian Carlos—his stage name—grew up in Anjar among the remains of the eighth-century inland commercial trade center built by Walid I, the sixth Umayyad caliph. Carlos's grandfather, a tailor, was among thousands of Armenians who fled the genocide in 1915. They came to Anjar, cleared the malarial swamps—hundreds died of disease—and built homes reminiscent of Armenia.

The Beirut–Damascus highway via Masnaa winds through sparsely populated mountain villages and culminates at an Italian-style deli serving delicious cappuccino. I got the feeling this is a last gasp of city air before travelers descend into the beautiful but impoverished Bekaa Valley. The narrow road down the pass had been battered during the summer war, and bomb craters, debris, melting snow, and overloaded trucks made driving risky, although billboards depicting Condoleezza Rice tutoring Lebanese politicians added wry humor.

Lebanese border control was routine, and as we traveled toward Syria through the depopulated border region, I dared to hope that getting a visa would be easy. At Jdeideh, military border control officials were friendly but not encouraging: visas are faxed from Damascus, they told me, and they, in Jdeideh, had no control over it.

"How long could it take?"

"Maybe two or three hours."

It took over ten hours and many ingratiating visits to the border commander. During that time, Carlos and I window-shopped in Jdeideh's overheated duty-free emporium, where only U.S. dollars buy consumer goods: tall pyramids of three-liter bottles of Smirnoff vodka (US $23) Gilbey's gin (US $19) and Johnny Walker red and black labels (US $28) indicated that, despite religious proscription, travelers appreciate a good deal on booze. For the less thirsty well-heeled, there were similarly inexpensive HDTVs, European chocolate, and CDs of Lindsey Lohan, Ricky Martin, Ying Yang, and Boys' Club.

While Carlos and I huddled over space heaters in the cold, cavernous border waiting room, we befriended three shifts of border officials and watched them issue visas to all travelers except Americans. Nevertheless, I was finally granted a visa, and by the time Carlos handed me over to Arkan in Baramka Square, he had thoroughly restored my faith in taxi drivers.

Iraqi refugees

Arkan, my translator and guide in Damascus, had been a colonel in Saddam Hussein's army, and he and his family fled Baghdad in late 2006. They were part of the flood of more than 4 million Iraqis displaced by Operation Iraqi Freedom, more than 2 million of whom have crossed into neighboring Jordan, Egypt, and even into struggling Lebanon.

Syria, with a population of 18 million, has taken 1.2 million Iraqis; that's the equivalent of Canada accepting 4.9 million refugees. (The then opposition leader Stephen Harper, who agitated for Canada to join the war, has been silent about admitting Iraqi refugees since becoming prime minister and has admitted fewer than 3,000 since 2003.) The vast majority of refugees are in the greater Damascus metropolitan area and Syria has been particularly hard hit since it has had little international help, principally because the United States and its allies consider it a "rogue nation" in the Axis of Evil.

Jordan, population 5.7 million, has admitted 800,000 Iraqis, the equivalent of France welcoming 8 million refugees, Germany 11 million, or the United States 40 million. Britain has admitted fewer than 500. Washington promised to take in 7,000 in 2007 but has admitted only 2,084. Kuwait and Saudi Arabia, among the most bellicose of America's pro-war Arab allies, have accepted a handful. Saudi Arabia has closed its border with Iraq and is fortifying a $2 billion fence.

Palestinians, again in no-man's land

By March 2006, Palestinians who'd fled Baghdad were arriving at Al Tanf border crossing in northeastern Syria. Refused entry to Syria, they remained in the strip of no-man's land—the barren desert buffer region between the Syrian and Iraqi borders—where there are no amenities and travelers are subject to interference by border police, local police, and the Iraqi army. A group of more than 300 Palestinians reported that Iraqi armored vehicles with armed guards were entering their camp, intimidating them with weapons, and threatening to force them back to Iraq. In November of that year, five Palestinians—three men and two boys—in search of diesel fuel for a generator were arrested by Iraqi security forces at Al Tanf. By March 2008 the size of the camp had more than doubled to an estimated 720, including 500 women and children.

An estimated 10,000 to 20,000 Palestinians remain in Iraq because they lack valid identity documents—or have nowhere to renew those they hold—and are refused entry to neighboring countries. The U.N. High Commission for Refugees has repeatedly appealed to the Iraqi authorities and the multinational forces to provide increased protection for the Palestinians, and according to a 2006 UNHCR report on the situation, has "also appealed to countries in the Arab region, in Israel, and in other resettlement countries, to provide a humane—if only temporary—solution for this specifically targeted group. These appeals have so far yielded few results."[2]

Additionally, during the 34-Day War, the then U.N. Secretary-General Kofi Annan reported that more than 140,000 Lebanese had entered Syria. One of these, a mother sheltering in a Damascus stadium with her family, who'd had nothing to eat or drink for days, told a CNN reporter, "I didn't escape Lebanon. I came to save my children, to see them grow up, and to send them back to fight Israel."[3]

Even I, a mother researching the roots of war, see that a truly equitable solution for Palestinians would settle much of the hostilities in the Middle East. And, as successive U.S. administrations forge ahead with unequivocal military and political support for Israel—and the American people tacitly approve it—former President Jimmy Carter and former Prime Minister Ehud Olmert agree with me! Tragically, it is only *after* they leave office that they summon the courage to say so.

Syria—"rogue nation"?

There's a saying, "Americans come to a new country for one week and write an article, for one month and write a book." Since I stayed in Damascus four days, I'm not in a position to do much more than present my impressions, with the caveat that these are more about the lens with which I view the world—including unconscious cultural bias—than how the world actually is.

Like many of my generation, I'd watched *Lawrence of Arabia* and thrilled to camel-mounted Lawrence commanding, "To Damascus!" as he and his followers galloped across the desert into the sunset. Things have changed since then...for one thing, camels would never survive the wide, modern Damascus streets bristling with traffic.

I spent my first night in an overheated Western-style high-rise hotel. As a single woman, I had to eat breakfast alone in my room. I checked out the next morning in favor of a sparse hotel near the Old City where I could chat with Syrians at breakfast.

Even under the thin layer of soot, Damascene architecture displays exquisite attention to detail: stone walls layered in horizontal stripes of black, pink, and white; residence doors with unique handcrafted trim;

intricate filigree iron and brick work; quarried black paving stones; the elegant iron buttress of the *souk*'s entrance and main walkways.

I covered up in another shapeless gown to visit the Umayyad Mosque with its gold-trimmed friezes and murals and vast marble prayer plaza. Then Arkan and I shared an apple-scented tobacco *narghili* (water pipe) at a local coffee shop.

I'd peeked through enough doorways of Arab residences—Iraqi, Palestinian, Lebanese, Jordanian, and Syrian—to understand that Arab exteriors are designed to disguise the richness of interior life. I was struck with how much America's extroverted culture misunderstands introverted Arab culture. Edward Said's book *Orientalism* eloquently discusses the pitfalls of Western stereotyping in this region, and the reverse phenomenon is undoubtedly just as marked and complex.

Is Damascus crammed with fanatics who "hate us for our freedom"? I can say that state-run or government-affiliated Internet cafés disallow users accessing certain websites. I had to find a privately owned Internet café to access my Hotmail account. Judging by the long wait in these places for an available computer, Syrians figured this out long ago. As for fanaticism, it is as tough to discern a Syrian fanatic as it is to discern an American fanatic. As far as I know, I met neither on the streets of Damascus.

My return trip to Beirut by Pullman bus (costing the equivalent of US $4) was quick—less than four hours including a stop at the Italian deli at the top of the pass—although I missed Carlos's amiable company.

MAYSAA ALI, Damascus

"A first principle"

Maysaa Ali is a devout Muslim and a schoolteacher who has lived in Damascus all her life. I met her through Arkan, my translator, and added her voice here as she clearly states what many in the West fail to grasp: that Western hegemony in the region is a major stumbling block to peace.

No Syrian would accept a foreigner who puts his foot on an Arab land, not Iranian, not American, not Russian. This is a first principle. Any

Arab, no matter from which Arab country, can own property in Syria; Iranians cannot, but Iranians are not Arab.

Syria has ties with Iran, but we don't accept that Iran has any claim to Iraqi land...even though they claim some Arab land inside Iraq as Iran's. We associate with Iran because of U.S. and Israeli pressure on Syria; we want somebody on "our side," and in this case, it is Iran.

We know that much of the weaponry the militias use was made in Iran, and they admit it; they don't hide it. Iran helps Arab countries because it is a neighbor and because it is Muslim.

Iran wants us to receive Iraqi people and has good political relations with Syria. We have advisors from there and we accept exchange students on scholarships, for example, and so on. Here in Syria, we have a lot of shrines and religious structures that are important to Iranians, and they make pilgrimages here. Iran may want to build something in Syria that I am unaware of, but I can't speak to that.

WISSAM, Damascus

"Lethal freedom"

Wissam, young, fresh-faced, and outspoken, was newly single. Her husband, a Shi'a, divorced her, a Sunni, out of fear for his life. At first Wissam was reluctant to speak to me, insisting that her English wasn't good enough, and she relied on Arkan to translate. Her passion to express her own thoughts, however, quickly took over, and she flew along in perfectly good English.

I am a biologist and I started working in the Ministry of Trade as a quality control specialist about one month before the invasion. I continued working there until we left for Damascus. I received a salary for the last three years, although I went to the office for a total of only four months because of shutdowns, lack of electricity, lack of work, and so on.

The living standards here in Syria are not as good for us as they were in Iraq. I cannot find work here. My brother and his friends—highly qualified medical doctors—cannot find work here either. Even Syrians face difficulties finding work with livable salaries, so Iraqis don't stand a chance. I might find a job selling in a store, but anything that actually used my education and skills would require papers to prove I'm not taking a Syrian's job.

My ex-husband is here too, and he works as mobile telephone communications engineer. The problem in our marriage was that he was a Shi'a and I am a Sunni. This is becoming more of a problem among Iraqis now, although it was never the case before when people intermarried. Now we are beginning to see this as big trouble.

My family and I left everything when we left Baghdad. I'm afraid that we will lose it forever—even if we are lucky enough to return to our original home. We spent our whole lives there, so we are losing not only material wealth but our memories, our history, our community, everything.

Syrians, Jordanians, and so on have their own countries and nations. We Iraqis are frightened now because we may lose our country. When television shows Egyptians, for example, honoring their country and raising their flag, I cry. The Kurds have a flag, too. But the Iraqi flag has been changed and it doesn't unify us anymore. Now we're frightened Iraq will be partitioned into four countries, and that that will divide us even more.

What is good in this terrible time is that our whole family and many relatives and friends are here in Damascus. Many live near us, so our sorrow is not that we feel isolated from our family but that we feel isolated from our country. Having to live here is abnormal. We are looked at as immigrants and not as nationals or landowners: this is important. We lived a decent, even upper-class lifestyle; our houses were big, we had more than one car, our children were college educated, and it was a good life—until the invasion. Now we live here just for security. We don't have hope or even a future.

I blame the U.S. administration—not the American people—for the destruction of our infrastructure, our society, our culture, our historical richness, and our independence. All we respected of our land and our people is gone, destroyed by the arrogance of the U.S. administration.

The Americans didn't bring us democracy, but instead brought a lethal freedom. There is the sense now that anybody can do anything and nobody will be punished. Is this the ethic of democracy, freedom without limitations? When it appears, life is run according to the rule of the jungle.

Before arriving in Syria, I had big problems with my husband and my divorce and the situation in our country. I cried 24 hours a day in Baghdad, and I thought I was the unhappiest creature in the whole world because I saw no light at the end of the tunnel. But in my office I found I was better off than most, because our family is well educated and we had a high standard of living. There are huge numbers of people who have no money and no food to eat. But they have to survive somehow. When I saw people living like that while I had a loving family and food to eat, I saw how well I was doing in comparison.

My friend's husband was a sheik in a mosque. She has four kids. Her first son, Omar, has a Sunni name and they lived in a Shi'a area. Some people kidnapped my friend's husband because he prayed in the mosque. He has been gone over four months and my friend felt unsafe so she left to live in a Sunni area. One day Omar was in the market and a Shi'a militiaman killed him. Now my friend has lost her husband, her son, and her home. There but for the grace of God go I....

The real disaster is that we are losing our country and our culture. A person without a past does not have a future.

What if, one day, Americans become just like us?

AYSER and MAMOUN CHALABI, Damascus

"Suggest to your government they establish a plan for refugees"

Ayser, her husband, Mamoun, and their son left Baghdad in late July 2004, soon after Mamoun recovered from his kidnapping. They welcomed Arkan and me in their small apartment in a new section that spread into the hills surrounding the city, generously fed us, and told their story.

Ayser

My husband, Mamoun, was an office administrator for an optometrist. As he left work one day, five kidnappers mistook him for his boss, the doctor. These five were dressed in Iraqi police uniforms, drove an Iraqi police vehicle, and forced Mamoun into this car. Within 15 minutes, they sold him to men that Mamoun described as a "gang of low-class thugs."

The first thing I knew about this was when one of the kidnappers telephoned me and demanded US $750,000 in ransom. We do not have that kind of money, and I told them that. They didn't believe me and told me that if I didn't find a way to pay them, Mamoun would die. I was frantic. Mamoun is 68 years old, and like anyone, he cannot take too much physical abuse. I tried to find some way to come up with the money but it was impossible.

Meanwhile, for four days, these gang members kept him in a basement room, beat him with wooden planks, told him he was a liar and that he *was* the doctor, and that he had the money to pay their ransom.

Mamoun

I could not take the beating anymore. They used a wooden plank and beat me around the head and the legs and on my body. I was dizzy all the time and getting very weak. Finally, while I could hear the gang and their women friends drinking in another room, I broke a small window and, with a sliver of glass, I slashed deeply into each of my wrists. I just couldn't stand the beating and saw no other way to escape. I knew that in kidnap cases like mine the hostage rarely escapes with his life—even if someone pays the ransom. Since there was no way Ayser could raise that sum for my life, I did what I could to end the situation.

Blood pumped from my wrists as I waited to die. After a few minutes, however, a gang member came into the room and found me. He wrapped my wrists in tape, drove me to the approach of Al Khindy Hospital, and dumped me within sight of the hospital entrance. It was very early in the morning and very dark, and I was too weak to call out and attract anybody's attention. I had just enough life left to raise my voice to scare off the dogs that were waiting to eat me.

At dawn, when it got light again, a young man passing heard my whimpers and carried me into the hospital. Hearing the news of my escape, Ayser came to the hospital.

As soon as I was released we packed up our things and left for Damascus.

When you go back to the United States, suggest to your government that they establish a plan for refugees—there are so many of us—that allows us to withdraw our money at Syrian banks. As it is, if I need money I have to travel to Baghdad. That is an impossible situation. It is also a dangerous one. If anyone recognizes me coming into the bank every few months they might know that I collect money and return to Damascus. What would stop them from kidnapping me again? Or, even quicker, simply steal my money and cut my throat this time. People die for much less these days.

FATIMA and FAMILY, Damascus

"Living here is a disaster for us"

Despite their dire financial straits in Damascus, Fatima included me in the family meal without hesitation and told her story. As she spoke, her family reminded her of parts of the story she'd forgotten and filled in for her when she cried.

Fatima

I worked in a large bank in Baghdad for 21 years, and I had to quit my job without any retirement to come to Damascus with my family. We rented our house in Baghdad's Adhamiya neighborhood to people we didn't know. Our house was over 300 square meters, with lovely furniture, and we had to pack up, rent it out, and leave. I cried so much leaving my home, a lifetime of family memories, all the material wealth we'd worked so hard for. But the area had become very dangerous. For example, my son Haman's life was threatened and four of my son Hassam's friends were killed. Haman had to travel 50 kilometers to school each day, and he'd run into various checkpoints and that was not safe. Now he attends the European-Syrian College and we pay US $4,900 a year for his studies. In Iraq, education was free.

Living here is a disaster for us. We are not earning much and we have many expenses, including rent for this small house we live in—eight of us squeezed into two small rooms; we don't have a car here, and we had two at home.

While we do not know the neighborhood and we do not have close relationships with our neighbors, they are friendly and compassionate. They are also frustrated with the presence of over a million refugees, as prices are rising all over the country. Syrians say that Iraqis deserve much better than they're getting, since their country is so rich with oil, agriculture, a good industrial base, tourism, and many natural resources. Syrians are more generous with their country than, say, the Jordanians, who are now prohibiting Iraqi refugees from entering.

Haman is very unhappy here. Many of his friends have been killed, and he cries for them.

Haman

I am 16 years old, and I left my home, I left my school, I left everything I'd ever known and loved. I had a friend who was 16 years old whose father had been killed in the war. He went to the market to buy vegetables for his mother and he ran into a small street battle. He turned into another street to avoid it, but too late: a bullet struck him in the heart and killed him. He was my best friend and we did many things together from a very young age.

Since I'd always been in school in Iraq I wasn't prepared for some of the subjects taught in school here. In Baghdad, I knew who the good teachers were and how to avoid the bad ones. Here, I knew nothing. I call my friends every day—some still in Baghdad, some in Jordan—and we compare situations. Those in Baghdad say that they are home at 1 o'clock in the afternoon. If there is electricity, they watch TV. If not, they sleep, then eat a bit, and sleep again. All the schools are closed and there is nothing to do; they cannot, of course, go outside or even risk going to a friend's house.

Here, some of the Syrian boys my age are friendly, some laugh at us, and some make problems for us. Even the teachers are similar. One teacher asked me on my first day of school if I was Iraqi. I said that I was, and he told me to get out of his class. A Syrian talked to that teacher and I learned that the teacher wanted me to speak in Syrian dialect. I told the headmaster, who said he'd talk to the teacher.

Fatima

Everybody who has the financial means to do so will leave Iraq. There are people who cannot leave because a family member is ill or in the hospital. Like people everywhere, Iraqis want stable lives. But that is impossible in Iraq right now. Despite all the hardship here, I know my family is safe. In Baghdad, we were afraid somebody would raid us: gangs, militias, even American troops. If a family member had to leave the house for a short while, he'd carry a mobile phone and the family would call every 15 minutes or so asking where he was, what is going on, and when he will return home. Those remaining at home would be apprehensive until that person returned. If he didn't answer the phone we'd be anxious: What could have happened? Where was he?

Before we left we spent a week packing and storing household goods in the attic. Some had never been used and were still wrapped; about five boxes of such things were stolen…and this in a neighborhood where everybody knew everybody else. We think gangs did this. They saw what was going on and took the opportunity to enrich themselves.

People who would never have thought before of joining the resistance or of becoming part of the insurgency are likely to do so now—because they must protect themselves and their families, and their minds are disturbed by all that is going on.

Remember the roots of this thing: it all started with so-called terrorism, which in turn was started by Al Qaeda, which was started by the American conflict with the Soviet Union in Afghanistan. That spread to Iraq, Sudan, Somalia, and now to Lebanon. Actually, under the guise of fighting terrorism, this fighting is increasing terrorism.

My husband was a colonel in the Iraqi army from 1970 to 1990, before Saddam invaded Kuwait. During the war with Iran from 1980 to 1988 he fought with Iraqis and no one recognized anyone else as sectarian—Shi'a, Sunni, Kurds, Turkmen, and so on. About 70 percent of his soldiers were Shi'a but they all fought as one for a single, undivided Iraq. Recently there has been discussion about partitioning Iraq into various areas divided at the rivers…similar to what happened in Palestine. What if *we* lost the ability to prove that we own *our* homes? We'd be in a situation similar to that of the Palestinians during the 1948 war when they were forced from their homes without the deeds—actually, some even have their deeds today, but they cannot regain their houses because other families live in them.

As a bank employee, I know that after the invasion we made three backups of every day's transactions: one copy went to the manager, one copy went to the department manager, and one copy stayed in the department. We have financial records, but we'd have to spend about six months getting things back into working order.

I worked at the main bank in Rashid Street, now enclosed by a high concrete barrier. It was difficult for me to get inside with all the barriers, security, checkpoints, and so on—and I was a bank officer. Despite daily explosions, I went to work every day. We had a mixed population of Shi'a and Sunni, even some Christian. Our director was a Sunni, and those who worked for him were mainly Shi'a, and after a while he was unable to manage effectively because he was afraid of the Shi'a and afraid he'd lose his job. He couldn't sign a piece of paper without thinking of potential trouble he might be getting himself into.

My brother taxis people between Baghdad and Damascus. Now, when he leaves Baghdad and his family he is scared of what might happen while he is gone. At the same time, when he's in Damascus he wants to rest up and regain the courage to return to Baghdad. He cannot afford to bring his family here. Instead, he takes food back to them.

My brother-in-law went missing after death squads took him from his bed. Two months later family members went to the morgue. We didn't see his body but found his picture in the database. We learned he'd been brought to the morgue the second day after his kidnapping. We asked where he'd been buried and were told an agency had buried him in Najaf. Imagine, a Sunni buried in Shi'a holy ground! We went to that agency and learned that in January and February—just two months—the agency had buried 4,307 dead.

My other son, Hassam, was studying communication engineering in Baghdad University. He had four best friends, two Sunni, one Shi'a, and one Christian. Their families had already left Iraq for Amman, and the four were living together in a house until they finished university. On the first day of final exams Hassam didn't see his friends at the university. He learned that they'd been killed in an explosion: apparently, after class the previous day they'd gone for lunch together. There had been an explosion in the restaurant. Three died immediately—they were not even recognizable—and the fourth died of his burns soon after.

That was in June 2006. For a month after that he stayed home and never left his room. He was in a desperate way, never shaved, barely ate. There is not a day when Hassam doesn't think of his friends. Here, people ask him about his life and he tells them about that experience. One can conclude that one's fate follows one, but Hassam's opinion is that life now is simply chaos.

Despite our bad circumstances, we are far better off than many in Iraq who cannot afford to leave. The new security plan treats those remaining in Iraq as insurgents. My brother, for example, is an airline steward who came to visit and wept about not being able to provide heating fuel for his family. He couldn't warm his little daughter and had to put her under blankets—in the dark, because there is no electricity. This, in a wealthy country with lots of resources: oil, agriculture, farming. Yet my brothers cannot be safe here, because they don't have the financial means.

WALEED, Damascus

"Everybody is locked down in their homes"

Waleed left his family in Baghdad to visit extended family in Syria. He planned to return to Baghdad the day after this interview, although he admitted that in his heart he was terrified of returning. I include it here for an account of everyday life in chaotic Baghdad.

My neighborhood, Amriya, mainly Sunni with a population of about 500,000, is one of the Baghdad's hot spots these days. This was a clean neighborhood with no insurgents (the American term) or resistance fighters (the local term). Yet, when I left a few days ago, the Iraqi army and police had surrounded it, and there was only one entrance and one exit. Also, the police and military forces—usually a combination of U.S. troops and Iraqi army and police—prevent people from leaving the area and perform house raids, detain people, and so on. Every day I see bombed Humvees, militias fighting it out on the streets, people killed by stray bullets, and the dead lying in the streets for days. There are many civilian casualties.

The government imposes curfews, yet convoys of 40 to 50 vehicles filled with people in police uniforms still enter the area and raid houses. How can this happen without the government—or the Americans— knowing about it? They claim that these people are wearing stolen police uniforms and renting police cars. But, tell me, how do 40 or 50 vehicles get through *all* of the many checkpoints? The general sentiment now is that when there are curfews there will be raids. So people stay at home and face the inevitable.

Why are people abducted from their homes? Why are over 50 bodies a day found here and there? Surely these people are targets for some reason, and they're abducted and gotten rid of in this way. During the raids, the forces detain anybody, often quite randomly or for false claims made by an enemy. My neighbors' son had been killed in 1993, yet the forces brought a warrant to arrest him—even though he'd been dead for over ten years! Without any evidence, people claim that somebody is a suspect and that person arrested. When the American troops leave the neighborhood, the Iraqi police loot houses and humiliate, beat, and abduct people.

My house is four kilometers from my parents' house, yet once I had to stay with them for two days because a bomb exploded only a few meters from a checkpoint nearby. Who could plant a bomb right next to the checkpoint without anyone noticing?

The government forces are not doing their jobs. If they see a car being stolen or a house raided or even someone murdered, they don't get involved. If they're at a checkpoint they should at least see *something*—unless they already know what is going on or they're too scared to intervene. The police don't do any investigating. Too often, *they* are committing the crimes!

But, of the two groups—U.S. troops and Iraqi police—I trust the Americans more. Previously the Americans were very aggressive with us, but recently they've become more humane. Some soldiers, though, are still impulsive. For example, if residents are ordered to stand against a wall and a man is afraid, and perhaps falls to the ground, he is shot; maybe the soldiers suspect he has a bomb or other weapon.

There is no reconstruction going on at all; just the opposite. We hear about billions of dollars spent on rebuilding, but nothing like this is happening anywhere in Iraq. At best, electricity is on for one hour with multiple blackouts during that hour. In our house we went without any electricity at all for ten days. Just ask any American pilot to describe the lack of electricity, and they'll say that at night they fly over a totally dark city, full of horror and fear.

People—mainly Shi'a—come from poor areas outside the city and take up residence in bombed-out government buildings in the city to create better lives for themselves. The government tries to persuade them to return to their original residences by charging rent. Then sometimes they take over houses whose owners have fled, and when the rightful owners return they refuse to move. Shi'a militias often support these quests to maintain the houses. Sometimes the squatters are paid reparations to leave. This is going on in some of Baghdad's most prestigious areas: Al Mansour, for example, has been destroyed as poor people moved in. Up until 2004 the original owners could reclaim their property, but this not possible anymore. Property owners going to court often fail, because in many cases militias run the courts too. So districts that used to be mixed, dominated by neither Shi'a nor Sunni, are becoming the opposite.

In the Sunni-dominated areas, the Shi'a leave for a Shi'a-dominated area and look for a place to live. Sometimes Sunni and Shi'a switch homes. There are even a few neutral areas where people switch cars before returning to their "safe" area. Sometimes even moving vans cannot travel all the way to the new place but have to exchange goods in the neutral area because militias may interrogate people about why a Sunni is in a Shi'a area or vice versa.

Even the markets are separated: Sunni, for example, cannot shop for food in a Shi'a area. If a Sunni tries to make a little extra money by delivering food or goods to a Shi'a market and has to go through a checkpoint, he runs the risk of being identified as a Sunni and abducted, ransomed for a high price, or killed.

The story about the young Haditha woman raped by American troops then killed along with all her family members was a big story in the United States. It was not so big here because her family had a sectarian background, came from outside Baghdad, and was not linked to government officials. It was a small and unimportant family from a small and unimportant town and not so interesting to this government. If the family had been linked to government officials it would have been a much bigger story, followed by demonstrations—although nobody has much of an inclination for demonstrations these days. Besides, demonstrations are expressions of American democracy, they're not Iraqi. One goes to demonstrations and speaks freely, but nothing changes. I think demonstrations are just as ineffective as the Iraqi parliament.

This is the "freedom" we've been sold: everybody locked down in their homes—if they still have homes. Streets are empty while people stay home to hide from the violence. Iraq finally has the fewest traffic accidents in the world, because there are no cars on the streets! Sometimes we hear that American soldiers died in traffic accidents, but we know this is absurd, because there is no traffic—except for American vehicles.

It is sad to say that things were not as bad in the old days as they are now. Then we had one dictator. Now we have ten dictators *and* terrible security. In the old days, the rule was clear: don't defame Saddam or the Ba'athists and you'll be safe. Now there are no rules! Today, when a person speaks, he must know the person next to him and he must understand the mood of the situation: Who is the person next to you? What does that person believe? A stranger must know the people around him and the people around him must know something about the stranger's background—or he must keep silent. But silence tells a story, too.

If someone is killed in the street no one does anything about it. The police do not remove the body, sometimes for days. Citizens do nothing about it either. Once I called the police to fetch a body lying in the street and they didn't come for over twelve hours. Then there are those who see who takes a body and target that person. I saw someone go to retrieve a body in the street, and just as he reached out, his mobile phone rang and the caller told him to leave the body alone.

My son was talking with a friend when someone shot and killed the friend. My son ran away. Later another friend took the body to the hospital, and afterwards, walking home very sad and covered in blood, someone called his mobile phone and said that his end will be just like his friend's. Shots were fired at the funeral. My son had been accused of the killing, but after those shots, people knew he'd not been involved in his friend's death. My son moved back into our home because he was so afraid.

This is a nightmare for Sunnis, since Shi'a militias dominate most hospitals and there are few safe choices. This means that if a family member doesn't come home, the family doesn't know what to do. Is their loved one lying in the street somewhere? Is he in a hospital? If so, is it a safe hospital? Who can they even ask? At the morgue they might see the actual dead body or just a photograph.

Instead of freedom, people are being slowly strangled.

Even on calm days in Amriya when there are no car bombs, shootings, or street battles, there is an air of expectancy as people await the next tragedy. Baghdad's nicest stores and streets are closed. Schools and universities are closed because the professors have left and students are unwilling to risk class anyway. The brain drain is huge, and education, our pride and joy, is nonexistent.

I want to get back to my family in Baghdad, but my heart beats fast because I fear returning. I have no hope for the future.

"TALET" and "WIDJAN," Damascus

"My daughter plays with her own reflection"

"Talet" and his wife "Widjan," both doctors, and their small daughter arrived in Damascus from Baghdad in late December to visit family who had fled their homes months before. Both planned to return to work in Baghdad within a week of this interview. Widjan had heard that her parents' home—where she'd grown up—had been damaged by a bomb dropped from a U.S. helicopter. She was still in shock and asked her husband to tell their story.

We were working long hours in Baghdad's hospitals and we decided to visit our families in Damascus. My 2-year-old daughter doesn't play with other children because of the security problem, but when we bought her new clothes for the trip, she played with her own reflection in the mirror.

I'm not sure that I want to return to Baghdad. My hospital is very near to Haifa Street, where there is so much bombing. My wife's parents' house was bombed, and the family very quickly packed up and all their belongings and furniture and fled to Damascus. Same thing with her sister and other family members, who up until then had resisted fleeing Iraq because they want to contribute their skills as doctors, administrators, and so on, to their country. But they couldn't justify staying and risking the family in the violence and chaos.

Iraq's standard of medical care was high before the war with Iran, the invasion of Kuwait, and the subsequent sanctions. Now, walking into any Iraqi hospital brings tears to my eyes. They are supposed to be places of hope, where loved ones heal. Instead, today they accelerate death.

During the 2003 invasion, I worked in the emergency department of the Surgical Specialties Hospital. We felt apprehensive when U.S. forces surrounded our hospital—which was already being looted by thieves, thugs, and gangs—but they protected the place very professionally. When we first saw them, though, they looked so different from our military personnel that we couldn't help but see them as alien, as coming from "outside." Coming from a closed country, Iraqis stared at these strangers with great curiosity and many mixed feelings: fear combined with looking forward to a better future...the dictator is no longer in power...these are American forces and things will change for the better.... Day by day, people began feeling better and shared feelings of jubilation and hope for the future. I can assure you that even those who are now in the resistance—the "insurgency" as they are known—were happy back then, because they felt hope and anticipated calm and peace.

Things have changed dramatically, and we are in a very grave situation. My opinion is that either the U.S. administration is unaware of what is going on or they don't know what to do...or they intend to ruin things. I think the second option is probably true, and they have no clue about what to do. What are the achievements since the invasion? Shi'a theocracy in the south; autonomous Kurdish state in the north—threatened by Iran and Turkey; western Sunni insurgency supported by Al Qaeda. I'm sure people will join Al Qaeda and the insurgency. The U.S. administration has brought nothing good, and people say to themselves, "We will have to fight those who invaded our country, killed and tortured our people, assassinated our scientists and those we call 'The Minds'—our intelligentsia and those who have the capacity to rebuild the country." Essentially, America hasn't provided anything good.

We all await Mr. Bush's new plan. The indications are not encouraging. We see no evidence that he has learned anything about our country and our people, and I'm sure he doesn't know how to handle things. His strategy seems to be backing the same weak Iraqi government. What are the achievements? Are Iraqis secure and protected? Do we have electricity? Running water? Iraqis living in Syria feel as if they are living fantastically, since they have electricity and running water again. The Americans say, "We've lifted your salaries from $3 to $250," but they don't mention that inflation in Baghdad is so high that even this raise is not enough to keep up.

Fuel is unavailable for purchase. People cannot leave their houses for fear of getting caught in improvised checkpoints manned by people and government officials whose loyalty is unknown or by members of various militias. I don't go anywhere in Baghdad without my wife and my small daughter with me, so that when we're stopped at a checkpoint the guards see I'm a family man. Every single man is stopped, and he doesn't know if he'll be abducted or left alone. Every Iraqi man takes a chaperone like his wife or his mom—even to the market—so that if he's stopped, his chaperone can beg for his release or his life.

Saddam's execution [infiltrated by hecklers] showed the government's weakness. Mr. Bush should be ashamed of backing a government that couldn't even control that small execution chamber. Those people who called out, "Muqtada, Muqtada," ought to have called out, if anything, "Iraq, Iraq," or "Liberate Iraq," or "Justice for Iraq." I believe that was a put-up job by a so-called elected government.

Surely everybody knows that the election was pushed by religious leaders and the theocracy they're setting up, and not by the people's will. If you asked people anything about their candidate, they had nothing to say; they didn't even know their candidate's party affiliation or where to find his name on the ballot. This is what people are learning about "democracy" and "elections."

On the other hand, information is so uncertain and foggy, for Americans and Iraqis, that no one *can* know just what is going on. Iraqis think, surely if the United States wanted stability, they could have it. There are already 140,000 troops on the ground, yet nothing positive happens. What will another 20,000 troops add?

As a man with a wife and child, I want a stable life with dignity and prosperity. I'm looking for a change in this government and the installation of a secular government that represents the spectrum of Iraq's population. Yes, it may be complicated, but we need this. I don't want those with turbans running things. That will not be a democracy. I hope Mr. Bush dramatically changes his strategy and really liberates Iraq, for the people he's put in power cannot even run a ministry.

We have ignorant people who don't know what to do now running the Ministry of Health. Guards at the hospital wear uniforms and hang pictures of [Shi'a cleric Muqtada] al-Sadr, [Ayatollah Sayed] al-Hakim, and so on, everywhere. The situation has never been worse. Medical personnel cannot do our jobs due to interference or abductions. We don't have medical equipment. Senior consultants and doctors have been abducted, assassinated, or are living in Syria, Jordan, or the Gulf States, so junior doctors don't get proper instruction from their mentors.

Recently a party of Saudi Arabian pilgrims was stopped on the border and four senior college professors abducted by "people wearing police uniforms" and "driving police vehicles." We haven't seen any results from the investigation that was supposedly conducted. Perhaps people are renting police cars, paying money for the use of these vehicles.

There are double standards dealing with the provinces, and people in Fallujah, Baquba, and Ramadi are having a terrible time, for they cannot get medical care. This saps one's motivation for work. I worked hard during my schooling, my internship, and my residency but I lack the motivation to return to Baghdad. I'm supposed to rotate to other hospitals, but I cannot, because some lie in regions that I am afraid to enter. Luckily, my name doesn't indicate an affiliation with either sectarian identity, for in Baghdad today people's names determine their future. The names Kharar or Sadjat, for example, mean you are Shi'a and cannot go into Sunni areas. Names such as Omar or Ragman mean you are Sunni and you cannot go into Shi'a areas. You cannot take a bus without risking your life. At night, Baghdad is dark and scary, but even after three in the afternoon people are afraid to go outside. Shops are closed. Electricity is on for about one out of every twelve hours, at best. In the hospitals, we use uninterrupted power systems, although elevators don't work much. One day some American troops entered a hospital where I was working and took an elevator that had been working intermittently, although its inside light was always off. As soon as the doors closed, they were in total darkness. They switched on their flashlights, and when they exited their faces were pale. I hope they shared this experience with their superiors.

So Mr. Bush's gift of a democratic government provides daily sectarian violence with 50 bodies a day dumped in our streets. Whose family members are these? How many widows do we have in Iraq now?

Nobody knows...and nobody is counting. This so-called democracy allows Mr. Bush to make television appearances and political gain by saying, "We're building democracy in Iraq." But this is a curse for Iraqis. The people in power are dictators. Each has a militia and each provokes violence and counterviolence. Each says, "We're not supporting Saddam," but Saddam never had a ministry for the Islamic party. Nor did he put pictures of religious leaders in the ministries, as we have now. Visiting the Ministry of Health now is like visiting a Shi'a mosque rather than a governmental institute. Inside the hospital delivery rooms we have large pictures of al-Hakim, and we cannot say, "Please remove this," for they will remove *us*. We cannot ask, "Why are you putting this up in a hospital?" Instead of seeing notices for scientific meetings or lectures, we see Fatwahs and holy doctrines from al-Sadr or [Grand Ayatollah Ali] al-Sistani. We cannot find notices for forums or announcements but see statements such as "Women must wear the veil," "Women must not wear trousers," and so on.

A U.S. medical contact wanted to send $300 to the family of a young child who'd been injured in a blast. I went to the child's house in Sadr City to explain this. As they asked about me, where I was from, and so on, I realized I was putting myself and my family in danger: since I brought them money, they suspected I had more money, and they might report this to those who kidnap wealthy people for ransom. I'd like to help this child, but I emailed my American contact and said I'd help people outside Iraq—like in Syria, for example—but not inside Iraq, because it is too dangerous.

Many aid agencies in Iraq face the same situation: they cannot do their jobs because of the bad security conditions. During the sanctions [in the 1990s] many aid agencies helped Iraqis, so after the invasion many Iraqis were friendly with the U.S. troops: children climbed into Humvees, troops gave them candy, and Iraqis spoke to the troops. But now, when we see a Humvee we stay at least 200 to 300 meters away, for we've learned that troops may start shooting randomly.

Nevertheless, the high incidence of civilian casualties now is not due to U.S. troops but to random sectarian violence. The Badr Brigade, loyal to and backed by Iran, targets certain people—scientists, intellectuals, and so on. I've seen online lists targeting doctors, engineers, university professors, and other influential people. These people are vulnerable because they do not join militias for protection. Those financially able hire bodyguards or leave Iraq.

People depend on militias because of the weak government, police, and army. And there is a double standard too: the Americans hit Fallujah and other Sunni areas but didn't deal effectively with the robbers, mobs, and gangs residing in Sadr City [the district of Baghdad controlled by al-Sadr]. At one point they surrounded Sadr City for about two days, then withdrew for political reasons. The Americans know that bad elements live in Sadr City, but they will not publicly declare the Mehdi Army troublesome.

Iraqi refugees are all over Syria. My wife and I overheard two young Iraqi men talking about their ruined futures. Violence forced both to quit college. One said he fled because American forces raided his neighborhood and took almost every young man. They were agreeing that education in Syria is expensive—about $2,000 per year.

One said, "Forget about college. Find a job here."

The other answered, "What kind of a job? Everything here is restricted for us."

WHERE ARE THEY NOW?

These families remain in Damascus although "Talet" received a job offer in the United States and, for the time being, has gone there to live. His wife "Widjan" and small daughter remain in Syria.

Wissam found work in Damascus as a biologist. Waleed returned to Baghdad. There is no news of him.

6—AFGHANISTAN

You were
never hidden
from my eyes[1]

PRESIDENT G. W. BUSH, Vice President Dick Cheney, Defense
Secretary Robert Gates, Deputy Secretary of State John
Negroponte and others sat at a table at the White House video-
conferencing with U.S. Ambassador to Afghanistan William Wood and
U.S. military and civilian personnel in Kabul. Bush told them, "I must
say, I'm a little envious. If I were slightly younger and not employed
here, I think it would be a fantastic experience to be on the front lines of
helping this young democracy succeed. It must be exciting for you…in
some ways romantic, in some ways, you know, confronting danger.
You're really making history, and thanks."[2]

More realistic views of Afghanistan's situation are considerably
harsher than Bush's romantic picture. Taiseer Alouni, the Al Jazeera
journalist who secretly shot footage of the Taliban blowing up the
Buddhas of Bamiyan, quotes Iranian filmmaker Maksein Makabaf, "I'm
now convinced the statues were not demolished; they crumbled out of
shame because of the West's ignorance towards Afghanistan."[3]

Afghan-born Dr. Qudrat Mojadidi traveled to Afghanistan with
promises from the U.S. Department of Health that included medical
supplies, renovations to the Rabia Balkhi hospital, upgrades to an
ob-gyn ward (named the Laura Bush Ward) and the wherewithal to
train Afghan doctors. After four months the supplies still had not
arrived, and Dr. Mojadidi—unable to change the financial conditions—
departed. In 2005 he said,

> I learned, "Don't trust the U.S. government." They know that if we don't
> invest they can't get rid of Al Qaeda. But if they knew they could get rid of

Al Qaeda without investing in Afghanistan they'd do it in a heartbeat. The Afghans had suffered for over 25 years, but after 9/11 we were suddenly going there to rescue women. What baloney! We could have done it before. But now the U.S. is affected by Afghan affairs they're doing it. I sincerely believe that if the U.S. knew tomorrow that Al Qaeda is not going to move across the border, they'd get out of Afghanistan, because it is very expensive for them there.[4]

The hard day-to-day reality for Afghan mothers and women is hardly a "fantastic experience." My overwhelming impression collecting the stories shared here is of the fierce dedication these women have for their people. They really are making, not only history, but tangible improvements every day, and largely on shoestring budgets, while much of the population continues to suffer from shortages of housing, clean water, electricity, medical care, and jobs.

After 30 years of war, Afghanistan has the highest maternal mortality rate in the world. Nearly one in seven women dies in childbirth. Gross domestic product per capita was estimated at $800 in 2004.[5] About 180,000 teachers serve a current school-age population of about 4 million, although 2 million more children should be in school. Many teachers are not highly educated themselves. A Ministry of Education official told me,

> The fundamental problem in Afghanistan is one of economics. If the poverty could be alleviated, the problems associated with it—lack of education, lack of decent health care, and women's access to resources—would be more accessible and, in turn, the cultural and social problems would be reduced.... My message to developed countries is: Understand the real needs of Afghanistan. We appreciate the money you send us, but it is not getting to the people. Right now we have a lot of street beggars: women, men, and children. There are many children around 7 or 8 years old working very hard at physically demanding jobs—if they can find them—to support their families.

"Righteous war"?

As I talked to American "military moms" and peace and anti-war activists concerned about the occupation of Iraq, I noticed a dearth of indignation about events in Afghanistan. Additionally, when pressed some told me this was a "righteous" war and that bombing Afghanistan was one way of "getting at" those responsible for 9/11.[6] (Not a single

9/11 hijacker was Afghan. The then FBI Director Robert Mueller acknowledged that "some" of those behind the Trade Center attacks may have stolen other peoples' identification but nothing was said about stealing nationality.[7] Saudi Arabia acknowledged that 15 of the 19 hijackers were Saudi citizens.[8]) I found that merely asking why the most sophisticated military in the world was bombing a developing country that even the CIA describes as "extremely poor, landlocked, and highly dependent on foreign aid, agriculture, and trade with neighboring countries" seemed to raise doubts about my motives. Questioning this logic was tantamount to taking a megaphone to the rubble of Ground Zero and declaring oneself a traitor to one's country and to the War on Terror.

The stories

I was unable to travel to Central Asia to interview in Afghanistan, so the stories presented here do not reflect my firsthand experiences in that country. The account by Robert Darr, however, is informed by three decades of travel into Afghanistan and presents a far deeper view than the one I, a woman visiting for three or four weeks, could offer. Nevertheless, all the voices shared here—of Afghans living in the United States, those who returned subsequent to the U.S. retaliatory invasion begun in 2001, and those living in Afghanistan or as refugees in surrounding countries—surfaced similar themes: the plethora of women widowed during the Soviet invasion, the civil war, the Taliban's reign, and the War on Terror; the dearth of health and education centers to service a population of more than 26 million; dismal poverty; and cultural mores that relegate Afghan women and girls to the home. Each of these stories explores these themes and presents a systemic view of the effects of war on ordinary families and communities.

The stories presented first were gathered in March and April 2008. The shorter vignettes were recorded in 2004 when I interviewed Afghan immigrants in a social center in Pleasanton, California. Most had survived the Russian occupation of 1979 to 1989, when Soviet forces supported the Marxist People's Democratic Party of Afghanistan government against the mujahideen insurgents supported by the United States, Saudi Arabia, Pakistan, and other Muslim nations.

ROBERT DARR, Mill Valley, California

"We assume we have the 'right' viewpoint"

Author of *Spy of the Heart*, Robert Darr, also known as Abdul Hayy, has traveled to and from Afghanistan many times since deciding almost 30 years ago to learn the languages key to its classical literature. His photographs of refugees and refugee camps show the psychological scarring of the children—now adults—exposed to war.

Too many Afghans have never known a time of peace and prosperity, decent social services such as education and medical care, or functional infrastructure, roads, and so on. They've grown up without most of the things we in America take for granted. Plus they have been exposed to so much indoctrination from the Islamist schools that have penetrated well into Afghan society. It is a pretty bleak picture, and our response to it has been to bring a foreign ideology in the form of democracy. People don't have the tools to think about something like Western-style democracy because they're wondering where they're going to get their next meal, or how they'll remain safe, or how they'll cope with the grief or the trauma or scarring that they live with—all of them. There is hardly a person who hasn't been affected by the wars there: first the Soviet invasion, secondly the war among the mujahideen and the destruction of Kabul and the complete breakdown of the law and order social structures there, and now finally the U.S. and NATO invasion of their country.

Many of the Afghan refugees who came to San Francisco Bay Area who had been professionals in their country—doctors, teachers, professors, editors of magazines, poets, and so on—tried to make a living hawking clothing and such things. This was quite a change for people of great pride and dignity. I met many people of great talent and skill, the cultural crème de la crème you might say, who had gone into exile. That still holds true today: some of the finest Afghan thinkers are outside Afghanistan.

I traveled into the remote areas of Afghanistan on horseback in the late 1980s and early 1990s. After that, I was contacted by the United Nations Human Rights Commission to look at the situation from Pakistan and set up a project. There were about two and a half million refugees from the northwest provinces around Peshawar and some near Quetta. Huge numbers of refugees needed employment, and by 1986 I'd organized a rug-weaving project and traveled around the United States with the Afghan Cultural Fair, introducing Americans to Afghan culture.

Afghanistan was the poorest place I'd ever seen. If there were roads they were very poor, mined, or washed away. Land mines are still a problem, and it is difficult to get rid of them; thousands have been removed, but back then, many people were injured or killed by mines designed to do just that; the larger mines laid on roads were meant to prevent supplies reaching the mujahideen who were very well organized by 1986. In fact, the Russian defeat took three more years, and Pakistan was supplying them with American weapons.

The Americans were trying hard to support the mujahideen without actually escalating the Cold War. Eventually they were giving very sophisticated weapons—Stinger missiles and so on—to the mujahideen. That was a disaster in some ways, because when the mujahideen were fighting the Russians they were more unified and they knew they had to be more unified to succeed. As the Russians began pulling out, the next war between different Afghan ethnic and sectarian groups began. It lasted seven more years until the arrival of the Taliban and, eventually, to the American invasion. That long war brought further breakdown of Afghan society and culture.

In cultures such as this—clan- and family-oriented—one sees and gets to know the headmen and tribal leaders first, making sure that they approve of the particular work one is proposing and establishing bonds that allow one to work with the different groups. So I had the funding and then I had to work with the local leaders. I had to figure out who was the true spokesperson from each particular refugee group and set up a project ensuring that each person I worked with had a project so that there was no sense of favoritism and so on. At that point, I began wearing local clothing and tried to learn more about local etiquette. I grew a beard, for example, because that is culturally appropriate for a dignified and trustworthy person; if you cover your head you are considered more polite. If you're wearing tight Western clothes they have a bit of a lewd appearance so I wore the loose, amorphous clothing, which is also incidentally more comfortable. That was very effective, because pretty soon I was having dozens of conversations with dozens of people, learning about what was going on in remote regions, and finally traveling there on horseback to see what was actually happening.

At this time I was also able to see the depth of the faith that allowed people to face so many of the things that were lacking in their lives and the many tragedies that struck them. People from the experiential Sufi tradition had the idea that religion sets forth principles that one needs to verify. One cannot just accept these principles on faith but only through personal verification.

The rise of the Taliban has changed all of this. In this generation of refugee children you can see the psychological scarring of children raised by organizations that are Islamist by nature. These are very narrow-minded, with rigid views of religion and supremacist tendencies built in. When they entered Afghanistan they discounted traditional Afghan values. They came in and said the way you are doing things is just plain wrong. The vast majority of the Taliban were from the ages of 15 to 25, led by and indoctrinated by older leaders with these narrow tendencies, and they had no understanding of how things worked, world events, Afghan literature and culture of the last 1,000 years, which was a culture of religious ethics and humanitarian values and an ecumenical perspective—they didn't even want to hear about it: "No, it is just wrong."

It's unfortunate that, in the U.S. there is a tendency to see only the surface, or propaganda side, of Islam. No one should take, for example, the Bible's story literally. It is literature. One should look at one's own house to see another's house. In other words, we should not look at our own country and culture, whether Christianity or Judaism, absolutely literally. On the other hand there is a big range and there are reformist movements that happen in every religion and have happened cyclically in Christianity and in Islam. There were great enlightened periods in Islam. Why did the Jews who went to Turkey from Spain not just settle in France? Because they were being wiped out by the Christians in Europe and treated terribly. So they went to a country that had a more enlightened view of the world, of other people, of compassion. So people forget—or have never learned—their own history, or the history of Islam or Christianity or whatever. One needs to see the stories in these various traditions as symbolic. But groups like the Taliban see these things literally and take them very seriously: No, that *really* happened....

In 2004, when I went to Afghanistan, the people were still in favor of the American intervention and were worried that the Taliban would come back—they knew the Taliban better than we did. Since then Afghanistan seems to be slipping back. Afghans have become increasingly pessimistic about their own country—and so have the Western powers. The Norwegian embassy closed its doors in February, 2008, which is what happened the last time Kabul fell into chaos—that is, the various embassies closed their doors. The Americans propose to increase the troop level and talk about their successes there. I'm of the view that we should give help to them, *but for what they ask for*. NATO went in and bombed without consulting sufficiently with local authority, and this is only going to make the Taliban stronger. The sad fact is that if we hadn't have been so involved with the military side of this operation, in time the majority of the people would reject the emptiness of the Taliban, as there is a lack of popular support for this kind of Islamism and fundamentalism. It is amusing that the Taliban outlawed music, dancing, songbirds, etc, for the Afghans are the most lively people. They love to dance and sing and do all the things that are now prohibited so how long, really, could a really draconian version of Islam survive? Unless it were linked to a political battle—and that is what has happened.

The Taliban are a Pashto movement, and the American and NATO attacks on the Taliban are gaining momentum because the Pashto majority is not represented in the government. They feel it is a puppet government that does not represent them, so they're fighting a kind of civil war to get fair representation. If one went just by numbers they'd have to have more than half the delegates. As it is, they have very little representation in the government. This is not a war of religion as much as the West believes but actually a war about representation, ethnicity, and strange borders created by Europeans—like the Durand Line [dividing Pashto territory between Afghanistan and Pakistan]—or even by Al Qaeda. Just as the early Americans revolted when they were underrepresented and went to enemies of the British for help, so too did the Pashto people, when they felt shut out, turn to these religious people. This is like a puzzle, pieces of which are about indoctrination, about a militant Islam, and much more complex issues such as the Durand Line.

We in the West assume we have the "right" viewpoint, the moral authority, or the detachment to impose our ideas. This has led to losing whatever gains we may have made, and it is very sad. The war in Iraq is outside of international law and ethics. We've created a war and we don't seem to get it that we need to know more before making these sorts of decisions to invade, attack, occupy, create borders. This will come back to haunt us…. Whenever we try to impose democracy anywhere, it is always a charade. It is hard enough for us to practice it in the United States, although the Pashto, in fact, have practiced a kind of democracy for the last 3,000 years. This was mentioned by Herodotus.

In Afghanistan, if the majority was given a political voice, I doubt they'd align with the Taliban zealots for very long. It doesn't fit their culture. We [in the United States] are sustaining the very ideological struggle that we are purporting to fight.[9]

ASMA ESCHEN, San Rafael, California

"Private military contractors are not helping"

I interviewed Asma days after she returned from her third visit to Afghanistan to plant thousands of pine, shade, and fruit trees to replace those destroyed during the country's three decades of war.

When I was a child living in Afghanistan my family went on picnics on a hill hear Kabul—the same hill that Khaled Hosseini talks about in his book *The Kite Runner*—and I have a photograph of me and my family there under a huge blossoming tree. When I returned to Afghanistan—after more than 30 years away—I returned to that place to plant trees and replace those destroyed during the wars. I also gave the villagers there a copy of the photograph to show them how lush the hill had been. We're hoping it will be that way again, and Bare Roots has traveled to Afghanistan each year since 2003 to plant trees.

This village was fortunate in that it wasn't destroyed during the Afghan civil war, but it was affected by the Taliban era. It is particularly beautiful, with a lovely river running through the valley floor on the east side of Shamali Plain, and many people visit it for its first-century aura and beauty. But Shamali Valley, comparable to California's San Joaquin Valley, where farmers produced all kinds of fruit and vegetables, was laden with land mines—from the Russian era, the civil wars, even Taliban times. Today, these are about 70 percent cleared, so agriculture is slowly coming back.

[Just north of Kabul, this lush valley was, until September 1999, one of the most fertile regions of Afghanistan and home to mainly ethnic Tajik farmers. Then the Taliban forced out nearly 180,000 people and conducted a scorched-earth policy as they retreated, poisoning wells, exploding irrigation ditches, destroying orchards, and shattering livelihoods.]

In 2003, no one was there and the area was desolate. The de-mining NGOs slowly cleared the area. What they do is put up signs designating areas that had mines—and there were thousands of such signs—and, as the mines are cleared, the signs are slowly being replaced by farmed land again. Since 2003, it is like night and day there: people are returning to their homes, the roads are being fixed, they're growing vegetables, restoring vineyards, and children are selling flowers on the streets.

When those people were forced out, some went to Mazar el Sharif; if they had families there they went to Iran; but the majority walked to Pakistan. They learn about the clearing of the mines and that they can return when the de-mining NGOs alert them with notices and word-of-mouth campaigns. Before they return, however, the NGOs try to get them into five-day seminars to educate them about the mines, what to look out for, what do it if you come across mines, who to call, and so on. The success rate for people who have done the seminars is excellent, and they've remained safe. Those that have not done the seminars have, unfortunately, not been quite as safe, and incidents with mine explosions have occurred. Then the person involved may lose a foot or hand or worse.

The good news is the projection that by 2013, only about 5 percent of the mines will remain. In fact, Afghans take this de-mining work very seriously...some have made careers out of it, going to Virginia to further their studies and then being sent to other places in the world to put their skills to work de-mining other regions like Somalia, Angola, Thailand, Zambia, Bosnia, and so on. For example, the Marshall Legacy Institute uses dogs to sniff out mines, and many Afghans work this way, with dogs, too.

If you ask my opinion, I'd say the Afghan civil war did the most destruction to the country. I have photographs of Kabul that show a city almost destroyed. When I ask the question Who did it?, I hear, "Well, the Uzbeks bombed the Pashto here and then they retaliated," or "The big warlords fought one another…" and so on.

Nevertheless, psychologically, Afghans are very determined and creative. For example, they're recycling the metal from the Russian tanks left behind and making things they need from these scraps. Schools are being built, people are smiling more. My impression is that there is a resurgence of a healthy society.

I am amazed at how resilient the Afghan people are. When we started the Bare Roots project, we believed the people had nothing, and we'd walk into a small courtyard and find fruit trees that were almost members of the family. The family would excitedly show us their apricot tree or rose bush. In terms of owning things, yes, they had very little, but they appreciated what they had. Remember, these people were very poor and had been in refugee camps, and when they came back to Kabul they'd been put into the northeastern part of the city and pretty much left to survive on their own without work or much assistance.

According to 2004 U.N. data, the number of widows in Kabul is about 60 percent of the total population. Today you see lots and lots of women and then very young or very old males. You don't see a lot of men between the ages of, say 18 and 55. Every family has a widow from one of the wars. During the Taliban era, Hazaras, Uzbeks, Tajiks, anyone not Pashto, was targeted, either killed outright or conscripted and killed that way.

Regarding the American military presence in Afghanistan, first, you don't see much of it in Kabul although the U.S. embassy is there—it is like a fortress, with many layers of security and barbed wire, security walls, and so on. You do see a lot of French members of ISAF [NATO's International Security Assistance Force, which operates in Afghanistan under U.N. mandate and will continue to do so in accordance with U.N. Security Council resolutions]. The U.S. military is mainly in the rural areas, while the Afghan police and national army and ISAF are in Kabul.

What I'm hearing is that security is still a huge issue. Before it was the Taliban with their Puritanism, but since then there has been a big rise in criminality, with a few who've decided to have power over others and they take people's land and property as well as their daughters.

My cousin lives in a tiny apartment with her three daughters—16, 14, and 12 years old—and when I asked her why she didn't get a bigger place, perhaps a house, she said, "Are you crazy? I don't know who might come and steal my daughters." Because there is a lot of this sort of activity with young girls being sold to Arabs or Pakistanis or Indians. This infuriates me because those girls are being sold and shipped to Muslim countries...we talk about Shari'a as a more conservative way, yet this is going on. There is little common theft in Afghanistan these days but there are these huge thefts of the whole person, young girls and women.

I tried to determine how much of this activity was the residue of traditional culture and indicated revenge between families—an eye for an eye is still the common way of thinking. It is a mixture. About the common theft, I noticed that when my group was distributing trees no one took anything that didn't belong to them. I asked a man who works with United Nations Radio why he locks his home. He said, "I'm not concerned about common thieves. There aren't that many, but I don't want Taliban or mullahs or big criminals coming into my home and seeing that I have young children to steal."

Afghanistan is going through the process of settling down after years of turmoil, even to the point of having their music shut down. Now there is a lot of loud music played on the street, and I hope that this too will settle down after this initial euphoria quiets. There is a sense of trying to figure out how much openness to have. On the other hand, the women were so crushed, and now they're being exposed to new TV shows and marketing.... But no matter what laws or policies are brought in, the man of the house, the male, will make the final decision. In my family we women never covered ourselves. We used a scarf but nothing more than that. In the family next door, of the same socioeconomic bracket as our family, the women had to cover up. Why? Because the man of the house said they would—and they did.

I returned to Afghanistan after 32 years and I recognized a lot of places. I visited where my grandparents lived and all the places that I knew.

Some were destroyed, some were intact. I still have an uncle and his wife, sons, and grandchildren there. During the Taliban era they went to Peshawar. My uncle lost his 17-year-old son in the civil war. One afternoon four boys including his son were walking on the street in Kabul when a rocket struck them and killed all four. My uncle said the civil war was the harshest time: all windows were sandbagged and the family lived in the hallways in case of rockets.

When I went there in 2003, every corner of Kabul had a cemetery and a *tandoor* [communal oven for baking bread]. These are gone now but my uncle told me that during the war they would get up early every morning, turn on the *tandoor*, and cook the bread for the whole block, to avoid rockets being rained on them. My grandfather was killed like this. The cemetery was created out of open space because there was so much death. And Kabul was divided up into quarters: the Hazara, Pashto, Uzbek, and Tajiks got their own areas. They've gone through a lot.

Today, Kabul is slowly coming back to life and greening. One thing though, the huge private military contractors are not helping there. They live in big fancy houses but they are getting a bad name because they tend to stay in their houses and don't connect with people. They gave us rules about not going outside Kabul, but we did it anyway. They are not helping since they are seen as making lots of money and telling us where we can't go, and to me they're not succeeding at their jobs if the security is still so bad. And they're being supported by USAID and our tax dollars. I wouldn't mind paying for it if it was effective, but it is not. If you want to work with people, go "people to people" and avoid the big government contractors because they're not doing the people any good.

RAHIMA HAYA, Fremont, California

"I try to bridge cultural misunderstanding"

Rahima represents the Afghan Women's Association and Berkeley Bamiyan Foundation and is involved in projects to promote literacy in Afghanistan and cultural understanding in the United States.

I left Afghanistan in 1980 and took my two small children—2 and 4 years old—to Germany. My husband remained in Kabul working in radio and TV, and he was targeted by the Soviets and the mujahideen. I was very worried about him, but I needed to rescue our kids. I left my house, my teaching job in a women's high school, my husband, everything. I'd been to college in Germany, so I had some contacts there and I could speak the language. My two brothers also left; one was a pilot and one was an engineer. My husband joined us two years later.

I started going back to Afghanistan after I set up a widows' project that helped these women to make a living. In 2001 I went back to start a literacy class so women could become self-sufficient. I'm pleased to report that one of the young women I taught to read and write recently opened her own 501(c)3,[10] and she too will be able to teach literacy to another 30 or 40 women a year.

We've heard on the news about the Taliban preventing women from getting an education—they locked all the schools with big, big locks, and that was it for educating women while the Taliban were in power. Along with this lack of literacy that followed this action was a huge increase in the number of widows across the country. Today there are close to 2 million widows, and many of these women have five or six children.

I was shocked when I went back to Kabul to see women begging on the streets, old women, young women, so many women.

I asked one young, beautiful woman, "Why are you here? It is very dangerous for you to be out here."

She said, "My mother has six other children and she can't feed them so I have to come here and try to make some money this way."

So she travels through the city, from north to south, to beg.

I've also seen them begging late at night after dark.

A lot of these girls were sold to others, and sometimes taken out of the country too. Sex trafficking is not uncommon here now. One young widow whose husband was dead had no one taking care of her, and her uncle sold her to some people for prostitution in Pakistan.

In Kabul, some people saw a lot of progress after the American forces came and their presence in the Kabul region at least hasn't been as negative as it is in Iraq, for example. There has been some general progress with schools being built and so on.

It is important for Americans to know how different the American and Afghan cultures are. I worked for a long time as an advocate for my local community in California trying to bridge some of this cultural misunderstanding. We cannot force Afghan culture to adopt new and very different ways, and I try to help the two groups understand one another in order for both to be successful. One misunderstanding for Americans is that Afghan culture is different from Arab culture. The Afghans are Muslim and became Muslim after almost 2,000 years of Buddhist culture with Buddhist stupas, monasteries, and the massive statues carved out of a sand rock at Bamiyan in the heart of Afghanistan. Nevertheless, Afghan women face a lot of challenges in the United States, too, with their children, their husbands, their health issues, and their way of life. We try to get them together to talk about these things. One woman I'm talking with is diabetic and has other health problems, and her stress level is very high: she has two children still in Afghanistan—20 and 21 years old—and she cannot get them here. In this case she came to the U.S. because her older son was already here and sponsored her to get here, but he couldn't sponsor his brother and sister so they remain there.

Another woman here has three young sisters back there and is very stressed because it is extremely difficult for young women to live alone over there without a male figure to protect them: it is frowned upon, no matter the reason.

There was a large group of Afghans who were able to immigrate to the U.S. after the Soviet era in Afghanistan but since 2001 it is very difficult for Afghans to get here.

FATIMA AKBARI, Kabul

"If a woman wants to do something she is capable of doing it…"

Fatima Akbari owns and operates Gulistan Sadaqat Company, a carpentry business and training center in Kabul. She is also involved in a food-processing business making jams and other food as well as literacy programs to educate widows. I interviewed her by telephone with the help and translation skills of Soraya Omar.

I left Afghanistan as a refugee during the Taliban era and went to Iran. I'd always been interested in skills that are unusual for women, and while there I learned to make furniture. It is not a very difficult craft for women, because much of the heavy work is done by machine.

After three years I proposed to the woman who had trained me that I start my own business. Since it is difficult for Afghans to open a business in Iran I started under contract with the agreement that I'd work for nine years. So I stayed in Iran and nine years later returned to Afghanistan and opened a business in Kabul. I brought all the equipment I'd need with me from Iran.

At first the people in Afghanistan made fun of me, saying this was work for men and that women couldn't do it, that I was ridiculous, and so on. I also started a food-processing business making jams and other things. Nevertheless, I persisted with carpentry and brought my family members who were widows into the business. Three months later Afghans were beginning to see that, in fact, not only can women do carpentry, we can make a successful business of it. They started respecting us and encouraging us, knowing that we were helping widows who, traditionally, have few skills yet have big families to support, often six or more children.

I started training and employing ten other women, all widows, in carpentry and in the food-processing work. At this time, I have about 60 trainees in the carpentry business. All together, in the food processing businesses, literacy programs, and so on, I have about 2,000 working women, mostly widows. I've been doing this for about four years.

We don't have adequate equipment or shelter. Right now we're working under a large tent and trying to get a permanent structure. We work throughout the year under these conditions, and this winter there was a very heavy snowfall and the tent collapsed. We had to stop work for a whole month and we also had to replace some of the equipment that was damaged. I got a temporary tent from one of our contractors, and now that their work is finished they will take back the tent. The organization B Peace is helping us write a proposal for a grant to raise funds that will allow us to purchase a permanent structure. We need to raise $90,000, which means knocking on many donors' doors for that amount of money.

I also want to expand the business into other parts of this country so that we can train more widows but right now we don't have enough equipment to do this. Another factor is that the equipment runs on electric power, and since Kabul doesn't have reliable electricity we use generators.

There are about 70,000 widows in Kabul alone and they have a very difficult time surviving and supporting their families. Most of these women are illiterate and have never worked outside of their homes. While there are a few small organizations trying to help these widows— find them jobs and improve their situation—it is a tiny drop in a huge sea. The widows are the most vulnerable people in Afghanistan, and they are a priority for all of us. I'm trying to get more widows involved in supporting themselves. Their ages range from about 18 to 60; some of these women were married at 14 years old, and many of the younger women lost their husbands in the Taliban era.

When I hire, I first of all hire women who are widows, keeping in mind that they are the most disadvantaged and often have no work at all. At the same time, carpentry requires energy, so I try to hire the most needy who can also do that kind of work. I pay them about $40 per month, so not very much, but it is enough to provide food for the family. (In 2006, our annual revenues were about $12,000.) Besides the charity organizations distributing basic food rather than teaching skills, there is no other system in the country that provides for this group of people, and of course, without an income, it is very difficult to survive. The numbers of needy in Kabul alone are tremendous: about 7 million people live in Kabul, and many adults and children beg on the streets. They manage to survive somehow, often by tiny businesses—for example, a child sells chewing gum after school and brings that little bit of money home.

I have been very fortunate in that my family is very open-minded and has always encouraged me to do whatever I wanted. They were always open to letting their daughters be involved in wider society, to be self-sufficient and self-supporting, and to be independent in their work. They gave us the option to do whatever kind of work we chose, and this has really helped me throughout my life and helped me be successful. Nevertheless, this is very unusual in Afghanistan, where the majority of Afghan families do not let their daughters have an education or work or have choices like what to learn. Often the girls are married off while they are young and they don't have any other option.

The message I'd like to share is that women who want to do something should never think that we cannot do it. If we are willing to try it, we are always capable of doing it.

FAZILA WISAY, Peshawar, Pakistan

"I have many dreams of a good future for my people"

I conducted this telephone interview with Fazila from Peshawar, Pakistan, where she currently lives and works with the NGO Afghan Women's Network, based in the Peshawar office since 2003. She also publishes a youth magazine, *Lives of Youth*.

Many young Afghan women don't have the courage to enter into and work in their larger society, so I work with them to develop these skills. I work with young girls because they have lots of issues associated with lack of education, forced marriage, and lack of information on health topics. I go to their homes, talk to their families, and if there are deeper problems I refer them to specialists in that field who can advise them.

In the case of young girls being forced into marriages with much older men, I talk with the family and explain that if a young woman doesn't want to marry someone, she should not be forced to do so, as it will create all sorts of future problems as well as make the woman herself miserable. I'm happy to say that I have been very successful in this area. Last year I had three cases of young women being forced to marry old men that they did not want to marry. I went and talked to the families and explained the problems associated with such actions. The families were convinced and changed their minds. The women were very pleased too and have gone on to engage themselves in other ways. The families and the girls agreed that if there is a man they would like to marry they will judge whether he is a good man and if he can support a family.

At that point, when they marry, they go and live with the man's family but stay in touch with their own families.

Education is poor here and there is very little attention on improving it here. In many cases refugees are not interested in returning to Afghanistan yet. First, the infrastructure is ruined in Afghanistan, and that is not the case here in Peshawar. Also, there is very little work there because there are so many refugees returning. According to U.N. Human Rights Commission, the refugees should stay here until the end of 2009. Besides, there are security problems and few homes to return to. They are doing well enough here. They can be educated in Pakistani colleges and universities, and many have their own businesses, shops, taxi services, and so on. Also, women can work outside the home here without a problem. They also have a lot more social freedom, and no one is watching over their activities, as would happen in Afghanistan. For example, I'm trained as a social worker and I can go wherever I want here. If I were in Afghanistan I'd probably be followed by some sort of security to see what I was doing, who I was talking to, and so on.

There are more than 2 million refugees outside of Afghanistan, but they get very little attention and almost no funding. Much of the attention toward Afghan people goes to those living inside Afghanistan, but the Afghan people here also need help, especially with health and education.

As a reporter for the magazine I went into the refugee camps where conditions were bad. Things are better now and especially for those living in the city.

There is a misconception about the Pashto people—most of the Afghan people here are Pashto—and that Peshawar is "dangerous" because of the Pashto presence. In fact, Pashto people are not, as the stereotype paints them, "terrorist" or "Al Qaeda." Here, we Afghans mix with local people, and there are no problems or discrimination among us. We can use the buses, go shopping, and go to restaurants and other public places just like any other residents. In fact, the local people see how hard Afghan women work to make their lives better for their families and they have a lot of respect for Afghan women.

My magazine is a monthly. It used to be in English but when I was in Afghanistan I understood that many young women couldn't read English, so I changed my mind about that and now publish it in Farsi. There are three of us working on this magazine, reporting on social topics, interviews with young people, and all sorts of things. We distribute it for free in girls' schools and publish over 200 copies.

At first the young women I worked with had very few social skills and were very uncomfortable speaking in public, or even in small groups, outside their families. Also, girls and young women in Afghanistan are discouraged from talking to boys and young men. Now, I'm happy to say, we are managing to change this. These girls and young women are doing so well that they can talk on any topics that interest them. They also join youth committees, have a student union, go to university, and so on. I've been working with these groups for many months, and now they create youth workshops and work well together.

Once a month I go into the schools and talk to the girls about health issues, including HIV-AIDS and how it is transmitted. Traditionally these topics about sexuality and so on are not talked about, but the young women are very interested in knowing how to protect—and improve—their health and the health of their families. I also talk about marriage and issues associated with it. Again, traditionally we don't talk about these things in our culture. At first when I started talking about these topics people were uncomfortable and unwilling to listen. But now they are demanding this sort of information. I share it in workshops, show movies, and get them talking among themselves. I also talk about birth control so that mothers can understand it. I approach these topics in many different ways. For example, I talk about the health effects on the mothers and the children of having very large families. I also try to guide the young women that I work with to understand how to talk to the people about this.

Health care here is not free, but there are facilities, the health care is good, and Afghan people have access to it.

People are reluctant to talk too much about the war. They had a tough time in the past. They are also not sure that they want to return to Afghanistan, because they are uncertain about whether the fighting is over and they don't want to give up what they've built here to return to what they perceive as uncertainty there. There are families living here who return there to see conditions.

My message to American women: Afghan women need lots of help, especially those living outside of Afghanistan. They are mothers, they have children, they struggle, and they need help.

AFGHAN VOICES FROM CALIFORNIA

Alia

"War affects everyone, especially the families"

I spent most of my life in Kabul. I left Afghanistan during the Russian occupation and spent five years in Pakistan before arriving in the U.S. I have nine children but only three—the unmarried children— were granted visas for the United States. My married children live in Australia, Germany, Canada, and Pakistan. I left one son in Kabul who was imprisoned for his political views. After some time in jail, he refused to see me anymore. I don't know what happened to him, but I surmise he is dead.

Adjusting to a new country at my age is difficult. I still have trouble speaking English. I also had a big drop in income since coming here and I have no transportation other than the bus that brings me to the (senior) center each weekday. Of my 25 grandchildren, six are in the U.S. and I've never seen the other 19.

I'd like to say to those who hear this story: No more war. We'd like peace. As a mother I know how war affects everyone, especially the families.

Shireen

"I still hope to hear from him"

I left Kabul nine years ago after the Taliban came to the door of my house, pointed to my younger son and demanded that he accompany them. When the family tried to prevent his kidnap another son and a son-in-law were shot dead in front of them. I have never seen my younger son since that day. I heard a rumor that the Taliban killed him, but I still hope to hear from him.

Twenty days after the Taliban's visit, driven by fear, I and most of my family left for Pakistan. A daughter and son-in-law remained in the house in Kabul. We lived in Pakistan for seven years before coming to Pleasanton with my husband and our two daughters.

Like Alia's, my family has been split by war and fear: four daughters live in Kabul, one daughter lives in Pakistan, and another lives in Azerbaijan.

Sometimes I get a phone call from one of them. They tell me they are getting along. Their husbands are working, at least.

Hanyama

"American people are different from American policies"

Hanyama works in the Afghan Women's Association (AWA) center and is a student at a local college. Her English is excellent, and her mother Rahima lets her tell the family's story, now and again adding a few words in Farsi.

Before we left Afghanistan, a friend of my father's came to our house and told my father that foreign people (Taliban) would take over our country, and that if we could move, we should. But my father was very patriotic and said that after 25 years of war, we—my brother, sister, parents, and I—could manage. My father died three years later. We've been in Pleasanton for four years.

I grew up under a communist regime, although it is not the communism that is depicted in American politics. Rather, it was more of a socialist political structure with communal ways of life. I liked it very much. The Russians spread propaganda about the United States, mostly in documentary movies showing the American lifestyle of big houses and very little caring about anyone outside of one's own group. Since I've been in the U.S. I have seen that some of that propaganda is true.

When the war came I saw many bombs labeled "Made in USA." Maybe they were mislabeled? I don't know. But many weapons were supplied by the United States and Afghans hated what was happening to our country with so many weapons and bombs.

When I came to the U.S. I had a twisted view, but I discovered that American people are different from American policies.

I was in class when the planes rammed into the World Trade Center on September 11. Classmates turned to another woman in class who looks more Afghan than I do and asked her, very aggressively, Why did your people do this? Their hatred toward us was scary, and I never let on that I was Afghan too. Intimidated by the hatred, that girl never returned to class.

Besides the prejudice in school, violent acts have been committed against the mosque in Concord [California]. And one of my new friends invited me to her house, but when her husband met me, she cooled down towards me. I learned that her husband didn't want a "Middle Easterner" in his house. [Afghans must often confront Americans' ignorance that their country is in Central Asia.]

I am studying International Relations so that I can return to Afghanistan and do something useful.

It bothers me that Americans believe Afghan women are uneducated. It's true that during the Taliban era women were not allowed in schools, but many conducted or attended classes in secret. Afghanistan has a long tradition of educated women; over 64 percent of those educated are women.

Shobobo
"A misguided bomb…"

I have lived in Pleasanton for 13 months. Before this, my family and I lived ten years in Pakistan.

One evening, during the Russian occupation, my whole family was together in our house, eating and drinking. Out of the blue a bomb dropped on our house. My husband was killed outright and a daughter-in-law was injured. The police came and asked us if we had enemies who may have bombed us. In fact, it was a misguided bomb that no one wanted to take responsibility for.

We left Pakistan from fear of the same thing happening, although one son and one daughter stayed in Kabul. I have a son and a daughter in Holland and one son here in the United States.

Bibi
"No safety for children"

I followed my older son to Pleasanton after seven years in Pakistan. I've lived here for three years.

In Afghanistan there is no safety for children. During the Russian occupation one of my sons was conscripted unwillingly. My sister-in-law's son was killed by a car bomb and another son disappeared.

Hawa
"He works in a gas station now"

My husband came to the United States as a young man to study electrical engineering. After graduating from JFK University he returned to Afghanistan and lived a good life working in a television station. After the Russians came he persisted in staying in Afghanistan. But when a bomb dropped on our home he said, "Now I'll go to the U.S." He sustained injuries to his back and neck. We went to the UN offices in Pakistan for our visas, but they were delayed for five months due to the American war on Iraq in 1991. My husband works in a gas station now.

Shafiqa
"Nothing changes when it comes to war"

People were very upset before the start of the latest war with Iraq. They suffered from their memories of Afghanistan and nightmares. Now Iraq is like Afghanistan in 1992. Iraq wants peace.

I can't watch TV anymore. Why? I don't feel like it. It shows the same thing over and over, always the same American point of view. Nothing changes when it comes to war.

Author's note: U.S. President Barack Obama, partially elected for his anti-Iraq-war stance, presents a disheartening direction for Afghanistan: sending in more troops and "finishing the job" started by the Bush administration. Meanwhile, the Taliban threaten that a course similar to that of G.W. Bush will reap the Democrats a fate "even more shameful and despicable" than that of the Republicans. And insurgent leader Abu Omar al-Baghdadi pragmatically guarantees America "free trade, including the trade of petroleum."

7—UNITED STATES

JANUARY 2004 THROUGH 2008—SAN FRANCISCO BAY AREA—
WASHINGTON, D.C.—FAYETTEVILLE, NORTH CAROLINA—CRAWFORD,
FT. HOOD, TEXAS

Broken-heartedness is the beginning[1]

OUNSELING GIs gave me an insider's view of the U.S. military. At first, however, I was overwhelmed by GIs' stories of harsh treatment at the hands of military personnel. I needed "balanced views" about the institution my son had joined, and troops seeking to get *out* of the military tend to be on one side of the equation. I turned to one who excelled at—and enjoyed—soldiering.

Glimpses that would make me less forlorn[2]

Lieutenant Julian Goodrum and I talked over lunch in an empty banquet room in a Maryland restaurant; he'd been there often enough that the staff knew he required quiet.

This man had been so good at his job that he'd received a direct commission—rare for enlistees—and many awards during 13 years of service, including the 176th Maintenance Battalion's "Soldier of the Year." His evaluation stated, "[he] is a truly outstanding junior officer.... In addition to his technical competence, he demonstrates great leadership potential.... Promote to captain and select for advanced military schooling."

Lieutenant Goodrum had excelled in Gulf War I. During Operation Iraqi Freedom he displayed what his superiors thought was too much concern for his men's safety. He also identified serious problems with his transportation battalion, which was obliged to cover thousands of miles and to perform grueling day missions: it had no radios, no maps, no heavy weapons, no armor, and no medics, and its first aid kits didn't

193

have the requisite supplies. Additionally, one of his young soldiers had been crushed to death between two vehicles in a long convoy. This stress surfaced and exacerbated symptoms of Post Traumatic Stress Disorder from Gulf War I, for which Goodrum had never been treated.

In 2003, Goodrum returned to the United States, where he isolated himself and tried, as military experts order, to "suck it up." His depression, racing thoughts, and inability to sleep increased. It "just accumulates until it overwhelms me. I was having a breakdown and trying to get assistance…. The smell of diesel triggers things. So do loud noises, crowds, and heavy traffic. I have a lot of panic. I feel like I'm choking."

One night he woke up choking his fiancée: "My nightmares were so intense that I had my hands around [her] throat. Another night she woke me up because I was kicking and violent in my sleep. Now I sleep on the couch until I get my nightmares under control."

When the military refused him medical care for depression and a psychological breakdown, Goodrum sought care from a civilian psychologist. This incurred a charge of Absent Without Leave (AWOL), which he vigorously denies. Nevertheless, if forced into a court martial, he may face prison time and a dishonorable discharge that will deny him U.S. Department of Veterans Affairs (VA) treatment for PTSD, care which he'll probably need for the rest of his life. He already owed tens of thousands of dollars in legal fees. "I loved the military and gave it everything I had. What the military is doing to me—and others—undermines the honor I've always associated with it."

"The thousand-yard stare"

I visited Ramon in Walter Reed Army Medical Center (WRAMC) in Washington, D.C. Until October 2004, he was a member of a U.S. military mechanized brigade. Then an Improvised Explosive Device (IED) exploded under the vehicle carrying him and an Iraqi man to a military base. Now his right leg is a $60,000 prosthesis, his left leg is deeply scarred, and he suffers from undiagnosed neurological damage to his hands.

This 21-year-old father of two girls shared the WRAMC ward with six other young men, all amputees. Most appeared in good humor, although one, about 35 years old, had the vacant look that veterans call "the thousand-yard stare"—and his left leg was missing at the thigh. When our eyes met I wanted to reassure him—"You still have your life"—but his look told me he may not want to settle for that.

Ramon grimaced through his physical therapy, his cell phone within reach of his wheelchair. "My wife often calls to ask how I am doing. I miss her and my kids." She can afford to travel from New York to visit only every few weeks. At his prompting, I admire his prosthesis—he reminds me several times that it costs $60,000. The hollow shape into which his bandaged stump fits is thick clear plastic. The mechanically articulating knee and ankle joints glide with silky smoothness. The foot, dressed in a sock and shoe, perfectly matches Ramon's other foot.

"I owe my life to an Iraqi man. If he had not insisted medics put the IV into my arm I would be dead. They thought I was beyond saving. My heart stopped twice—once before and once during surgery—but here I am. I didn't know I was supposed to die and just kept fighting so I'd see my family again. That Iraqi man prayed for me and insisted our medics treat me. Our baby was 3 weeks old when I was deployed. She's 9 months now and never knew me with legs. But my 5-year-old is scared of…[he gestures to his legs]. I have to coax my own child to kiss me. That is harder to me than losing my legs and almost losing my life."

Iraq War veteran Logan Laituri tells of a soldier trapped under an overturned Humvee in Baghdad. The triage medics found his injuries were fatal. Consequently, as they're trained, they refrained from attending to him. The soldier understood what this meant and quietly watched them attend his buddies while his own life seeped away.

Veterans tell me medic is the toughest job in the military; now I know why.

What is PTSD?

During the American Civil War, it was known as "soldier's heart"; World War I dubbed it "shell shock"; in World War II it was described as "battle fatigue" or "war neurosis." In 1980, Post Traumatic Stress Disorder (PTSD) was entered into the Diagnostic and Statistical Manual of Mental Disorders (DSM) III for the first time. In 1994, DSM IV described it as a psychological condition experienced by a person who has faced a traumatic event that caused a catastrophic stressor outside the range of usual human experience, such as war, torture, rape, or natural disaster. These stressors are different from the "ordinary stressors" such as divorce, failure, rejection, and financial problems, which can lead to "adjustment disorders."

Embraced by the scientific community, PTSD was found to be a serious problem for veterans *and* a public health problem for the general population. With the high prevalence of civilian assault, rape, child abuse, and severe accidental and violent trauma, PTSD may affect an estimated 10 million or more Americans at some point in their lives. It is prevalent in countries where social upheaval or natural disasters are common.

Nevertheless, the U.S. military command has yet to fully acknowledge PTSD. Military mental health providers survey, study, and report the effects of combat on soldiers. Military commanders listen, nod, read reports, and agree on medications. Then they go back to their core business: deploying troops, fighting battles, winning wars. For the military is a bureaucracy whose focus is the ability to engage anywhere in the world at any time; its function is operating the machinery of war smoothly and efficiently, and its supply line is its ability to prime enough combat troops. From the point of view of can-do military bureaucrats, PTSD is a nebulous, unquantifiable, qualitative distraction difficult to distinguish from shirking. Simply put, as Goodrum learned, troops must "get over it"…or "suck it up."

Military mental health practitioners are not discouraged from surveying troops and studying the disorder. If anything, they have unprecedented access to war's psychological effects on troops.

The Department of the Army's Mental Health Advisory Team studied services to troops evacuated from Iraq's combat zones from August 27 through October 7, 2003. They found that combat stressors include seeing dead bodies, being attacked or ambushed, and knowing someone who was seriously injured or killed. Operational stressors include uncertain redeployment dates, long deployments, being separated from family, and lack of privacy. The ratio of health provider to soldier in Iraq was 1 to 830; in Kuwait the ratio was 1 to 986. The ratios by area of responsibility ranged from zero providers per 4,025 soldiers to 1 provider per 673 troops. And, while assistance from chaplains and behavioral health providers was available, one of the greatest hindrances to soldiers asking for help is the military itself: soldiers may recognize that they need mental health care, but they are reluctant to ask for it. Reluctance stems from the danger and resources involved in transporting a soldier to counselors, inability to get time off work, fear of retaliation within the military, and fear of being seen as weak. The report indicates the ubiquity of psychotropic medication and states that "forward-deployed psychiatrists indicate that filling prescriptions... forces soldiers and units to arrange at least two convoys: the first for the soldier's medication evaluation and prescription, and the second for medication pick-up at the nearest pharmacy."

An examination of operational, doctrinal, and organizational maintenance concluded that 81 percent of the psychiatrists and/or nurses spent less than half their time providing prevention activities. Additionally, clinical charts were inconsistently maintained, documentation did not reliably accompany patients through the evacuation chain, outpatient evacuee charts were disorganized (often containing inconsistent documents) and clinical documentation did not reliably arrive at the receiving facility (only 44 percent included clinical documentation with the patient's medical chart).[3]

This disorganization surfaced after Dick Cheney voiced his fantasy of the war as "a cake-walk" that Iraqis would greet "with flower petals and candy" and before Donald Rumsfeld declared that shortages of armor and supplies in his "lean and mean" army of the future were due to going to war "with the Army you have, not the Army you want."[4] The disorganization was widespread when, during a press conference five days before Christmas 2006, President Bush urged Americans, "I encourage you all to go shopping more."[5]

There is a particular set of criteria used to diagnose PTSD.[6] Nevertheless, while counseling troops as the wars ground on, I heard a trend in service people's interactions with the military or the VA: formerly mentally healthy troops, now suffering from syndromes that fit the criteria for PTSD, are being diagnosed with Personality Disorders. (DSM IV defines this as "An enduring pattern of inner experience and behavior that deviates markedly from the expectation of the individual's culture, is pervasive and inflexible, has an onset in adolescence or early adulthood, is stable over time, and leads to distress or impairment.") Oddly, according to the recruiters who sign them up, new recruits enlist with clean bills of mental health. They "do their jobs" under conditions where "accidental and violent trauma" and "social upheaval or natural disasters are common"—yet, when they manifest signs of PTSD, they are diagnosed with a pre-existing condition that, incidentally, the military is not responsible for treating.

"Resist! Ask me how!"

Along with a small peace group I protested the war outside Ft. Hood, Texas. My sign displayed the GI Rights Hotline toll-free number and the words: "Resist! Ask me how!"

While local police threatened to arrest us, an army captain approached and asked me what I was doing.

"I'm offering free, accurate information to soldiers who stop and ask for it."

"You know, we're protecting your freedom and security."

"I appreciate your efforts. After 9/11 the United States had the opportunity for a constructive response yet we choose war. Now I feel it's my responsibility to work with the troops who enlisted to serve their country...."

"I've been over there, and the situation is nuts."

"I've been over there too, and I agree with you. But the occupation is deepening the tragedy, and hundreds of thousands are dying. One soldier who stopped here is preparing for his fourth redeployment to Iraq. When I told him that there are people who care about him, he cried. Captain, you know about IEDs and car bombs, unscrupulous militia members throwing kids in front of military vehicles, and you know that exhausted, angry troops commit atrocities. You know better than I do that we're destroying people's lives and communities."

"Yes, some soldiers are overextended. Well, good luck to you."

Overextended...

As a counselor, I talked to many troops who are not cut out for military life. That they are there is not a mistake: it is a result of sophisticated marketing campaigns. Lt. Gen. Robert Van Antwerp, commander of the U.S. Army Accessions Command, stated, "[We must] make the U.S. Army message distinctive and powerful...and deliver [it] in ways that reach eligible recruits."

Accordingly, in 2007, the U.S. Army paid McCann Worldgroup $200 million to run direct-response television, radio, print, and online advertising campaigns. The spots, including a Spanish-language version, emphasized how the Army makes young men and women stronger—mentally, emotionally, and physically. This "Army Strong" campaign replaced the $150 million "Army of One" campaign, which in turn replaced the decades-old "Be All You Can Be" campaign launched in 1981. That campaign was dumped after focus groups with 87 male and 27 female soldiers indicated

> a wide gap between the promises of Army advertising and the actual performance of the Army in keeping its promises…[many soldiers] expressed disillusionment, frustration, and anger [with the ads that] appear to damage soldier morale, commitment to the military, and reenlistment potential. For both ethical and pragmatic reasons it is suggested that future advertising be designed with a concern for both effectiveness and honesty and that future advertisements should be concerned with increased sensitivity for the immediate and long-term effects on both the target audience of potential recruits and the unintended audience of active duty soldiers.[7]

The commitment to honesty and sensitivity doesn't trickle down to zealous military recruiters pressured to fill quotas or face deployment themselves.

Recruited…

James wanted to be a medic. His military entry test scores were good enough that he could train as a medic. When he went to the recruitment office to sign up, suddenly James' test scores were not good enough; alas, he'd have to be an infantryman. James refused to sign. But all day long more gullible recruits were bullied into enlisting in the infantry. When James threatened to leave without signing, his recruiter discovered that, miraculously, James *had* passed his test. (Caution: Recruiters are under no obligation to follow through on any guarantees to enlistees regarding Military Occupation Specialties. Once the recruit signs the recruiter's job is finished and the enlistee may believe there is no recourse.[8])

Robert was 17 years old when he enlisted "to learn to be a man." Despite Robert *and* his military commanders recognizing Robert's inappropriateness for the soldier's life, they lectured him about his fitness as a man and lied that his single mother was sick and tired of his feminine ways and didn't want him in her home. After Robert attempted suicide, drill sergeants shadowed him 24/7. He went AWOL, refused to return to Ft. Benning, and won't discuss his humiliation at the hands of noncommissioned officers (NCOs). Today, his mother lives with the specter that her son may kill himself.

Eden sent registered letters to his commanding officer, his congressperson, and his military recruiter stating he retracted his interest in the National Guard. His recruiter simply ignored Army Recruiting Regulation 601-56, 3-1c, which states that "recruiters will not threaten, coerce, manipulate, or intimidate those wishing not to continue with the military, nor will they obstruct separation requests." Instead, he called Eden's home, his workplace, and his grandmother threatening that Eden would "be paying legal bills for the next 20 years…if he's lucky enough to avoid a ten-year jail sentence."

Janet awaited an Entry Level Separation with bandages on her wrists while military leadership decided whether to release her. Before enlisting, the psychologically fragile 20-year-old told her recruiter— over an alcoholic beverage in a Texas bar—that she'd attempted suicide at least once. He said, "All that stuff doesn't matter, the military will get your head right. You'll have a ball. You'll get a life." It took three days in the service for her to realize it wasn't the life she wanted. When she tried to leave, a drill sergeant seized her at the gate and verbally abused her. She slit her wrists. As medics bandaged her the drill sergeant threatened, "If you try this stunt again, we'll deploy you to Iraq without training." Two drill sergeants slept in a front office with her every night until her discharge.

Hazed…

Kenny was older than most of his NCOs and didn't take well to the concept that when told to "jump" his response should be "how high?" He quickly became a target. During one beating, set upon by eight troops, including his sergeant, one attacker told him, "You're now part of the biggest gang in the world." Kenny was recommended for a medical discharge. When his NCO disregarded this, Kenny went

AWOL. Later, he turned himself in, faced court martial, was sentenced to 30 days in the local community jail, and received an Other Than Honorable discharge.

Mohammed enlisted to provide a better life for his family. As an Arab-American he was fair game for fellow recruits who called him "rag head," "sand nigger," and "hajji" and accused him of "spying for the enemy." They'd enter his sleeping quarters with weapons slung over their shoulders and tell him he'd be "the first *Ay-rab*" they'd shoot. He said, "It amazed me that the military enlists anybody these days: addicts, gang members, bullies. These folks bring their lifestyles and ideologies with them and find a receptive environment. I enlisted with a commitment to do my best. What I found was a nasty environment where I couldn't thrive."

Lars, of the U.S. Marine Corps, was regularly beaten on his permanent assignment. He says his mistake was not figuring out how to belong to the "Military Mafia"—"the guys who've been in for a while, look out for each other, play by their own rules, and, even if they commit court-martialable offenses, they cover for one another and don't let the brass know." When he sassed an NCO, he was ordered to do push-ups, kicked in the ribs while he did so, and forced to low crawl so that his face was torn up and his eyes were caked with mud and grit. After hours of this, he was unable to lift his arms the following day to salute, incurring more punishment.

Fortunate...

Justin's leg was injured in an ambush in Iraq, and he had a full leg cast up to his thigh. It was still in a cast when he deployed to Fallujah in April 2004. He told his mother he was a liability in combat: he had no agility, he was unable to defend himself or fellow combatants, he was losing his sharpness as a soldier, and it was "just a matter of time before something bad happened." His anguished mother spoke about this on NBC television. An outraged medical doctor saw the show, recognized that Justin shouldn't be in combat, and complained to the military. Within 48 hours Justin was on his way to Germany via Kuwait.

Stop-lossed…

Joe was stop-lossed in Afghanistan for one year. He finished that year, and he and his unit packed their bags and were in formation, about to board the helicopter, when they were told they were extended for another four months. The troops were devastated: they screamed, cried, and attacked one another. After a week they settled down, although low morale and feelings of betrayal were common.

Christopher says, "I was stop-lossed; I went from the happiest I'd ever been because I was going to be released from this prison called the army to the most depressed, sharpest, most anguishing downward spiral that I could imagine…." He'd already been diagnosed with depression, anxiety disorder, and adjustment disorder, but still he was ordered to redeploy. After he tried to kill himself, he received a General discharge and his official discharge papers state "Serious Misconduct." He lost his GI bill, and if a future employee requests his official military documents, this note will hamper his prospects.

Evan spent a week on a scaffold in downtown Bellingham to protest the military's stop-loss and Inactive Reserve policies, which, he says, "Substitute for conscription in a political war, under the pretense of a nonexistent national emergency, and are destroying our military readiness as well as the lives of our young men and women."

(According to a civilian tally, more than 80,000 troops have been stop-lossed.[9] The Department of Defense tallies 7,000.)

…and previously healthy

Daniel suffers from PTSD due to his deployment to Iraq. He has been on the VA wait list for treatment for over two years. Two of his friends, on the same wait list, have died in the interim, one an alcohol-related death, the other through reckless behavior. Daniel has been moved to three different VA offices in three different states—in Michigan, Minnesota, and Wisconsin—none of which has delivered care.

Matt started self-medicating with alcohol while in the military. He is now an alcoholic who can barely hold down the only job he feels eligible for: pizza delivery man. He is concerned that his job contaminated him and his military buddies with depleted uranium;

the military and the VA state that no useful tests exist to determine this. Matt says, "Depleted uranium and Gulf War Syndrome are to the Global War on Terror what Agent Orange is to the people, veterans, and landmass of Vietnam…except DU is everywhere: it can be found on my hair and on yours, it has even been found on the surface of NASA space shuttles."

Sharing the stories

Some parents interviewed on the condition that I respect their policy of "not exploiting their child's death." Nurit Peled-Elhanan of Israel is one such parent. The same request was made by the family of a Palestinian suicide bomber and by Dr. Bacevich, a military officer in Vietnam and staunch opposer of the War on Terror. I share Sue Rosenberg's story, as her son Joshua was killed in the attack on the World Trade Center, the designated impetus for the Global War on Terror, and I acknowledge the following people:

Dustin Brim died from Non-Hodgkin's Diffuse Large Cell B Type Lymphoma, which attacked his kidney, caused a mass to grow over his esophagus, and collapsed a lung. He had served as a mechanic and worked on disabled army vehicles, including tanks, which his unit repaired and retrieved or destroyed with explosives on the spot. Most of these vehicles had been on the battlefield and are laden with depleted uranium and other toxins. Dustin's mother, Lori Brim, and other parents, hundreds of sick soldiers, legislators, research scientists, and environmental activists say the cause of their problems is exposure to depleted uranium, a radioactive metal used in the manufacture of U.S. tank armor and weapon casings.

José Couso, a TV cameraman for Spain's Tele 5, died after a U.S. tank shelled Baghdad's Palestine Hotel; it was well known that numerous international journalists resided there.

Alexander Arredondo was killed in Najaf. When military personnel arrived at his family's home with the news, his father, Carlos Arredondo, set fire to the military vehicle and burned himself in the process. After he recovered from his burns, Carlos toured the United States with a flag-draped coffin on a flatbed to protest war.

Patrick McCaffrey was shot to death near Camp Anaconda by Iraqis he was training. His mother, Nadia McCaffrey, caused a national stir when she allowed media to photograph her son's flag-draped coffin returning from Iraq: she'd broken the rule about never showing images of our war dead. She co-founded Veterans Village to honor her son (www.veteransvillage.org).

Casey Sheehan died in Najaf. His mother, Cindy Sheehan, refused to go quietly into the dark night of grief after Casey was killed; her expressed anger energized the peace movement.

Rachel Corrie was crushed to death by a militarized Caterpillar bulldozer trying to protect a Palestinian family's home from demolition. The day after Rachel was killed, the same bulldozer demolished the house. Rachel's parents, Craig and Cindy Corrie, implored the U.S. State Department to investigate Rachel's death, to no avail.

"Jennifer," a New York firefighter, donned her uniform on 9/11, her day off, and rescued victims at Ground Zero. She'd recently traveled to Israel and the West Bank, discovered that injustice and inequality, and was determined to do something about it. Then her son-in-law, a Marine, was killed in Iraq and Jennifer lost hope.

SUE ROSENBLUM, New York

"We deserve better than that"

Sue is a member of 9/11 Families for Peaceful Tomorrows. Her son Joshua died in the World Trade Center attack.

Joshua, at 28, was the youngest of my five children. He worked for Cantor Fitzgerald and had gone to work that Tuesday morning to finish some work before leaving for Bermuda, where he was to be married on Sept. 15th.

On the morning of the 11th, I left home to run some errands, and it wasn't until my husband phoned that I learned of the attacks. We returned home and watched the news, horrified, as the towers collapsed. Before the North Tower fell, I shouted, "Run, Josh, run!"

Later I learned that, because Cantor's offices spanned the 101st to 105th floors, the plane's impact directly below made it impossible for anyone to survive. Six hundred fifty-eight Cantor employees died that day: more victims than the New York police and fire departments put together.

My daughter Ruth, and Gina, Joshua's fiancée, tried to get information through Cantor's branch offices. The next day my husband and I drove to Hoboken, where Josh and Gina lived. I cannot describe what I felt when I saw the smoldering remains of the World Trade Center across the river.

Joshua's remains have never been recovered.

Initially, I wanted to blame someone or something for the senseless terrorist attack: First President Bush and his administration for failing to heed the intelligence they had. The 9/11 commission made it clear that a blind eye had been turned and that one government agency blamed another. Then the airlines: why did it take this horrific event to make them secure cockpit doors? Then the flight schools: why did no one question the validity of a man who learns to fly a plane but not land one? One question led to another, and after a while I stopped asking.

So what caused this to happen? In one word: hatred.

My husband was devastated by Joshua's death and never recovered. I, on the other hand, tried to turn my grief into some positive action by speaking to groups, especially children, about what hatred can do and how we must work toward peace.

If the memory of the 9/11 victims is to have any meaning, their deaths must mark the beginning of the end of the cycle of violence.

September 11, 2001, was used as an excuse to catapult this county into a useless war that has claimed far too many lives, both military and civilian. It needs to STOP and stop NOW!

I have experienced a mother's worst nightmare, and I live with pain 24/7. Not a day goes by when 9/11 isn't in the news in one way or another. I've been asked many times how I have managed to get through this, and this is my reply: It has been so many people reaching out to me, most of them strangers, that has allowed me to believe that God does exist. He has reached me through the love, care, kindness, and concern of people I have never met. Thankfully, goodness and humanity are alive and well. Like Anne Frank, I believe people are basically good.

RACHEL AVILA, California

"We're trying to help them and they're shooting us"

Rachel Avila shared her story just before her son Ryan was due to return to the United States after his first tour of duty in Iraq. A week later she called to say Ryan had been badly injured in Baghdad when an explosive-laden vehicle exploded under Ryan's tank. Another soldier had been injured and one killed. Ryan was evacuated to the Burn Center in San Antonio, Texas. His injuries included shrapnel in the face, eyes, skull, and brain and burns on his arms and hands.

Ryan's father died when Ryan was 13, and he had several tough teenage years. After high school he couldn't figure out what to do. I was worried and suggested he actively decide on what he wanted to do with his life, that he couldn't simply expect something just to happen. One day he called a military recruiter, and just like that, they processed him into the army in January 2003. He deployed to Iraq in October. When his original six-month tour was extended I wasn't sure when to expect him home.

Until he moved into southern Iraq we were in regular contact. On Mother's Day he mentioned he'd completed four patrol missions that day. In the past, he'd told me how upset he was with "these people"—Iraqis—and that he was beginning to hate them. He'd say, "Here we are trying to help them and they're shooting us."

At the same time, I think the military has been good for his growth and maturity. He writes that he now realizes how good he had it at home.

After his unit moved into southern Iraq where communication equipment was less available, I didn't hear much from him.

I tried to keep busy and immersed myself in work. I wrote to Ryan almost every day. I prayed. I talked to friends. I exercised. I didn't sleep very well and often woke up from nightmares. I paid attention to the news and educated myself about what was *really* going on. I was very frustrated and upset with how things were handled.

I was surprised by our invasion of Iraq. When we went into Afghanistan after 9/11 it made some sense. But suddenly we were talking about Saddam Hussein, and that didn't make any sense. We weren't finished with the first mission, yet we started another. Why?

I feel we are in Iraq for oil—and to support friends of this administration.

I listen to young people who are so pro-military and pro-president, and I wonder how they will feel if the draft is reinstated and they find themselves in the military. Another thing: why are our soldiers paid so little in comparison to civilian contractors? I've had to mail Ryan supplies that the military doesn't supply, things like bug spray, ointment, even sunglasses and goggles for sandstorms.

In 2004, when Ryan was scheduled to leave Iraq in nine days and be home for 30 days, he called to say that his tour of duty was extended another four months. What made it more painful was that he was shopping online for T-shirts and so on and shipping them home so he'd have clothes to wear when he got there. They were arriving in my mail, and I knew Ryan wouldn't be home to wear them. Very upset, I sent an email to my elected senator, Dianne Feinstein, to find out why my son and other armed forces personnel were extended. I felt this was unacceptable in light of Secretary of Defense Rumsfeld and his generals telling the American people the military doesn't need more troops to fight the rebels. She responded with a generic response that "the regime of Saddam Hussein has been defeated and removed from power…we must take the lead in rebuilding the Iraqi nation, in stabilizing its new government, in providing interim security to prevent the emergence of tribal hostilities, that Iraq is no longer a producer of weapons of mass destruction…that the United States should work closely with the United Nations and our allies in the reconstruction of Iraq."

I was furious, because this was the same answer I heard every day from the president. If Iraq produced WMDs, where are they and why haven't they been found? After all, WMDs were the stated reason for invading Iraq. The president calls Iraqi rebels "thugs," but *we* look more like thugs than Iraqis do. Why are we forcing our form of democracy on a country that already has a strong philosophy and religion? We're there for the wrong reasons. If Iraq were not rich in oil, the United States wouldn't be there. It's obvious to me that GREED for Iraq's oil is the main reason we are there.

Corporations like Halliburton and its subsidiaries and the policies of President Bush and his puppets are resulting in the deaths of our troops and allies, along with innocent Iraqi people. We're spending millions of dollars while citizens at home are unemployed, lack health care, are hungry, and are getting substandard education because schools lack money or must close.

What has happened to our elected officials?

"ANNE," California

> "Now that my family is involved
> I understand what colors our world"

"Anne" requested anonymity. Her son "Bob" was with the Army's Armored Cavalry in Habbaniyah, about 60 miles north of Baghdad.

"Bob" and his twin brother enlisted for four years in the Army after a very enthusiastic recruiter came to our home. They went with a friend and his father for induction. The father balked at having his son inoculated with anthrax vaccine, and that the boy didn't go to basic training. Bob received the shots and has served since before 9/11.

His brother left after his first tour while Bob re-upped for four more years. He does office work, guards detainees, and transports goods.

We're not a traditional military family, although my nephew, my brother's son, is with the Airborne and very gung ho. He wants to be president of the United States one day and believes he must have a military background. My brother is a rabid Bush supporter who believes in this war, although he may have felt differently if he'd served in Vietnam. I oppose actions for empire, so my brother and I don't talk politics—he supports my son, though, and I appreciate that. I believe this action in Iraq is motivated by profit and not by what is good and right. While I agree that Iraq's former regime was not good, the United States isn't the world's arbiter.

In my opinion, Bush hasn't looked presidential since 9/11. I see him as a megalomaniac and a puppet in the hands of more powerful and experienced people. As for his statement "Bring it on," I notice that no one in his family or his cabinet members' families is over there.

Couldn't Iraqis be every bit as passionate about their homes, land, and philosophy as we are about ours? Wouldn't we fight just as passionately as they're fighting if our land was invaded? If we hadn't bombed their schools, roads, and hospitals in the first place we wouldn't need to rebuild them—not that we are rebuilding anything there. The news about mistreatment and torture at Abu Ghraib wasn't a surprise to me. This is what war does to people. But after that news I emailed Bob and told him that, while I can't [judge] his situation, he must remember he's dealing with human beings. Most soldiers are not trained for policing detainees, yet they're forced into horrible circumstances that harden their hearts while doing what they're told to do. Nevertheless, my communications with Bob indicate a disturbing trend toward casually demeaning people.

His letters mention that U.S. soldiers who are fired upon leave detainees tied to poles. A month ago I was receiving 20-page letters from him, but now they're only one or two paragraphs. I ask him about his state of mind and he replies, "Okay...just a bit depressed being in this place." He says he doesn't have the heart to write more.

His life has changed for the worse, and that makes me sad. He'll never forget these life-changing events. He'll never be able to ignore things that go "boom" in the night. He can't "un-ring" that bell.

I feel hopeless about the world situation. Now that my family is involved I understand what colors our world—and it's not good.

"Bob's" letters home

March 31, 2004

Today is full of sadness. We lost five of our greatest men: I may have not known them personally, but none deserved to die.

I was going to OP8 [Observation Post 8] when I heard a loud explosion followed by 50 Cal gunfire fired from a truck. As I left for X-ray to let Cpt. S. know that we had a unit in contact, the radio went nuts.

Bulldog, the engineer unit, called for a "sit rep" [situation report] from that convoy: several men severely wounded. Centurion X-ray pushed an element of engineers, an Apache, four scout trucks, and the QRF [Quick Reaction Force] medics to provide care at the explosion site. Next report was three dead and two expectant, meaning they wouldn't survive.

The medics and Centurion tried to get a helicopter in the air to evac, but that got scratched: the military doesn't put a bird in the air unless someone has a chance of surviving. The final total was five dead. From the radio transmission I heard that the Humvee was blown apart. If it was anything like other IED incidents, there wasn't much left of the vehicle. All day long missions have been recovering the vehicle, conducting area searches, and seeking those responsible.

[We] recovered the vehicle with three HEMTT's [Heavy Extended-Mobility Tactical Trucks] an M88, and a Low Boy truck. A Mortuary Affairs Unit from TQ [Transition Quarter] recovered the bodies. There was another explosion as the convoy headed to the site. It turned out to be unrelated and no one else was hurt.

April 1, 2004

Happy April Fool's Day. It's the fool talking from Iraq. Today has been good: no one killed and unexploded IEDs found. Despite the obvious—that someone put them there—we discovered them before they detonated.

The vehicle hit yesterday was an M113 light armored tank, basically an aluminum can on a track: the largest almost-intact piece was the rear ramp. Next largest piece was the engine block, but pieces were so small that the recovery crew didn't need the M88 to lift anything. Over 500 lbs of explosives had been set; that could have disabled an M1 Abrams tank. The memorial service for the five dead is Saturday.

Some of the funny things that we see daily will crack you up. Not long ago I saw two Joes jogging. They continued running north until they heard some celebratory firing then they turned right around. For us the firing was nothing new. But these Joes were from Fallujah and Fallujah has a bunch of scared soldiers right now.

April 3, 2004

I've been OP8 for almost a week and I'm bored.

Yesterday Centurion X-ray kept calling up and asking if we had any audio or visual on explosions or gunfire. Their acquisition machine was so sensitive it picks up birds flying and planes taking off from TQ and reports them as massive explosions. But it's good to have a warning device.

In certain spots on the wire you can see where the little bastards put a board over the wire to cross. I'd love to catch one of those idiots. I'd be proud to notch one detainee on my belt.

Today we had the funeral ceremony for the five engineers killed last Wednesday. We've lost around 20 soldiers and officers since we arrived here Sept. 18th last year. Col. C. of Devil 6 was here for the occasion, along with the 1st Engineers LTC and higher-level people. It's sickening that they only come here when it involves death; they never pop over to see their toughest guys in action.

Heck, in Fallujah, they're scared to do any nighttime missions. That's why IEDs go off a few miles outside the gates each morning and why giant truck bombs rock Champion base and Camp Junction City. It's both good and bad to be with the heavy hitters like 1-34 Armor Task Force.

Last night Apache shot a guy with a HEAT [High Explosive Antitank] round from a tank. He was toast, didn't have a chance. He and two buddies had approached our wire when Apache OP spotted them and fired. They may—or may not—have been setting an IED. Despite excessive force, we accomplished the job.

April 7, 2004

Things have been wild around here. Marines and Army are getting killed all over Iraq [but] no one from our task force has died since last week so we're breathing sighs of relief.

Our mortar platoon, Arch Angel, received an RPG while waiting for EOD [Explosive Ordnance Disposal] at a possible IED site. I've heard rumors we'll have another seven to eight months in this hellhole. I can't believe our brigade commander did this to us.

Ever since the weather warmed up we've had trouble from Ramadi, Fallujah, and Kaldiyah, including protests and killings. I can't wait to be done with all of this. Other reports tell of Marine convoys hit, attacks on patrols, and so on. These poor guys returned to Iraq after they'd served in the initial invasion—they just can't win!

Last night we had 59, then 57, then 51 detainees at Ramada Inn which is just a tiny compound but it was just insane last night. Eight were from an attack on Attack Company. We heard battles raging outside the wire and a floating bomb blew up our pontoon bridge OP. We expected action but not so much. Four of our newest Lt's were here when we brought in our eight new bad boys. Second Lt. M. wants new stuff done so we can monitor detainees easily. A Marine Lance Corporal

(E3) was there as a Civil Affairs guard and Attack's soldiers did the paperwork. The place was crammed with people, good and bad.

Here's the story about the new bad guys. Attack arrived to search a building in Kaldiyah and these eight guys were readying for a surprise attack. There was more shooting from Attack than from the Iraqis who tried to scatter. One guy tried hiding under something but he was too big. When a Bradley started unloading 25mm rounds in his direction he wasn't hit but he was caught. He had a machine gun within reach but didn't use it. An Army corporal was ready to shoot him but didn't because it's prohibited by the laws of land warfare.

All eight were brought in for a not-so-nice American welcome. They were blind folded with first aid cravats. Some detainees had cotton in their ears so they could shoot us without harming themselves. I thoroughly searched them and I found that one guy, call him Fat Boy, had fuses for grenades and the other had bullets. Our soldiers yelled at them, questioned them, and so on. After 20 minutes standing, Fat Boy fell over, just took a bad left dive to the cement floor.

April 8, 2004

Last night, when I arrived at Ramada Inn, I heard wild screaming coming from the other side of the wall. They'd put Fat Boy in a stress position that makes anyone cry with madness. [He] was yelling in Arabic "Fuck the Americans." We promptly gagged his mouth. I had to kick one guy in the ass a good couple of times because he talked to other detainees, even with his mouth taped! Another guy tried biting one of the MI personnel and was placed on his knees; he cried. The guy who puked on the wall the night he was brought in from the Attack raid was also put on his knees on hard tiles. We had three guys begging for their sanity last night. Another guy from that group needed to use the toilet so I [took] his bottle of water figuring he wouldn't pee if he didn't have water; he had to suffer for his stupidity. It was an entertaining evening.

April 14, 2004

Man, things have been crazy around here lately! For me it's been 91 Iraqis deep and rockets flying overhead. I can't believe the stuff that's happening!

Fallujah and Ramadi are in ruins.

Last night and this morning there were two big missions aimed at Kaldiyah and Ramadi. I have a mission to Ramadi for the combat patch ceremony for brigade. I'm hoping that Col. C. will tell us during the ceremony when we'll leave Iraq. I've been doing late night patrols and OP8 and *I feel as if this place will drive me insane.*

There was a huge mission kicking off in Ramadi with tanks rolling through and one could shoot at anything that looked suspicious. On the 24th I'll be going to Ramadi for an official ceremony to put on our patches. It'll be great to show I was involved in this experience, deployment, the ceremony itself, and that I've had experiences that most people never have. I've been at the front and center of ceremonies with the unit colors. It's a good feeling to be seen and recognized. It's nerve-racking too because top brass watches our every move. The guys in combat infantry/mortar-man MOS [Military Occupational Specialty] will get their badges; that's a great honor.

April 15, 2004

We're losing our services and supplies: fuel, water, and food. All the supply lines are compromised because of increased attacks on coalition forces. Convoys are getting hit on the highways and back routes. Everyone's scared to bring fuel up so we're cutting back on everything. But, if there's no fuel we can't cook. We're eating MRE [Meal, Ready-to-Eat] lunches and soon will eat the same for dinner.

We're hurting pretty badly, plus we'll be receiving 600 more soldiers from 1st Armored Division. The water guys who deliver water for showers aren't showing up so we don't have regular showers. Life is getting hard around here.

Love, "Bob"

ADELE KUBEIN, Oregon

"Don't worry, mom, there'll never be another war"

After her daughter M'kesha's experience in the War on Terror, Adele became an anti-war activist and the Pacific Northwest contact for Military Families Speak Out.

M'kesha and I are very close. We're both liberal and somewhat cynical about government, and we both disagree with war. She joined the National Guard six years ago and her contract stipulated she'd never be involved in combat.

I was very concerned about her joining, but she told me, "Oh, Mom, don't worry, there'll never be another war. I'm going to build roads and fight fires and save money for college."

She's with Bravo 52 and has had a very rough time.

When she left the United States she had a broken leg and plates and bolts in the bone to assist healing. She walked with a stick and she told me that they wouldn't deploy her like that. But they did. They sent her to Mosul in April 2003, as the initial invasion ended.

She was traumatized by what she saw in that country. Bombs and weaponry had decimated the countryside. Iraqi tanks and armored vehicles, strewn in the road, still had bodies in them. She asked why the bodies hadn't been removed and learned that people were afraid to approach because of chemical contaminants and depleted uranium from U.S. ammunition: "Just don't breathe the red dust," she was told—but she was not given a mask or protective equipment.

M'kesha said Bravo 52 was undersupplied in weapons, armor, and basic support; the company had no water for days at a time, no ammunition for days at a time, and ate just one meal a day.

She'd been told, "You'll build houses and orphanages. The Iraqis will love you; they'll greet you with flowers and candy." Instead, she was mounted behind a gun on the back of a Humvee. Not only has she seen combat—despite her contract—she's killed people.

My family is Arab, from Jordan. My father came here years ago and I have Jordanian relatives in the United States and in Jordan.

After M'kesha killed Iraqis she didn't want to see members of my family. "I've killed people. How can I ever come home? How can I ever look in people's faces? I'll always see the look in the face of the first man I killed and how he looked as he died."

The irony is that when they arrived in Iraq and convoyed from Kuwait to Mosul, they were escorting military contractors who had the best of everything. Contractors Kellogg Brown & Root [KBR], a subsidiary of Halliburton, had all the best equipment and military protection and did none of the work, while military personnel took all the risks fighting, shooting, and killing. After KBR set up the kitchens many troops got sick from tainted meat. On average, troops dropped about 30 pounds in weight, and many were gaunt.

M'kesha and several other troops contracted a liver disease. When her liver stopped functioning she was medevac'd to Germany. She recovered somewhat, but at least two troops with the same disease died. Several other people in Bravo 52 died of heart attack and stroke. Remember, these were National Guardsmen, many in their 50s, out of shape, not combat ready, and not expecting to see combat.

From Germany M'kesha returned to Mosul, where she was blown off the back of her Humvee by an exploding mortar round. That reinjured her leg, and she went to Ft. Carson, Colorado, for another round of surgery to repair it. She was on active duty while she waited. While there she discovered she was pregnant. Turned out that the antimalarial medication neutralizes birth control; no one thought to tell the female soldiers this important information. She refused to have an abortion, saying, "After so much death, I want to be part of continuing life."

The United States has a pattern of mistakes in the Middle East. Yet the Bush Administration's agenda is so radical it outdoes all previous mistakes over there. September 11 was a rude awakening to many Americans, and now we're playing catch-up.

I don't agree with this war. There was no reason for it and there was no contingency plan for what happens afterward—the result of which we're seeing. It is starting to look more and more like the Vietnam War.

M'kesha's letters home

April 21, 2003

Things have been pretty crazy, over all one helluva experience. I've been kissed, blessed by Shiites, shot at, my hand shaken by a hundred Kurds, and my truck struck by AK-47. I've literally had shit, rocks, cans, and bottles thrown at me and been beaned with a slingshot. In return, I've nailed people with sand-filled Coke cans tossed from moving vehicles as they've thrown shit at me.

Somebody tried to run over me and I saw someone run over a kid. I've seen an Iraqi shot in the face, been in firefights in the middle of the night, and seen every kind of military aircraft. I've been in every kind of fucked-up convoy except for one going into a minefield.

I've been lost in Saddam's hometown of Tikrit and found my way back, run a convoy, and repaired a truck in the middle of a riot.

People have tried stealing my tools as I worked. I've almost killed children who ran into the road to pick up MREs thrown by soldiers in vehicles ahead of me.

I've been wounded, medevac'd, and I've run amok. I've taken pictures all over Iraq and terrified whole stretches of Iraqis who seem afraid of me and my tattoos. Perhaps they think I'm demon-possessed? Normally they flock to American women, crowd around, touch them, kiss them, and try to buy them. But they sidle around and look at me sideways.

It isn't mayhem all the time, often it's pretty dull and routine, interspersed with random and incredible violence. Once our guys accidentally set the munitions dump alight and ignited in three hours what was supposed to take three years to use: mortars and missiles were flying everywhere; one guy was blown up.

Arabs have strange trinkets, animals, and toys hanging off their trucks and on their dashes. There are dingle balls and fringes hanging from windows, stickers all over cars, and everything is painted in brilliant Gypsy colors. Men dance in the street; little girls line up and wave like crazy while their brothers flip us off and throw rocks. Young women are starting to throw away their black shawls and *hijabs* and wear scarves of brilliant colors like belly dancers. One carload of women blew kisses then whipped their scarves off and waved them at me out their car windows. Maybe they thought I was a guy.

Cities here are a mixture of rubble and incredible architecture. Baghdad is still burning in places and people are taking down Saddam's walls and rebuilding with the bricks.

The drive from Kuwait was a study in the complete destruction of cities, infrastructure, fuel lines, and all sorts of shit. Swaths of highway were littered with carcasses of tanks and artillery, burnt hulls of cars lining the road, and great pits burnt into the asphalt.

Sunset catches light over the sand and turns the sun into a bloody orb and adds eerie desolation to highways free of civilians, where gutted buses and stripped and burnt chassis lie. Dead bodies still rot in tanks because of depleted uranium.

Things are going bad fast. We had ten attacks yesterday alone. One guy was killed and three others seriously hurt. It's not just the infantry getting hit, and losing our guys is hitting us hard.

My helicopter was shot. We made it but I had a serious moment when that damned bird started dropping. I love the ground.

Runs to Dohuk are cancelled except for vital parts. As people realize we're at war the mood around camp gets serious, somber, and sketchy.

Things are very bad here, worse than before. We're attacked nightly by Iraqi freedom fighters who have found a stock of rockets and launched them from a few miles away. Infantry is hard hit.

May 31, 2003

Nights here are a trip in the rainy season; even the rain is desperate. But I feel at home, as if the land holds no hostility toward me.

I walked in the desert last night and there was a pack of wild dogs barking. The moon was hidden by clouds, and as I danced in the rain, my rifle thumped and beat against my calves and my boonie cap fell back and was held by a string against my throat. The rain fell in great, big drops and the wind whistled across the debris in the sand.

Someone was out there shooting the dogs. Those are the ugly moments interspersed with the beautiful. I heard two shots. I hope the dogs got away.

If I didn't distance myself from the world I'd be more upset than I am.

I miss my own dogs, my truck, my home, and my people. Yet if someone offered me a ride home tomorrow I'd turn it down. My crew is here and the kids need me.

I have angry moments, frustration, all the usual things, but I've also found something. I cannot describe the joy I have in living, even in the bad moments I find something beautiful around me. I hold on to it with all my power.

I may not be able to change the situations I face or the world here but I hold true to things that make me who I am. I will change. I'll return home a different person but I'll not let go of my joy in life. I will not let go of my ability to find beauty in squalor. I can't explain the faith that surges through me but I know that I will return whole. I will not let this tear me apart.

September 3, 2003

A young, beautiful Iraqi girl saw me walking up the street. I was greasy and my rifle and toolbox was slung over my shoulder. Instead of running like most wise women do when they see soldiers, she paused. I guess she saw me as a sister, because I could see her friendliness. She seemed happy to gain my attention and I was in awe of her fearlessness. We stopped and exchanged a dozen sign-language-augmented words. Her name is Dunyia, and she laughed when I told her my name. Later her mother told me Mageesha is Iraqi Arabic for "to sweep out."

The night before we left, Dunyia found me—itself noteworthy as women *never* leave their courtyards—and took me home for dinner. Her family speaks English, and her mother told me Dunyia had been watching me order the men around as I worked as a mechanic.

Dunyia and I talked a lot. She liked my necklace. Afterwards, alone in my room, I made her a choker like mine. In the morning as we rolled out to convoy, I stopped at her house, jumped out, stormed the gate, put it in her hands, and fled back to my truck before I got in trouble.

The dog packs have shifted. Now there's a young female German shepherd who runs to me to play; she bounces off me, bats me with her white paws, and gently nibbles me. The Iraqis are horrified, and I threaten to shoot them when they stone her. They say the dogs will turn on me and tell me I'm as filthy as a dog. I smile and reach for my rifle. I hate the men who look at me like that. Abuse of women here is tragic. Going home and seeing whole women, women who aren't soldiers, will be great.

The other night I and others were on the scraper when a firefight started. We kept working until bullets whizzed past and one hit the scraper below me. I killed the drop-light, finished tightening the brake line, and got down giddy and crazy with laughter.

There are mortars on the other side of camp. No big deal. Those guys have bad aim. They put mortar tubes on bricks, light 'em up, and hope they go; most land without exploding.

I love you, I miss you, and I will be so happy to see you.

"SANDY," Missouri

"Life is so precious and war so dumb"

"Sandy's" son "Jonathan" is career military based in Germany and currently deployed to Iraq. Her husband is a Vietnam War veteran and her father a World War II veteran.

Jonathan spends his working day among the Iraqi people talking, making contacts, looking for the enemy. He doesn't interrogate anyone but writes reports about who he has talked to and what he has heard. This is his first posting in the intelligence field and his first opportunity to work among Iraqis. He is aware of various construction work, improving water filtration systems, sewer systems, building schools and so on.

The day Jonathan arrived in Iraq was stressful for me. Although he's 37 and career military, Iraq is his first combat mission. I turned to my friends for support and they asked me what they thought Jonathan or his squad—50 men and women—might need over there. Then they packaged up 50 parcels and sent them to Baghdad.

When he first arrived in Baghdad, he said he didn't know if he could use his gun against the people. Jonathan is a very compassionate person and understood the difficult position of the Iraqi people. He has two children of his own, and seeing Iraqi children playing in streets covered in garbage and sewage breaks his heart. Last Christmas he was down in spirits as he missed his own family. I sympathized and then reminded him that he had a job to do and he'd better pick his chin up off the ground and get on with it. That helped him! He said he felt better for my stern words.

Jonathan has been invited into the homes of Iraqis and shared their meals. His translator is an Iraqi who is a U.S. citizen, lives in the United States, and volunteered to return to Iraq to help our troops. Jonathan says that most of the people he comes into contact with are pleased we're there; they say they have fresh food in the markets for the first time in years. At one home Jonathan was introduced to the young daughter who was born blind. Jonathan asked me to make her a quilt as a gift. When he delivered it the family was astounded that Jonathan's mother—someone far away who doesn't know them—did such a thing. His unit volunteered to do minor repairs on a local orphanage and he also worked at another orphanage with 70 young girls in Mosul. With the help of local quilters we sent them 70 quilts, shampoo, toothbrushes, toothpaste, and so on.

March 2, 2004, was a bloody day in Iraq when simultaneous bombs exploded into crowds of Shi'a Muslims celebrating a religious holy day: over a hundred people were killed. They were desperate for blood, and

I suggested Jonathan donate blood—especially as he's a rare blood type. He doesn't know if that's acceptable, but he'll try.

He's had some close calls. Once, a rocket-propelled grenade flew right over their Humvee before it exploded. The occupants were badly shaken. Another time, a Humvee right behind him struck an IED. Jonathan's vehicle shot off over a hundred rounds at the suspect, although they don't know if they made contact. He believes some of these opportunistic bombings, lobbed grenades, and IEDs are carried out by local, desperately poor people who are paid cash for shooting our troops.

I was so saddened by 9/11 and I've tried to understand the frame of mind of people who plan such events. I wish I knew more so I could understand how people could think so little of their fellow human beings and of their own lives. I don't understand man's inhumanity to fellow beings. If they just let us mothers talk to each other across the world maybe we could convince them that we're all God's people and to treat each other as such. But now that we're in Iraq, we must do our job. It won't happen quickly, but perhaps things will calm down in a year or so. I don't see things from a political perspective, but I believe there'll always be difficulties between a civilian administration and the military, because both of them have an agenda. A couple of weeks ago President Bush was in this town and he went to buy a fishing pole in the big sporting goods store here. In a town about 30 miles away a family was burying their son who'd been killed in Iraq. Townspeople were very angry that President Bush didn't pay his respects at that funeral.

Jonathan said, "Mom, the President can't just change his mind any time he wants. His itinerary and security is worked out weeks before hand. He can't just rush off wherever he wants."

The following is an exchange between Jonathan and a quilter who mailed boxes to his unit.

The quilter:
Dear "Sandy,"
I haven't mailed a package to Jonathan yet. In my enthusiasm to help, I purchased and boxed a lot of "goodies." Alas, postage cost $60.00! I'm disabled and live on Social Security and couldn't afford it. Heartsick and tearful, I put the box in my car. That weekend my 28-year-old

son went into hospital with an acute asthma attack and almost died. Hospital staff resuscitated him, but I rushed there with Jonathan's box still in my car. Late that night my son awoke and was hungry for "real" food. I took some from the box. My grandchildren visited and I fed them from the box too! God took something bad and turned it around. I felt bad about not shipping the box to your son but I helped my own son's family in their time of crisis.

God Bless your family and our troops!

Jonathan:

I was moved to tears by your email to my mother: that box was meant for a more important destination. I think God was helping me do my job: protecting the American people. Not only protecting them from tyrants who would harm them, but allowing them to live free, provide for their families, and not worry about someone taking away something they've worked for. Seeing the way Iraqis live, I am thankful for what we have in America.

Today, in Iraq, I saw children trying to avoid puddles of raw sewage and piles of trash in a vacant lot where they were playing. It's because of this my soldiers and I ask that you help us do our job and complete our mission with Honor and Integrity. It means more to us than a box from home if you take future items that you wish to send us and give them to your grandchildren in our name. That's our small way of giving something back for all the support, love, and prayers that sustain us through our duties. We'll be honored and grateful if you do this.

PAT GUNN, Washington

"Our children are suffering"

Pat's son Jason served with the Army's 137th Armored Brigade. He was badly wounded in an attack, and after weeks of recuperation he was sent back to combat in Iraq.

Jason drives Humvees. He was driving with three other soldiers when an IED exploded under them. The sergeant died outright. Jason was badly cut by shrapnel on the left side of his body, an artery was severed, he lost his hearing, and when he was pulled from the vehicle his uniform was smoldering. His severed artery was treated immediately in a MASH [Mobile Army Surgical Hospital] then he was flown to Germany for long-term treatment.

We heard about this when an Army captain called from Germany, saying, "Jason was injured today. It's not life threatening." A tank commander called from Iraq a short while later verifying this.

That was Saturday. I kept in touch with the hospital as my husband and I went through the process of getting passports, buying tickets, and preparing for Germany. I called my congressman to get things expedited and was told that unless Jason was dead or dying there was nothing much he could do to help. Even finding the exact address of the hospital was difficult

We arrived there on Thursday. We stayed in Fisher House, which is something like a Ronald McDonald House [charity-run lodgings where families stay when their children are in a hospital far from home], and didn't have to go through security checks every day.

I think the hospital personnel was very surprised to see us. You are invited into a military hospital; you don't just walk in as in a civilian hospital. There was a cluster of medical personnel around Jason when I first entered the ward, so I struggled to get near him stopping first to put on gloves because he had some kind of skin infection. I sobbed the whole time.

All I could think of was getting Jason home. I felt he'd recover a lot faster in his own home amidst his family and friends. Jason is one of a set of triplets, and both his brothers followed him into the military. Justin was in Korea. Jerome was injured in boot camp and left. They both know about military life. I do too, because I was in the Navy for six years. I knew home and family was the best place for him at that point.

He was so medicated that he was content to just lie there and not get up. But it was important that he try. After ten days, the hospital released him.

For five weeks I changed the dressings on his wounds, some of which were very deep holes in his flesh, and I had to wet the gauze before packing these wounds, then wet it again to remove it. At one point I was on my knees tending to him and he was looking down at me, and I realized how grateful I was that he was still alive. As part of my protest against this war I've met a number of mothers whose children have been killed over there. I see what war and their children's deaths have done to them.

My son, although badly wounded, at least was still alive, and I had the opportunity to nurse him back to health.

He had to use a cane to walk out of our home and return to the military.

Once back in Germany, it was just a matter of time before the military figured he was ready for duty again. Imagine our shock—and his— when we learned he was going back to his combat unit in Iraq.

Something went on back there where they got him to sign a stack of papers saying he felt fit enough—emotionally and physically—to return to Iraq. I know he was suffering emotionally and traumatized, yet he signed the papers stuck in front of him. I asked him on the phone whether it was true that he'd signed of his own free will. He was very guarded and didn't respond directly.

He said, "I'm back where I belong." Yet just the day before he'd told me there was no way he was getting back on a plane to return to Iraq.

I'm very worried. At the hospital, I met a young fellow who is the only survivor of a helicopter crash. When the Marines told him it was time to go back he became suicidal. I opened a congressional inquiry about why Jason was being sent back against medical advice, but because he signed his papers, there's not much the doctors can do against the military.

Now I just get one- or two-line emails from him. He never says much. His voice on the phone is dull and automatic. He changes the subject whenever I ask how he's doing.

I've participated in many anti-war rallies and given some interviews. One pro-war reporter of a local newspaper asked for an interview and then, instead of listening to me, screamed at me, [negated] everything I said, and shoved his opinions down my throat. He simply refused to listen to anything that balanced his strong opinions. I don't know what he's even doing in that job, he's so bad at it.

Unfortunately, that attitude is quite common in this country. People don't know how to listen to one another or to listen to different opinions, and they don't know how to respond if someone disagrees—even if the disagreement is presented in a manner conducive to dialogue.

This is exactly how our foreign policy is handled. This war should never have been started. The United States should have found a better way to resolve the conflict. We have a real mess on our hands...and our children are suffering grievously or dying.

RITA DOUGHERTY, New York

"I'm furious with Democrats and Republicans"

Rita's son Ryan graduated from West Point Military Academy in 2005 with a degree in nuclear engineering. He trained stateside, went to the air base at Vilseck, Germany, in 2006 and deployed to Iraq in August 2007.

On October 18, 2007, Ryan was inside a Striker [armored vehicle] blown up by the improved version of the IED, the EFP [explosively formed projectile]. Strikers are impervious to IEDs but not EFPs, concave-type devices that, when detonated, punch the Striker's underbelly and turn the inside into a virtual blender with shrapnel.

Of nine solders inside, one died immediately, one had no visible injuries, and the others sustained various injuries. Ryan was severely injured on the left side of his body; the soldier next to him was similarly injured but on the right side of his body.

The electricity shuts down when Strikers are hit like this so the hatch didn't open. As soldiers screamed to open the door Ryan banged his body against the hatch until it opened and they fell out into the street. Ryan said he was semiconscious but completely calm. He saw the blood and knew it was bad but remained calm as medics applied the tourniquet around his leg. Luckily, they were not far from the medical cache.

His left leg sustained soft-tissue damage from the shrapnel ripping out chunks of flesh. His tibia was shattered; his buttock was totally blown off, he lost a third of his large intestine, and he's still loaded with shrapnel that can't be removed because that would do further damage.

He has an external fixator on his leg from mid-thigh down to his ankle. The nerves that control the flexing of his left foot were destroyed but may grow back. For now he has no feeling there.

I heard about the explosion as I walked with my daughter and checked my phone messages. My son's voice said, "Mom, I'm so sorry. I'm really messed up. I'm so sorry. I love you."

I called my sister, who said, "He's alive and they've saved the leg."

He received immediate medical care in Baghdad, then went to Landstuhl, Germany, for extensive surgery. I went there where everybody was U.S. military and took great pains to ensure Ryan was comfortable, had access to email, and so on. I flew back with him by military medical plane to Walter Reed [Army Medical Center].

Walter Reed was seven weeks of hell, right from the start. At Andrews Air Force Base a kind of school bus with the seats missing picked up the wounded on stretchers. Ryan was stuck in the back of the bus kind of hanging off his gurney; with the arm that had the intravenous feed in it, he hung on to a strap, almost like a subway train, because the gurney was angled precariously.

Ryan asked a soldier, "Are you sure this is stable?"

The soldier said, "Just suck it up."

Another kid who looked about 12 years old didn't have a visible injury but looked like a deer caught in the headlights. I tried talking to him but he just stared at me. The nurse, who never left his side, heard the reply given to Ryan and told the soldier who said it, "He was just blown up in Iraq. How dare you to say 'suck it up'? You have no idea what he has had to suck up!"

Another nurse told the first one to leave the young-looking soldier and sit somewhere else. She refused, "I have orders to be by his side. He's on a suicide watch."

At Walter Reed, they removed all the medical packing on Ryan's leg and repacked it. I noticed most of the people around me were rude army people and rude civilians. One woman talked to me about my "wounded warrior" and handed me a blanket and a bag with toothbrushes. They love to push all the stuff on you—and it is handy to have it—but they seemed unaware that this stuff isn't why we're there. I said something about that, and the woman responded, "Well, freedom isn't free."

I responded, "'Freedom isn't free?' Do you believe that crap? Do you think this war is about freedom? It's about oil; it's about keeping a few people wealthy...the reason my son is lying here has nothing to do with freedom."

I was at the hospital twelve hours a day caring for my son, and it occurred to me that the military puts up family members because there's nobody else there to take care of your child.

Friday they gave him another blood transfusion. By Sunday he'd developed a fever. In Landstuhl he'd received an antibiotic to fight sand germs but Walter Reed personnel took him off it. As his fever spiked the fluid dripping into the wound bag, which had been a cloudy, yellowish color, was now red, as if blood was just running through his leg right into the wound bag. He was sweating so much that the bed was drenched.

He told me, "I feel horrible. You have to get a doctor in here."

I called the intern—on the weekends no doctors are available—"My son is very sick; he needs treatment before surgery tomorrow. His fever is 103 and the blood from the transfusion appears to be running right through him into the wound bag. We're really frightened."

He says, "It's a Sunday night; what do you want to do?"

"I want to do whatever needs to be done. You're the doctor. He needs to be looked at."

He said, "We don't do surgery on a Sunday night because it means getting a doctor out of bed...."

"So you're telling me that needing surgery here on a Sunday night is like buying a car on a Monday. You just don't do it?"

He answered, "Yes, kind of," and walked out of the room.

Ryan was crying and said, "I don't want to have survived Iraq to die here. Call the chaplain; they know the people to contact."

The chaplain raised hell until a doctor came and they did another transfusion and gave him more antibiotics. I left at 3 o'clock in the morning and realized that this is why the military pays hotel costs for families: the wounded need somebody to advocate for them. Later I asked a psychologist about the wounded who don't have family, "What happens to the guys who come here who don't have an advocate, who don't have intellectual sophistication, who go into the military because they have no other options?" He replied, "Those are the guys that you see walking around talking to themselves, living on the streets, and going through the garbage."

As Ryan got stronger and was supposed to go to physical therapy, they gave him so much medication that he was unable to get up out of the bed, sit in a wheelchair, do anything like that. It was horrible. It was slowly killing me to see what was happening to him.

As I mentioned, he couldn't flex his foot due to nerve damage. In Landstuhl he'd had a boot that maintained a neutral position so the Achilles tendon wasn't further damaged. They removed this at Walter Reed, wrapped it with something like an ACE bandage, and tied that to the fixator to hold it straight. They said this was "better," but Ryan's foot was so numb he couldn't feel how tight it was. A couple of days later I got a look at his foot and it was black. I said it didn't look good and they replied, "That's what happens…the skin on the outside dies off, then the new skin grows. There's nothing to worry about. That's perfectly normal."

I was worried about his circulation to that foot. They'd check his pulse and say, "He's got a really strong pulse. There's circulation, there's blood coming to the foot. It is fine." But the necrosis got worse and I said, "There's something wrong with this. This isn't working."

So they put on a device that was supposed to put the pressure on the other side [of his foot]. Then that side turned black. This went on for two weeks: They tried one device then another—nothing worked—but they argued that [the latest device would prevent] more surgery.

I said, "At least he'll have a foot to do the surgery on, because with what you're doing this whole foot is just going to rot off. What you're doing isn't making any sense—I'm not a medical person, I'm a librarian—but logic tells you if you're doing the same thing over and over again, and his foot turns black with the pressure, something is wrong."

Once he started physical therapy and blood was reaching the extremities, he did better. But the megadoses of painkillers and medication didn't help. He'd do an exercise then nod out. Or he'd miss therapy because the media wanted to use him as poster boy for articulate wounded warrior, West Point graduate, or officer.

We got him into St. Vincent's hospital in Manhattan to a doctor who'd be able to save the foot. She took one look and said, "I'll do what I can. But if this necrosis has gotten to the bone…."

She amputated the little toe and part of the foot about which Walter Reed doctors had said, "Don't worry about it, it's perfectly normal."

He's still doing physical therapy, and he was invited back to West Point to tutor physics; he'd graduated first in his class and they wanted him back.

In Walter Reed we were worried about his physical state, now we're concerned about his mental state; he's kind of a prisoner in this house, can't easily get around after 4 o'clock, and is left to his own devices. He's fairly independent, he's weaned himself off a couple of the medications, and he's on crutches and pretty strong. I go there on the weekend, we shop for food, and I cook. During the week he heats up frozen food.

He got a grant for a car that accommodates the fixator so he could get around, have a cup of coffee, and talk to people his age.

But the Wounded Warrior Unit personnel told him he couldn't use the car. He was upset about that and was told, "If you're going to make a big deal about this, we'll label you an uncooperative patient and you may be out of the Army with no benefits or anything else."

You know, he did what he was supposed to do and got banged up doing it and he saw horrible things. He's doing his best to get well, he wants to get involved with something, stay busy and mentally active, and take care of himself. Now he's told he can't have a car to travel the short distance to West Point, especially when there's snow on the ground.

All this politicization of the military has an effect on morale. The army, supposedly apolitical, is now politicized and taking orders from the executive branch.

Ryan is getting beaten down; he's getting ready to throw in the towel.

I was 10 years old when my brother was in Vietnam in '68, '69, at the height of the Tet Offensive, for 15 months. I wrote him every day, lived, ate, and breathed war, went on my first peace march when I was 12 with the Vietnam Veterans Against the War, and over the years I've written letters to people in government. I never wanted Ryan in the military but he said, "I can do this, it is peacetime, and it's a way to see the world." After 9/11, I begged him to leave, and he "No, Erin [his sister] can use the money for school." I didn't think they'd send him to Iraq because they'd invested a lot of money in training him as a nuclear scientist. Now I know people who are going back for their third tour to Iraq.

I'm as furious with the Democrats as with the Republicans. At Walter Reed I wrote to representatives Schumer, Clinton, and Pelosi... the Democrats we put into Congress to change things. Pelosi says impeachment is off the table. What does she think we put her in there for?

Ryan thought about getting his graduate degrees from West Point but he's souring on that.

WHERE ARE THEY NOW?

Sue Rosenblum

Sue's husband Richard passed away in April 2006. Gina, Joshua's fiancée, left her job at Cantor Fitzgerald. Sue has new grandsons and a grandnephew named for Joshua. Sue works full time at a performing arts center in Ft. Lauderdale and reports, "Through a lot of hard work, I have come to terms with Joshua's death. The pain never goes away but by accepting it I'm achieving some serenity. I help parents cope with the suffering attached with the loss of a child and this work for peace remains, aside from my family, foremost in my life."

Rachel Avila

Ryan underwent several surgeries, particularly for his eyes, and lost the sight in one eye. He enrolled in community college in 2008 and is in a program that addresses the learning disorders accompanying his brain injuries, including occasional memory loss and inability to concentrate. Rachel says, "He's doing okay. It's slow but he's working at it and I think he'll be all right."

Adele Kubein

M'kesha's life is slowly improving, although her leg gives her constant pain. Since she never received the medical care she required at the time of the injury and she expects the pain to continue, she is considering amputation. Her four-year-old son has dyspraxia (inability to use language) and there is a chance that whatever M'kesha was exposed to in Iraq caused his disability. The family has been on a waiting list for two years for help from agencies. Adele reports, "My daughter is beginning to heal mentally. She is facing the horrors and rising above them. She is contented with her home and her garden, and she is kind to people. She is the best mother I have ever seen under very difficult circumstances of constant physical pain, mental distress, and a very demanding child. I have no doubt that we will emerge from hell into the light ... ."

Christopher, Daniel, Lars, Matt, and Kenny

Listen to their stories on Raising Sand Radio's archives of the Winter Soldier Hearings 2008 at www.raisingsandradio.org.

8—Where do we go from here?

Go to your broken heart.
If you think you don't have one, get one.
To get one, be sincere.
Learn sincerity of intent by letting
life enter because you're helpless, really,
to do otherwise.

—Jack Hirschman, "Path"

MANY MOTHERS I TALKED TO in the Middle East were puzzled about why American mothers *allow* their children to volunteer in the U.S. military. Many suggested to me that if American mothers just said "no," their kids wouldn't enlist in the first place. It seemed pretty simple to Lebanese moms Fatima in Kfar Kila and Zuhre in Kolilah, who, independently of one another, urged me to tell American mothers not to send their sons to the Middle East, where they were likely to be killed.

This key cultural misunderstanding arises because each group considers a certain way of thinking "just plain common sense." In fact, it is loaded with cultural assumptions.

Essentially, individualist cultures—the United States and Britain are prime examples—hold the individual as the primary unit of reality and the ultimate standard of value. That 18-year-old Americans can make legally binding choices independent of parents and family, including the choice to enlist in the military, is characteristic of American individualism. It is so sacrosanct that many parents, even if they disagree with their child's enlistment, will not fight it—*even if a recruiter secured it fraudulently*. These parents often assume that the military will teach the child "self-discipline," underplaying that other skill the military will teach their child: to kill.

Collectivist cultures—Iraqi and Palestinian for example—hold the group, family, and clan as the primary unit of reality and the ultimate standard of value. It is inconceivable to Middle East mothers that a son would enlist without a prolonged family discussion or would ignore advice from the head of the family. These mothers find it incredible that deep within the 670-page No Child Left Behind Act (NCLB) is a provision requiring U.S. secondary schools to provide military recruiters access to school facilities, contact information for every student, and the right to aggressively pursue students through mailings, phone calls, and personal visits—*even if parents object*. (Many American parents don't know about this aspect of NCLB. Those who do know and do object must actively "opt out" of the process. Although there is a vigorous "NCLB Opt Out" counseling movement, since access rules were tightened in favor of military recruitment in April 2008, opting out is harder.)

These cultural differences are instructive when they surface in hot-button issues. Individualist Americans find honor killing, for example, a barbaric custom perpetrated against an individual woman that simply must be stopped. On the other hand, collectivist Iraqis and Afghans, even those who do not condone honor killing, recognize how it developed in a culture where family and group pride and dignity are preeminent over any single family member—and that stopping it is not simple.

Middle East mothers, in turn, recognize more clearly than American mothers how entrenched militarism has become in American entertainment, politics, economics, and education. How many in the West can acknowledge the pervasiveness of militarism? (I define militarism as an ideological commitment to war as a virtuous condition embodying the values of honor, duty, country, and sacrifice, maintaining and promoting an ever-stronger military force to aggressively defend national interest, even at the cost of other social priorities and liberties.) For members of a group seldom see their own culture clearly, let alone engage in constructive critique—for example, how would a fish describe water.

So it is that Jerusalem activist Nurit Peled-Elhanan's statement about Israeli mothers is true for *most* mothers: "They cannot think clearly about the situation because they are *in* it. Very few mothers can go against [everybody]...*it is very hard to do.*"

Nevertheless, there are inspiring precedents. Russian mothers have formed a movement against the brutal hazing rampant in Russia's armed forces. Hundreds of thousands of new recruits every year face grossly abusive treatment at the hands of more senior conscripts. Dozens die annually, and thousands sustain serious—often permanent—damage to their physical and mental health. Hundreds commit or attempt suicide and thousands run away from their units. Natalia Zhukova is the head of the Soldiers' Mothers Committee and a leading activist in the decade-long battle to halt these practices. When Natalia and mothers like her learn about hazing on a Russian military base, they enter the base, face down the senior officers, and retrieve their sons. By modeling to ordinary Russians that human rights activism improves lives, these mothers are building a constituency for human rights in Russia.

China's Tiananmen Mothers covertly challenge official claims about what happened in that square in June 1989, when, by conservative estimates, more than 1,000 people may have died. Despite persistent persecution, interrogation, and threats of violence, detention, and house arrest, these mothers share information and collect and distribute funds to affected families. Every year they commemorate their loved ones' deaths by secretly laying flowers in the square; an Internet component places virtual flowers in an image of the square. Despite heavy government vigilance, in June 2007 a small advertisement saluting mothers of students and workers killed in the 1989 Tiananmen Square crackdown appeared in a Chinese newspaper. It stated, "Paying tribute to the strong mothers of June 4 victims." Chinese police are investigating how the advertisement got into the newspaper.

Madres de La Plaza de Mayo (Mothers of the Disappeared) have gathered in front of Argentina's Presidential Palace for over 30 years in memory of their children and grandchildren who disappeared during "Operation Condor." An estimated 30,000 people disappeared and another 50,000 were murdered during this program in the name of the "safety and security of the nation." It reached its peak in the 1970s when Henry Kissinger and the United States supported five Latin American nations in campaigns against their own citizens. Tortures included waterboarding, forcing families to watch or listen to their loved ones being mutilated, and coercing friends to conduct torture on those they knew. Pregnant women were kept alive until their babies were born, then the mothers were murdered; military families adopted the children.

The hand that rocks the boat...

But how do mothers (and others) examine prevailing, usually unconscious, cultural assumptions? Ensconced in the interpretations of reality that have shaped our minds, often from birth, we tend to accept only one worldview as "correct"—and to believe that *everyone* recognizes this as true.

The following are commonly held American assumptions about war, debunked here not because this will change minds overnight—or ever— but because surfacing these unexamined "givens" allows individuals and groups to recognize their own situations and create a common basis for discussion.

Assumption: Soldiers do not use excessive force

Webster's dictionary defines "excessive" as "exceeding the usual, proper, or normal." However, civilian and military cultures hold different understandings of "usual, proper, or normal." Training in the rigorously authoritarian and hierarchal military includes group chanting of "Kill, kill, kill" and "Blood makes the grass grow"—phrases the average civilian never utters—but it excludes specific orders to destroy, pillage, and rape. While no seasoned leader believes that excessive force will not occur in the fog and fear of combat, the tendency is to underestimate or deny it.

War veterans willing to talk about the less palatable aspects of military service describe excessive force as SOP (standard operating procedure). Iraq war veteran Jason Moon recounts that "We were told that we could kill up to 30 civilians if one insurgent target was hiding in the group...if it was thirty or more, we'd have to call it up to our chain of command...."[1] Winter Soldier Hearings 2008 presented similar testimony from dozens of veterans. Responding to the Hearings in a press release, Department of Defense spokesman Lt. Col. Mark Ballesteros stated, "Such incidents are not representative of U.S. conduct. When isolated allegations of misconduct have been reported, commanders have conducted comprehensive investigations to determine the facts and held individuals accountable when appropriate."[2]

By all nonmilitary accounts issued from Fallujah in April and November 2004, excessive force was the norm. Speaking of these attacks—conducted in response to the grisly killing of four private military contractors—U.S. military spokesman Lt. Col. Barry Venable said, "The combined effects of the fire and smoke...will drive them out of the holes so that you can kill them with high explosives."[3] The "collateral damage" was a city destroyed and a population of 300,000 displaced into the desert through the long winter.

Americans hearing of excessive force in Fallujah may have trouble believing that these events actually occurred, as they are seldom reported widely. Independent journalist Dahr Jamail describes a few scenes:

> U.S. troops sprayed chemical and nerve gases on resistance fighters, [and] residents have been burnt. Eyewitness Ahmed Abdulla, a 21-year-old student...described shops bombed [and] bodies with arms and legs lying near them.... Doctors [who] spoke of the initial raid on Fallujah General Hospital at the beginning of the siege [were] instructed by U.S. and Iraqi forces [and the] Iraqi health minister...that if anyone disclosed information about this raid, they would be arrested or fired from their jobs.[4]

But excessive force—and denying it—didn't begin, nor will it end, with Fallujah. In a *60 Minutes* interview with CBS News anchor Mike Wallace in 1969, a participant in the My Lai massacre described killing men, women, children, and babies. When asked why he did it, the soldier replied, "Because I felt like I was ordered to do it, and...at the time, I felt like I was doing the right thing.... The mothers were hugging their children...waving their arms and begging...we kept right on firing."

Ironically, political leaders publicly extol excessive force. We have heard Israeli prime minister Ehud Olmert threaten to "bomb Lebanon back twenty years" (a threat directed at *Lebanon*, that is civilians, not Hezbollah combatants), while Lebanese Sheikh Hassan Nasrallah has threatened attacks on *Israeli cities* (that is, civilians, not just on Israeli Defense Force combatants). It is worth noting that Ehud Olmert stepped down as Israel's prime minister in September 2008. While Israelis sorely criticized his lackluster leadership during the war—Hezbollah publicly claimed victory—it was charges of financial corruption that forced Olmert's resignation.

Prior to the invasion of Iraq, President Bush gave Iraqi president Saddam Hussein and his sons 48 hours to leave Iraq before military action began "at a time of our choosing" and promised "the United States will instill 'shock and awe.'"

Americans expect such bravado in their public officials. And public officials respond in kind. On primary election day 2008 in Pennsylvania, Presidential candidate Hillary Clinton stated that, if elected president, she would respond to a nuclear attack by Iran (which doesn't have nuclear weapons) on Israel (which does) with a promise to "totally obliterate them," ("them" includes Iranian civilians). How many Americans consciously recognize this as a "commitment to war as a virtuous condition"—that is, endemic militarism—and shiver with dread at Hillary Clinton's new role as Secretary of State?

Instead of Ballesteros or Venable acknowledging the nature of war—and allowing Americans to understand exactly what our citizens are engaged in and debate whether it is worth the long-term cost—they deny it or reiterate the standard "few rotten apples" theory. Their stonewalling undermines American democracy and every standard of good leadership.

Assumption: The Uniform Code of Military Justice holds soldiers to a higher standard than civilian law

While the Uniform Code of Military Justice may be a more rigorous code than civilian law, it is military brass—or civilian leaders—who interpret and apply the code.

During the Vietnam War, Lt. William Calley was the only person—out of 26 officers and soldiers—charged in the much publicized massacre at My Lai and was found guilty of the murder of 22 Vietnamese civilians and sentenced to life in prison. President Nixon ordered Calley released pending appeal; he ultimately served four and a half months. Moreover, in *The War Behind Me*, Pulitzer Prize winning reporter Deborah Nelson found that U.S. military officers had "amassed nine thousand pages of evidence implicating U.S. troops in a wide range of atrocities" in Vietnam. My Lai was just one massacre among many.

Sgt. Kevin Benderman, on the other hand, was punished for speaking out against the war in Iraq. During his 2005 court martial Benderman was acquitted of desertion but found guilty of missing troop movement and sentenced to 15 months in jail and a dishonorable discharge. He writes:

> Having watched and observed life from the standpoint of a soldier for ten years of my life, I always felt there was no higher honor than to serve my country and defend the values that established this country. My family has a history of serving dating back to the American Revolution, and I felt that to continue that tradition was the honorable thing to do. As I went through the process which led to my decision to refuse deployment to Iraq...I was torn between thoughts of abandoning the soldiers...or following my conscience, which tells me: war is the ultimate in destruction and waste of humanity.[5]

The assumption is that Benderman's resistance is prejudicial to good military discipline: if we let *him* get away with it, we'd have to let them *all* get away with it "when they don't feel like fighting."

But Benderman's act was revolutionary in that he took his Oath of Enlistment seriously and refused to participate when the oath would have been transgressed. The soldier interviewed by Mike Wallace about events at My Lai was truthful too: he was implicitly "ordered to do it." It just took four decades, until 2008, for this to surface with a copy of the original order, Directive 525-3, stating that free-fire zones were demarcated within which civilian killings were not discouraged.[6]

Assumption: Orders to shoot noncombatants are illegal, and a soldier is duty bound to disobey

Troops are theoretically duty bound to disobey illegal orders, but in reality do *not* refuse to carry out such orders. Dr. Stanley Milgram's experiments, designed to explore ordinary people's reactions to situations involving conformance and authority, may explain why.

During his first set of experiments, 65 percent—or 26 civilian participants out of 40—administered the experiment's final (simulated) 450-volt electric shock to a screaming victim (played by an actor, unbeknownst to the participants). While many were very uncomfortable doing it, the majority did not refuse. Milgram states:

> The legal and philosophic aspects of obedience are of enormous importance, but they say very little about how most people behave in concrete situations. I test[ed] how much pain an ordinary citizen would inflict on another person simply because he was ordered to by an experimental scientist. Stark authority was pitted against the [participants'] strongest moral imperatives against hurting others, and, with the subjects' ears ringing with the screams of the

victims, authority won more often than not. The extreme willingness of adults to go to almost any lengths on the command of an authority constitutes the chief finding of the study and the fact most urgently demanding explanation. Ordinary people, simply doing their jobs...without any particular hostility... can become agents in a terrible destructive process. Moreover, even when the destructive effects of their work become patently clear and they are asked to carry out actions incompatible with fundamental standards of morality, relatively few people have the resources needed to resist authority.[7]

The cost of not resisting authority can be devastating.

Paul Meadlo was an impressionable farm boy when he was drafted to serve in Vietnam. His mother said of the "nervous stuttering wreck" who returned home from that war, "I sent the Army a nice boy...and they turned him into a murderer." During the My Lai massacre, Meadlo faithfully obeyed Lt. William Calley's orders to shoot—even while "crying hysterically and pleading with others who were not firing [at the Vietnamese civilians] to join in." Paul Meadlo believed he could be shot if he disobeyed an order. After all, Lt. Calley had threatened and kicked him in the past when he'd failed to follow orders.[8]

Jeff Lucey was a lance corporal in the 1st Truck Platoon of the 6th Motor Transport Battalion when he was ordered to shoot two Iraqi POWs.

"Pull the fucking trigger, Lucey!" someone had shouted. His gun was shaking, but he looked into the eyes of one of the guys. When the order to shoot was repeated, Jeff obeyed.[9]

Jeff watched the men die, then removed their Iraqi dog tags. After he returned home he began wearing the tags around his neck. He told his father these were not trophies but tokens of honor for the two men he had killed who did not have to die. Jeff's parents found the dog tags among the belongings he left on his bed after he hanged himself in their basement.

The tragedy of these young men, and tens of thousands more like them, is swept under the rug. That is, until the next round of war....

Assumption: People who cooperate instead of resist will not be treated harshly

Holocaust survivors might disagree with this assumption. So might U.S. government officials who cooperated by performing their assigned jobs and were treated harshly for it.

Bunnatine Greenhouse, chief contracting officer and chief overseer of contracts, had worked in military procurement for 20 years for the Army Corps of Engineers (the agency managing reconstruction work in Iraq). In 2005, she was demoted for "poor job performance."

Her lawyer, Michael Kohn, said, "The Army's action was an obvious reprisal for the strong objections she raised in 2003 to a series of corps decisions involving the Halliburton subsidiary Kellogg Brown & Root, which garnered more than $10 billion for work in Iraq. She is being demoted because of her strict adherence to procurement requirements and the Army's preference to sidestep them when it suits their needs."[10]

Army Major General Antonio M. Taguba was forced to retire after being tapped to conduct a thorough investigation of events at Abu Ghraib Prison and reporting that interrogators and other intelligence personnel were encouraging the abuse of detainees. "[I was] accused of being overzealous and disloyal [and] ostracized for doing what I was asked to do...."[11]

Assumption: The Oath of Enlistment protects combatants, civilians, and the democratic process

The U.S. armed forces require of every enlistee the oath that "I will support and defend the Constitution of the United States against all enemies, foreign and domestic; that I will bear true faith and allegiance to the same; and that I will obey the orders of the President of the United States and the orders of the officers appointed over me, according to regulations and the Uniform Code of Military Justice." All the way up the chain of command—from privates to colonels—this oath was cited as a reason for resisting the war in Iraq.

U.S. Marine Corps enlistee Cameron White and Army enlistees Jeff Englehart, Joe Hatcher, and Tom Cassidy stated the Oath of Enlistment as their reason for opposing the war. All expressed concern that the Constitution of the United States was imperiled by Bush and Cheney's espoused reasons for invading Iraq. Englehart said, "During the looting [of Baghdad], my buddies and I were expressly told, above all, to protect Baghdad's oil ministry. That's when I first started thinking about defending the Constitution of the United States against domestic enemies."[12]

First Lieutenant Ehren Watada, an artillery officer stationed at Ft. Lewis, Washington, became the Army's first commissioned officer to publicly refuse orders to fight in Iraq on grounds that the war was illegal and violated the Constitution and War Powers Act. Watada stated, "My moral and legal obligation is to the Constitution and not to those who would issue unlawful orders."[13]

Colonel Ann Wright resigned from the U.S. Foreign Service on March 19, 2003. In her letter of resignation to then Secretary of State Colin Powell, Wright wrote, "I believe we should not use U.S. military force without U.N. Security Council agreement to ensure compliance. In our press for military action now, we have created deep chasms in the international community and in important international organizations."[14]

All these individuals attempted to live up to the military's highest professed standards, yet all were rewarded for their integrity by being forced out of the service, harassed, or prosecuted.

What do we want?

I am of European colonial descent and acculturated to think like a "westerner." Acculturation may seem inevitable, but contemporary times demand more of us than comfort with the status quo. We can change. For example, when I read that "U.N. monitors in Lebanon say 26 civilians have been killed in explosions in southern Lebanon since the war ended in August 2006, most of them from leftover Israeli cluster bombs,"[15] a part of me thinks, well, considering 4 million cluster bombs were dropped in a country of 4 million people—one cluster bomb per person—26 dead isn't *that* many. This part of me represses the terror of 4 million cluster bombs and the anguish of 26 families, and implicitly accepts the public rationale for dropping them: that Israel has a right to defend itself. Essentially, it reconfigures my thinking to make sense of nonsense, and uses culturally specific mental tools to soothe my compromised morality. But this reflex makes it increasingly difficult for me to look clearly at the world around me and its appeals to my humanity.

Responsible leaders would encourage the American people to grapple with the limitations of their worldview and to understand an increasingly complex world. They would encourage educational curricula that respect the variety of human cultures. Instead, our leaders, even when they know better, package reality according to the public's entrenched mindset.

- As a candidate for U.S. President, Hillary Clinton evaded the true issues of the War on Terror when she stated in a stump speech in late March 2008, "We have given [Iraqis] the precious gift of freedom and it is up to them to decide whether or not they will use it."

  This gross oversimplification "dumbs down" the situation for the American people, and the result is, effectively, a lie. Independent journalist Nir Rosen countered Clinton in a radio interview shortly after her statement:

  > I was in Iraq during the 2003 election. We [the United States] denied them freedom, we denied them sovereignty, we denied them their own government. We imposed a series of dictators on them: Garner, Bremer, Allawi. We created—caused—a civil war in a country that had never experienced a civil war. [As for] the "precious gift of freedom," there's freedom to kill whomever you want, there's freedom for militia. The Americans are not agents for freedom in Iraq. And there is no Iraqi government. Iraq is [like] Somalia, with different warlords controlling different areas.[16]

- Madeleine Albright's worldview—the American version of "realpolitik"—judged economic sanctions "worth" the lives of 1.5 million Iraqis, 500,000 of them children, because it served her sense of the greater good. The assumption, unspoken but implicit, is that the greater good privileges "us"—westerners and Americans—over "them"—Iraqis, Lebanese, Syrians, Palestinians....

- Conservative partisan political talk show host Rush Limbaugh "supports the troops" with daily broadcasts—including "exclusive access to American Forces Radio."[17] He opined concerning events at Abu Ghraib Prison:

  > This [abuse and torture of prisoners] is no different than what happens at the Yale University Skull and Bones initiation, and we're going to ruin people's lives over it, and we're going to hamper our military effort, and then we're going to really hammer [the troops] because they had a good time. You know these people are being fired

at every day. I'm talking about people having a good time.... You every heard of emotional release? You heard of the need to blow some steam off?[18]

This way of having "a good time"—waterboarding, posing for photos next to tortured corpses, raping women, sodomizing young boys, and forcing men to fellate and masturbate one another—is similar to the "good time" had by South African Defense Force troops who floured women before raping and killing them. Limbaugh offhandedly legitimizes activities prohibited by the Geneva Conventions, undermines democratic values, and turns brutality into a joke. Moreover, he insults the integrity of every service member struggling to maintain his or her humanity in inhuman situations.

What is required is a completely new approach to educating the populace. Students become wise not just through the accumulation of knowledge, but through knowing *how* to think—and how to feel. Young people will become leaders of a generative future by learning to confront leaders who, beneath the rhetoric, act on principles of unilateralism and "might makes right."

The world is a dangerous place, say Bush, Cheney, and Rumsfeld, and thanks to worldviews like theirs, carried to their logical conclusion, it is becoming more so. Instead of partisan ideology people require constructive ways to confront danger. Fear-mongering, threatening "shock and awe," and minimizing abuse as "blowing steam off" won't do it.

Leaders who want to keep us "safe" could acknowledge that excessive force is a standard element of war. This would present the nation the opportunity to consider how, for example, troops who become desensitized to aggression and killing turn off that training—if this is possible—when they return home. That would help, for example, Americans like Henry Berry understand why four Army Special Forces soldiers, recently returned from combat in Afghanistan, killed their wives in North Carolina in June and July 2002. Instead, Berry, manager of an Army family support program, found it "mind-boggling. To be absolutely honest, I was completely caught off guard."[19]

We can avoid being caught off guard in the future by understanding that such tragedies are logical by-products of war. As Americans, we must factor in the full effect of war *before* our leaders scare us into the next one. The data is available. The latest study of killings by military veterans shows

> an 89 percent increase—from 184 cases to 349—in the six years following the 2001 invasion of Afghanistan—in the number of homicides involving active-duty military personnel and new veterans. About three-quarters of these cases involved Iraq and Afghanistan veterans. More than half of the crimes involved guns while the rest were stabbings, beatings, strangulations, and bath drownings. Twenty-five offenders faced murder, manslaughter or homicide charges for fatal car crashes resulting from drunken, reckless, or suicidal driving.

The study, which the *New York Times* called "conservative," "most likely uncovered only the minimum number of such cases, given that not all killings, especially in big cities and on military bases, are reported publicly or in detail."[20]

The more direct recipients of our military destructiveness—those the recent crop of leaders dub "the axis of evil," civilians living in "rogue" or "failed" states, and "Islamofascists"—are demoted to "collateral damage" rather than murdered, maimed, bereaved, displaced human beings. At this time, despite our leaders telling Americans that "they hate us for our freedoms," most ordinary people around the world, including in the Middle East and Central Asia, don't hate us. Many say, "We like the American people, but we don't like their government." But this is wearing thin. How could it not, when so few Americans face the fact that each one of us is implicated in, for example, economic sanctions against Iraq, the inexorable theft of Palestinians' land and birthright, and the looting—corporate and otherwise—of Iraqi oil resources and historical heritage?

Support the troops?

Dick Cheney "had other priorities" when he took a series of draft deferments that resulted in other men serving in his place in the Vietnam War. President Bush had priorities other than showing up in the Texas Air National Guard from 1968 to 1974.

Since the end of the draft in 1973, most Americans have priorities other than military service: fewer than 2 million active military serve more than 300 million Americans. After the United States instituted the volunteer military, says Vietnam War veteran Dr. Andrew J. Bacevich,

> cheering the troops on did not imply any interest in joining their ranks. Especially among the affluent and well-educated, the notion took hold that national defense was something "they" did, just as "they" bused tables, collected trash, and mowed lawns.
>
> The stalemated war in Iraq has revealed two problems with this arrangement. The first is that "we" have forfeited any say in where "they" get sent to fight.... [T]he will of the commander-in-chief prevails.
>
> The second problem stems from the first. If "they"...get in trouble, "we" feel little or no obligation to bail them out. All Americans support the troops, yet support does not imply sacrifice. Yellow-ribbon decals displayed on the back of gas-guzzlers will suffice, thank you.[21]

Indeed, the mother of G. W. Bush unabashedly displayed this self-entitled worldview on *Good Morning America* in 2003. Dianne Sawyer asked for her views on U.S. troop deaths, then numbering 140. First Mother Barbara Bush answered, "Why should I waste my beautiful mind thinking about the dead? Why should we hear about body bags and deaths? Oh, Dianne, it's not relevant. So why should I waste my beautiful mind on something like that?"[22]

The "war to end all wars"—World War I—did nothing of the sort. From 1914 to 1918, more than 65 million men mobilized. Up to 10 million men lost their lives on the battlefields, and 20 million more were wounded.

The death toll for World War II was over 72 million, including about 12 million related to postwar famines in China, Indonesia, Indochina, and India (often omitted from casualty compilations); more than 25 million of these deaths were military, 40 million civilian, and 5.5 million from the Holocaust.

Yet, in the wars up to and including World War II, from 75 to 80 percent of riflemen did not fire their weapons...even to save their own or their buddies' lives. Once the U.S. military recognized this, it immediately improved training techniques to develop a reflexive "quick shoot" ability that improved firing rates to 90 to 95 percent by the Vietnam War, reports Lt. Col. Dave Grossman in his book on the psychological costs of war, *On Killing*.

In military training today, Grossman says, "every aspect of killing on the battlefield is rehearsed, visualized and conditioned...combining manufactured contempt, denial, and contempt for the victim's role in society (desensitization) and humanity, and practicing on man-shaped silhouettes."[23]

In the same time period, the military also determined that youth between the ages of 18 and 20 make the best soldiers. They are easy to condition psychologically during this developmental stage when individuals establish stable personality structures and a sense of self; they're also idealistic and vulnerable to the siren song of patriotism. Add signing bonuses that seem like small fortunes and the perennial glamour of jumping out of helicopters, and *voilà*, our nation has plenty of volunteers. Only in basic training do they learn that they no longer have the same civil rights other citizens enjoy.

David Chu, the Pentagon's Undersecretary for Personnel and Readiness, opined in 2005 that "the government was spending too much on benefits for Americans who have served in the military [and that] the money would be better spent on bullets and bombs," said a report in Salon.com. "The amounts have gotten to the point where they are hurtful," Chu stated. "They are taking away from the nation's ability to defend itself."[24]

Deputy Assistant Director for National Security Matthew S. Goldberg testified before the Committee on Veterans' Affairs:

> [D]epending on the future force levels deployed to OIF [Operation Iraqi Freedom] and OEF [Operation Enduring Freedom], if the Congress chooses to fully fund medical care for veterans of those operations, VA medical costs explicitly associated with those operations could total between $7 billion and $9 billion over the ten-year period 2008 through 2017.... The costs of disability compensation and survivors' benefits could add another roughly $3 billion to $4 billion over the same period.[25]

What happens if Congress chooses *not* to fund veteran care? Belt-tightening coincides with a dramatic rise in suicide rates among troops. The federal Centers for Disease Control and Prevention stated that the overall suicide rate nationwide during 2001 was 10.7 per 100,000. In 2002, the Army reported an overall suicide rate of 11.1 per 100,000. In 2003, the military-documented suicide rate for soldiers in Iraq was 13.5 per 100,000.[26] In 2006, the Associated Press reported that "the number of U.S. Army soldiers who took their own lives increased last year to the highest total since 1993, despite a growing effort by the Army to detect and prevent suicides."[27]

Based on extensive research, a CBS News investigative unit reported that more than 6,250 U.S. veterans took their own lives in 2005 alone. Four months after they submitted a Freedom of Information Act request to the Department of Defense asking for the numbers of suicides among all service members for the past twelve years, they received a document revealing that, between 1995 and 2007, almost 2,200 *active-duty* soldiers had taken their own lives.[28]

...or support the contractors?

The government avoids admitting the high costs of supporting the troops by keeping their plight out of the public eye—and by relying on Private Military Companies (PMCs). Accordingly, under the unwatchful eye of the American public a lucrative PMC industry—annual contracts range from $10 to $20 billion, perhaps even up to $100 billion—increasingly deploys well-armored mercenaries to hot spots around the world, including, after Hurricane Katrina devastated New Orleans, on American soil. During the 1991 Persian Gulf War, one in every 50 people on the battlefield was a U.S. civilian under contract; by the time of the peacekeeping effort in Bosnia in 1996, the figure was one in ten. The public companies that own private military contractors say little if anything about them to shareholders.

Blackwater USA, notorious for using armed helicopters in Baghdad's Nissor Square on September 17, 2007—killing 17 and wounding 24 Iraqi civilians—has "more than $500 million in government contracts," says Jeremy Scahill in his book on the company, "and that does not include its secret 'black' budget operations for U.S. intelligence agencies or private corporations/individuals and foreign governments. One U.S. Congressmember observed that 'Blackwater could overthrow many of the world's governments.'"[29] In fact, Blackwater may be better resourced than many world governments: it recently purchased five Super Tucano fighter planes from Brazil.

Blackwater and other PMCs recruit well-trained personnel around the world. A South African mother recounts that her son, conscripted into the South African Defense Force, had few marketable job skills, but today, he supports his family as a PMC mercenary in Iraq. Discharged U.S. service members can earn around $600 to $800 per day for short two- or three-month contracts in these private forces. The monthly pay for active U.S. troops—a grade 4 enlistee with less than two years' service receives $1,699.50 monthly; a grade 7 receives $2,339.10—does not begin to compare with the remuneration of Blackwater hirees, yet troops report that they are frequently called to protect PMC contractors and convoys. Terri Everett, Senior Procurement Executive in the Office of the Director of National Intelligence, stated in 2007, "Seventy percent of the U.S. intelligence budget is now going to private contractors. There is every reason to be concerned about the amount and significance of contracting being done by the U.S. government."[30]

At the 2008 Winter Soldier Hearings, Captain Luis Carlos Montalvan, formerly an Iraq Security Force subject matter expert with the conservative American Enterprise Institute, described corruption and graft in Iraq—from Paul Bremer III's Coalition Provisional Authority to high-level Iraq government officials—that includes, among other ruses, hundreds of thousands of "ghost" Iraqi forces, each one drawing a salary that funnels directly into cronies' pockets. The much heralded "troop surge" amounted to an enormous surge in corruption earning for contractors, officials, and PMCs. Montalvan puts part of the onus of responsibility on General Petraeus, who "failed to implement any systems of accountability for contractors who were given billions of dollars of American taxpayer [money]. And he has not been held accountable...nor have U.S. contractors in Iraq."[31]

Hail to the chief dissenters

Prominent figures who do not espouse a militaristic worldview are the role models our future leaders need.

- Dr. Martin Luther King responded to fellow clergy who criticized his civil rights activities as "unwise and untimely" in these words:

  There are two types of laws: just and unjust. One has not only a legal but a moral responsibility to obey just laws. Conversely, one has a moral responsibility to disobey unjust laws. I would agree with St. Augustine that 'an unjust law is no law at all.'... Any law that degrades human personality is unjust...an individual who breaks a law that conscience tells him is unjust, and who willingly accepts the penalty of imprisonment in order to arouse the conscience of the community over its injustice, is in reality expressing the highest respect for law.[32]

- The U.S. State Department sent theologian Michael Novak to the Vatican to make the case for war, arguing that "military action was justified under traditional self-defense principles and not [a] new concept of preventive war." Pope John Paul II, maintaining his strong position—"No to war!"—described war as a "defeat for humanity" and urged world leaders to resolve disputes with Iraq through diplomatic means.

- Army Major General Antonio M. Taguba lost his job because he adhered to the highest principles of his training: "loyalty, duty, honor, integrity, and selfless service." He said, "When we get to the senior-officer level we forget those values.... We violated the laws of land warfare in Abu Ghraib. We violated the tenets of the Geneva Convention. We violated our own principles and we violated the core of our military values. The stress of combat is not an excuse, and I believe, even today, that those civilian and military leaders responsible should be held accountable."[33]

- Dr. Philip Zimbardo, Stanford University psychology professor emeritus, was one of 300 faculty and 3,500 students who objected to the appointment of former U.S. Secretary of Defense Donald Rumsfeld as a Distinguished Visiting Fellow at the Hoover Institution located on Stanford University campus. Their petition states: "We view the appointment as fundamentally incompatible with the ethical values of truthfulness, tolerance, disinterested inquiry, respect for national and international laws, and care for the opinions, property, and lives of others to which Stanford is inalienably committed."[34]

    The professor clarifies: "Many of us believe that Donald Rumsfeld, in his role as Secretary of Defense, has behaved in ways that are dishonorable, disgraceful, and always disingenuous. [He] authorized a list of interrogation methods that violated the Geneva Convention and the Convention Against Torture used on detainees at Guantanamo Bay…and Abu Ghraib Prison. Rumsfeld does not uphold the 'ethical values' of the school."

Zimbardo's study known as the Stanford Prison Experiment found that situational forces can "make monsters out of decent men and women." From these experiments with ordinary, healthy young men he formulated his theory: rotten apples come out of rotten barrels. The Chairman of the Independent Panel to Review DoD Detention Operations, James R. Schlesinger, cites in the panel's final report that "psychologists have attempted to understand how and why individuals and groups who usually act humanely can sometimes act otherwise in certain circumstances. [Zimbardo's SPE is] a cautionary tale for all military detention operations."[35]

Dr. Zimbardo was also an expert witness for Abu Ghraib low-level fall guy Sergeant Chip Frederick. In his book *The Lucifer Effect: Understanding How Good People Turn Evil*, he points out:

> There is absolutely nothing in [Frederick's] record...that would predict that [he] would engage in any form of abusive, sadistic behavior. On the contrary, there is much in his record to suggest that had he not been forced to work and live in such an abnormal situation, he might have been the military's All-American poster soldier on its recruitment ads...as a superpatriot who loved his country and was ready to serve it to the last drop of his blood. He could have been the best of apples in their good barrel.[36]

Frederick, the low man on the totem pole, nonetheless became a scapegoat.

During an interview on *60 Minutes II*, Brigadier General Mark Kimmitt said, "It is inconceivable that high-level leaders were ignorant of these actions [at Abu Ghraib]." In fact, "evidence exists that General [Richard] Myers personally called Dan Rather" eight days before the interview, requesting that CBS "delay broadcasting the segment...to avoid danger to 'our troops' and to the 'war effort.' CBS complied [and] put off showing the piece for two weeks.... The request showed that the military brass was well aware of the 'image problems' that would be created."[37]

Lt. Col. Steven L. Jordan was named in the Taguba report as one of several officers "directly or indirectly responsible for the abuses at Abu Ghraib." Jordan supervised the interrogation task force at Abu Ghraib and served under Col. Thomas M. Pappas, who was granted immunity from prosecution so that he could testify against Jordan. On April 28, 2006, Jordan became the highest-ranking Army officer to face charges relating to the abuse, including mistreating detainees, lying about abuse, and dereliction of duty. He was found guilty of disobeying an order not to talk about the investigation, and the jury recommended a criminal reprimand, the lightest possible punishment. In January, 2008, Jordan was cleared of any criminal wrongdoing and given an administrative reprimand instead.

Prior to Jordan's reprimand, Marine Corps Maj. Clarke A. Paulus had been the highest-ranking officer convicted in relation to prisoner abuses in Iraq and Afghanistan. He was found guilty in 2004 of dereliction of duty and the maltreatment of a prisoner who was found dead at a Marine-run jail in Iraq. Paulus was discharged from the military but served no jail time.[38]

9—Just the facts

"There is nothing new in the world except the history you do not know."
—Harry Truman

ESPITE THE MILITARY and political establishment's skewing of the facts, ordinary Americans can understand how the current system affects our world and can make connections between research data and real life.

The material costs

- The Bush Administration transacted a $63 billion package of arms transfers and military aid to Gulf Cooperation Council states; additionally, over the next decade, $13 billion in arms grants will go to Egypt and $30 billion to Israel (equivalent to a payout of $4,500 for every current Israeli resident).

- The United States is the world's top military spender, with over 46 percent of global expenditures. The next biggest spender is the U.K., with 5 percent.[1]

- The 2008 appropriations bills included $506.9 billion for the U.S. Department of Defense and the nuclear weapons activities of the Department of Energy, plus an additional $189.4 billion for military operations in Iraq and Afghanistan. This amount doesn't include costs to society—payouts for loss of life, injuries, and so on. Nobel laureate and former chief World Bank economist Joseph Stiglitz estimates the overall cost of the Iraq conflict to be $3 trillion. Moreover, he states, "We were very conservative in our book [*The Three Trillion Dollar War: The True Cost of the Iraq Conflict*]. When we say $3 trillion, that's really an underestimate…. For the past five years the Bush administration has repeatedly low-balled the cost of the war."[2]

- A recent RAND study reports that "Nearly 20 percent of military service members who have returned from Iraq and Afghanistan—

300,000 in all—report symptoms of [PTSD] or major depression." It estimates these societal costs "two years after deployment range from about $6,000 to more than $25,000 per case." If the economic cost of suicide is included, the study estimates the total society costs "range from $4 billion to $6.2 billion.... One-year estimates of the societal cost associated with treated cases of mild traumatic brain injury range up to $32,000 per case, while estimates for treated moderate to severe cases range from $268,000 to more than $408,000. Estimates of the total one-year societal cost of the roughly 2,700 cases of traumatic brain injury identified to date range from $591 million to $910 million." Not a single U.S. elected official is acknowledging this reality.[3]

• An investigation by the progressive think tank Institute for Policy Studies found that the U.S. government budgeted $647.5 billion for the defense budget in 2008 (more than the defense budgets of the rest of the world's nations combined) and $7.37 billion for climate-related programs.

• For the five years ending in 2008, stock market earnings per share in the defense industry grew at an average annual rate of more than 31 percent, a trend reflected in share and stock prices. The AMEX Defense Index, created in September 2001 with a base value of 500, stood at 1180 in December 2008, having been at 1778 in 2007.[4]

• Exxon Mobil Corporation posted record profits for three years in a row, culminating in $40.6 billion in early 2008, the largest annual profit by a U.S. company ever. Its net income of $11.7 billion for the final three months of 2007 beat its own mark of $10.71 billion in the fourth quarter of 2005. The previous record for annual profit was $39.5 billion, which Exxon Mobil posted in 2006.[5]

• The American Council on Education states that in 2004–05, average American student loan debt was between $26,119 and $29,000—and as high as $165,000. Private lenders provided about $14 billion in private loans, a 734 percent increase from a decade earlier—with higher interest rates and less flexible payment options than federal loans. In 2006 Congress cut $12.7 billion from student loan programs, the largest cut in history.

- While more than half of all discretionary federal spending is now directed to the military, the nonprofit Food Research and Action Center states that "government officials are projecting the number of Americans receiving food stamps will reach a record 28 million [in 2008]. Over the past year, more than forty states saw the number of food stamp recipients rise. A 10 percent jump in food stamp recipients was recorded in six states: Arizona, Florida, Maryland, Nevada, North Dakota and Rhode Island. In West Virginia, one in six residents now receive food stamps."[6]

- At a White House news conference on September 20, 2008 President George Bush formally proposed a vast bailout of financial institutions in the United States, requesting unfettered authority for the Treasury Department to buy up to $700 billion in distressed mortgage-related assets from the private firms. He explained, "This is a big package, because it was a big problem." This raises the national debt ceiling to $11.3 trillion while placing no restrictions on the administration other than requiring semiannual reports to Congress, granting the Treasury secretary unprecedented power to buy and resell mortgage debt.

...and worse

- There is an epidemic of sexual assault in the military and among military subcontractors, but exactly how many female service members have been victimized is hard to establish. Helen Benedict writes in Salon.com:

  Comprehensive statistics on the sexual assault of female soldiers in Iraq have not been collected, but early numbers revealed a problem so bad that former Defense Secretary Donald H. Rumsfeld ordered a task force in 2004 to investigate.... Last year, Col. Janis Karpinski caused a stir by publicly reporting that in 2003, three female soldiers had died of dehydration in Iraq, which can get up to 126 degrees in the summer, because they refused to drink liquids late in the day. They were afraid of being raped by male soldiers if they walked to the latrines after dark.[7]

- Women face this hazard from the very beginning of their association with the military. In the San Francisco Bay Area, for example, U.S. Marine Corps recruiters arranged a "sleep over" for potential recruits. Two young women were presented alcohol that night, then raped by recruiters. At least one of these young women was a virgin and contracted an STD from the assault. When the women sued, the USMC paid the plaintiffs—with federal funds. In other words, the American taxpayer footed the bill.[8]

- The *New York Times* reported on May 18, 2007, that the number of contractors killed in Iraq was at least 917, and more than 12,000 wounded in battle or injured on the job.[9] By early 2008, the death toll among U.S. troops was 4,468; wounded, 31,187; injured, 9,984; ill, 27,890, VA treated, 299,585; claimed disability, 245,034.[10]

- The death toll among Iraqis since the invasion is difficult to establish with certainty, especially since official U.S. policy, as expressed to Fox News by then Secretary of Defense Donald Rumsfeld in November 2003, has been "We don't do body counts on other people."[11] Once again, we see which people "count" in the worldview of our leaders.

- A survey conducted by Johns Hopkins in Baltimore and reported in the prominent British medical journal *The Lancet* in 2004 found at least 98,000 Iraqi civilian deaths up to October 2004. "The second survey, in the summer of 2006, interviewed a separate but also randomly chosen sample of 1,849 households and found in excess of 655,000 deaths up to June 2006, of which 601,027 were said to be from violence rather than natural causes. This amounts to 2.5% of Iraq's population, or more than 500 deaths a day since the invasion."

In 2007 the British polling firm Opinion Research Business (ORB) asked 1,720 Iraqi adults if they had lost family members by violence since 2003. Sixteen percent had lost one, and 5 percent had lost two. Using the 2005 census total of 4,050,597 households in Iraq, this suggests 1,220,580 deaths since the invasion. Taking into account a standard margin of error, ORB says, "We believe the range is a minimum of 733,158 to a maximum of 1,446,063."

Frederick Burkle, a professor in the public health and epidemiology department at Harvard University, believes the number of civilian casualties may be higher than the Johns Hopkins figure. Burkle, who ran Iraq's ministry of health after

the war until he was fired by the United States and replaced by a
Bush loyalist, says the survey ignored the occupation's indirect or
secondary casualties—deaths caused by the destruction of health
services, unemployment, and lack of electricity. "Two surveys by
nongovernment organisations found a rise in infant mortality and
malnutrition, so why are those figures not reflected in the second
study that appeared in *The Lancet?*"[12]

On the other side of the debate, the *Lancet* report was attacked
in the January 2008 issue of the *National Journal*, a right-leaning
magazine aimed at Washington policy makers.[13] President Bush
has consistently pooh-poohed any Iraqi fatalities over the
30,000 figure he off-handedly put forth in December 2004. But
to comprehend how wildly unrealistic and irresponsible these
leaders have been, recall George W. Bush and Tony Blair's words
in their Address to the Peoples of Iraq, delivered April 10, 2003,
at the White House.

Bush stated: "The United States and its coalition partners
respect the people of Iraq. We are taking unprecedented measures
to spare the lives of innocent Iraqi citizens.... And I assure every
citizen of Iraq: Your nation will soon be free."

Blair followed with: "We will continue to do all we can to avoid
civilian casualties."

- While a grisly comparison, estimates of Iraqi deaths during
  Saddam's regime amount to an average annual rate that does
  not exceed 29,000, that is, a maximum of a million over 35 years
  (100,000 Kurds in the Anfal campaign in the 1980s; 400,000 in
  the war against Iran; 100,000 Shi'as in the 1991 uprising called
  for by George H. W. Bush, who then abandoned the resisters to
  their fate with Saddam; and an unknown number executed in his
  prisons and torture chambers).[14] On the fifth anniversary of the
  toppling of Saddam's statue, Ibrahim Khalil, one of the Iraqis in
  the crowd that day, said, "If history can take me back, I will now
  actually kiss the statue of Saddam. I am sorry that I played a part
  in pulling it down...that was a black day for Baghdad. We got
  rid of Saddam, but now we have 50 Saddams. I ask Bush, 'Where
  are your promises of making Iraq a better country?'"[15]

Contact these organizations for more information:

Afghans4Tomorrow: www.afghans4tomorrow.org
GI Rights Hotline: www.girightshotline.org
Iraq Veterans Against War: www.ivaw.org
Institute for Policy Studies: www.ips-dc.org
Israeli Committee against Home Demolition: www.icahd.org/eng
Middle East Children's Alliance: www.mecaforpeace.org
Military Law Task Force: www.mltf.org
MotherSpeak: www.motherspeak.org
Parents Circle–Families Forum: www.theparentscircle.com
Palestinian Counseling Center: www.pcc-jer.org
Raising Sand Radio: www.raisingsandradio.org
SOS Children's Villages: www.sos-childrensvillages.org
Swords to Plowshares: www.swords-to-plowshares.org
Veterans Village: www.veteransvillage.org
Vets 4 Vets: www.vets4vets.us

Notes

INTRODUCTION

1. IED: improvised explosive device. RPG: rocket-propelled grenade.
2. Joe Garafoli. "Hey, Nick, Your Mom Is Here." *San Francisco Chronicle.* April 3, 2004. (www.sfgate.com/cgi-bin/article.cgi?file=/c/a/2004/04/03/MNGIQ609LN1.DTL – last reviewed February 2008.)
3. *Le Monde.* Paris, France. Magazine cover article for week of May 24, 2004.
4. Lara Dutto and Claudia Lefko, interviewed on Raising Sand Radio October 15, 2007 (www.raisingsandradio.org).
5. Stop-loss is the involuntary extension of a United States service member's active duty that retains that member beyond the initial end of term of service (ETS) date.
6. Winter Soldier Hearings 2008. Iraq Veterans Against War (ivaw.org and www.raisingsandradio.org).
7. Tina Susman. "Poll: Civilian Death Toll in Iraq May Top 1 Million." *Los Angeles Times.* September 14, 2007. (www.commondreams.org/archive/2007/09/14/3839/ – last reviewed January 2008.)
8. Kari Lydersen. "War Costing $720 Million Each Day, Group Says." *Washington Post.* September 23, 2007. (www.commondreams.org/archive/2007/09/23/4049/ – last reviewed January 2008.)

1—IRAQ

1. Rahim al-Maliki. "If you do not love Iraq." This Iraqi poet was among 13 people killed in a suicide attack at a Baghdad hotel on June 26, 2007. He was filming tribal leaders about their decision to join U.S.-led forces in the fight against factions linked to Al Qaeda.
2. Sean Loughlin. "Rumsfeld on Looting in Iraq: 'Stuff happens.'" CNN Washington Bureau. Saturday, April 12, 2003. (www.cnn.com/2003/US/04/11/sprj.irq.pentagon/ – last reviewed January 2008.)
3. BBC News. "Looters Ransack Baghdad Museum." Saturday, April 12, 2003. (news.bbc.co.uk/2/hi/middle_east/2942449.stm – last reviewed January 2008.)
4. Alexandria Zavis. "Ancient Civilization...Broken to Pieces." *Los Angeles Times.* January 22, 2008. (www.latimes.com/news/nationworld/world/la-fg-antiquities22jan22,0,3195624,full.story?coll=la-home-world – last reviewed January 2008.)

5. Elizabeth Day and Philip Sherwell. "Looters Strip Iraqi National Museum of Its Antiquities." *Telegraph*. April 13, 2003. (www.telegraph.co.uk/news/main. jhtml?xml=/news/2003/04/13/wirq13.xml – last reviewed July 2008.)

6. Stacy R. Obenhaus. "During the Persian Gulf War, Did the Coalition Air Attack on Withdrawing Iraqi Forces Constitute Permissible 'Just War' Conduct?" Perkins School of Theology. Southern Methodist University (religion.rutgers. edu/courses/347/readings/just_war.html – last reviewed January 2008.)

7. Robert Fisk. *The Great War for Civilisation*. Knopf, Borzoi Books, 2005.

8. Bert Sacks. "Sanctions in Iraq Hurt the Innocent." *Seattle Post Intelligencer*. August 7, 2003. (www.commondreams.org/views03/0807-01.htm – last reviewed January 2008.)

9. Rahul Mahajan. "We Think the Price Is Worth It." Fairness and Accuracy in Reporting. November/December 2001. (www.fair.org/index.php?page=1084 – last reviewed June 2008.)

10. "We the Children: End-decade review of the follow-up to the World Summit for Children." UNICEF. (www.unicef.org/specialsession/documentation/documents/a-s-27-3e.doc – last reviewed August 2008.)

11. "Three Years of Slaughter in Iraq." (www.rsf.org/special_iraq_en.php3 – last reviewed January 2008.)

12. The Foreign Claims Act, (10 U.S.C. § 2734–2736), or FCA, is a United States federal law enacted on January 2, 1942, that provides compensation to inhabitants of foreign countries for personal injury, death, or property damage caused by, or incident to noncombat activities of United States military personnel overseas. Although the U.S. government's scope of liability under the FCA is broad, certain classes of claimants and certain types of claims are excluded from the statute's coverage. Procedures for adjudicating an FCA claim are substantially different from the general procedural pattern for other types of claims against the government. Chapter VIII, part B, of the Judge Advocate General's Corps Manual prescribes the requirements for the investigation and adjudication of FCA claims.

13. "ACLU Files Lawsuit to Require Department of Defense to Comply With FOIA Request on Human Costs of War." ACLU press release. September 4, 2007. (www.aclu.org/natsec/31540prs20070904.html – last reviewed January 2008.)

14. Nermeen al-Mufti. "Iraq: Free for All." *Al Ahram Weekly Online*. (weekly. ahram.org.eg/2004/707/re5.htm – last reviewed January 2008.)

15. "Prosecutors Shun Excuses for Accused GIs." *USA Today*. August 8, 2006. (www.usatoday.com/news/world/iraq/2006-08-08-iraq-case_x.htm – last reviewed August 2008.)

16. Mike Ferner. *Inside the Red Zone: A Veteran For Peace Reports from Iraq*. Greenwood Publishing Group. 2006.

17. Dexter Filkins. "The Fall of the Warrior King." *New York Times*. October 23, 2005. (www.nytimes.com/2005/10/23/magazine/23sassaman.html – last reviewed January 2008.)

18. Katarina Kratovac. "Iraq Struggles with Cholera Outbreak." Associated Press. October 5, 2007. (www.commondreams.org/archive/2007/10/05/4328/ – last reviewed January 2008.)

2—ISRAEL

1. Khalil Gibran. "Broken Wings."
2. Conal Urquhart. "My Crime Was to Protest at Israeli Assassinations." *Guardian* (U.K.). January 5, 2007. (www.commondreams.org/headlines07/0105-05.htm – last reviewed January 2008.)
3. The Israeli-Palestinian Interim Agreement on the West Bank and Gaza Strip (known as Oslo II, signed on September 28, 1995) divided the West Bank into three areas, each with varying degrees of Israeli and Palestinian responsibility. The Palestinians were given complete civilian and security control over "Area A," which initially consisted of the seven major Palestinian towns—Jenin, Qalqilya, Tulkharem, Nablus, Ramallah, Bethlehem, and Hebron. "Area B"—comprised of all other Palestinian population centers (except for some refugee camps)—remained Israel's "overriding security responsibility." Israel retained sole security and civil control over "Area C," which includes all Israeli settlements, military bases and areas, and state lands.
4. Phyllis Bennis interviewed by Max Elbaum. Centre for Research on Globalisation's *Colorlines Magazine*. December 15, 2000. (www.globalresearch.ca/articles/BEN108A.html – last reviewed January 2008.)
5. Uri Davis, an Israeli scholar and author of numerous books, identifies four classes of citizenship: Class A Jews have full rights; Class B Non-Jews lack equal access to state resources; Class C Non-Jews or "present-absentees" who held property prior to 1948 are denied property rights; Class D Non-Jews are refugees or their descendants who will never be citizens.
6. David Cohen. "Israel: apartheid-style law passed by Knesset." World Socialist Web Site. August 13, 2003. The "Nationality and Entry into Israel" law, passed by the Israeli parliament (Knesset) by 53 to 25 votes in 2003, prevents Palestinians living in the Occupied Territories of the West Bank and Gaza Strip from residing with their Israeli spouses in Israel and from obtaining Israeli citizenship. (www.wsws.org/articles/2003/aug2003/isra-a13.shtml – last reviewed January 2008.)
7. Joel Kovel. *Overcoming Zionism: Creating a Single Democratic State in Israel/Palestine*. Pluto Press, 2007.
8. From Ramat Rachel's website. (www.ramatrachel.co.il/ – last reviewed January 2008.)
9. B'Tselem. (The Israeli Information Center for Human Rights in the Occupied Territories) "Forbidden Roads: Israel's Discriminatory Road Regime in the West Bank." Information Sheet, August 2004. Prohibited use: includes 17 roads or sections of roads in the West Bank totaling over 120 kilometers upon which Palestinians are completely prohibited (even crossing these roads to reach other roads that are not prohibited is forbidden). Partially prohibited use: includes ten roads or sections of roads in the West Bank totaling over 245 kilometers upon which Palestinians are allowed to travel only with the "Special Movement Permit at Internal Checkpoints in Judea and Samaria." Issued by the Civil Administration through the District Civil Liaison (DCL). This also permits special buses to travel between checkpoints that block off major cities. Restricted use: includes 14 roads or sections of roads in the West Bank totaling over 365 kilometers that can be reached only via an intersection

with a checkpoint because the IDF blocks other access roads from Palestinian villages adjoining these roads.

10. For online maps of semipermanent checkpoints see Israeli Checkpoints in West Bank and Gaza at www.jatonyc.org/checkpoint.html#checkpoint and www.jatonyc.org/checkpoint2.html (last reviewed December 2007).

11. Michael Finkel. "Bethlehem 2007 A.D." *National Geographic*. December 2007.

12. Central Bureau of Statistics of Israel.

13. Online Ynet News, September 5, 2005.

14. Haroon Siddique. "Homes in Illegal Israeli Settlements for Sale at London Expo." *Guardian* (U.K.). November 16, 2007.

15. See Peace Now: Settlements in Focus. (www.peacenow.org/policy.asp – last reviewed January 2008.)

16. Isabel Kershner. "Israel Angers Palestinians With Housing Plan." *New York Times*. December 24, 2007. (www.nytimes.com/2007/12/24/world/middleeast/23cnd-mideast.html?ex=1199077200&en=c8730aa93357825f&ei=5070&emc=eta1 – last reviewed January 2008.)

17. Bat Shalom is a women's group that envisions peace rooted in the needs, rights, values, and histories of both the Israeli and Palestinian people. (www.batshalom.org – last reviewed January 2008.)

3—WEST BANK/PALESTINE

1. Kamal Nasir. "The Story." Kamal Nasir, born in Birzeit in 1925, was deported after Israel occupied the West Bank in 1967 and was assassinated by the Israelis in Beirut on April 10, 1973.

2. "Facing the Abyss: The Isolation of Sheikh Sa'ad Village—Before and After the Separation Barrier." B'Tselem Status Report, February 2004.

3. Report of the International Labor Office Director General. ILO, Geneva. International Labor Conference, 89th Session, 2001. (http://domino.un.org/unispal.nsf/fd807e46661e3689852570d00069e918/8bf5e5d4e43142e485256b6f006deece!OpenDocument – last reviewed January 2008.)

4. UNRWA. Balata Refugee Camp.

5. "Official UNRWA Palestinian Refugee Camps, November 1993." (www.mideastweb.org/mrefugees.htm – last reviewed March 2008.)

6. Research findings indicate that the percentage of female suicide bombers who acted out of nationalist motives was more than twice as high as those who acted out of religious motives. In addition, some of them had academic education and/or were married with children.

7. Marc Sageman. *Understanding Terror Networks*. University of Pennsylvania Press, 2004.

8. Barbara Lubin interviewed on Raising Sand Radio. December 2007. Middle East Children's Alliance (MECA): www.mecaforpeace.org.

9. Joel Kovel. *Overcoming Zionism: Creating a Single Democratic State in Israel/Palestine*. Pluto Press, 2007.

10. Quoted in *ibid.*
11. Ari Shavit. "Survival of the Fittest." *Ha'aretz.* January 2004. (www.haaretz. com/hasen/pages/ShArt.jhtml?itemNo=380986&contrassID=2 – last reviewed February 2008.)
12. Mayroun, with a population of 290, located six miles southwest of Safad, was obliterated in 1948 and the Jewish settlement of Meron built on its 238 acres. For a list of close to 400 Palestinian villages that disappeared after 1948, see Walid Khalidi's book *All That Remains* or www.jerusalemites.org/crimes/destroyed_villages1948/index.htm (last reviewed January 2008).
13. Uri Davis. "Martin Buber's Paths in Utopia: The Kibbutz: An Experiment that Didn't Fail?" *Peace News,* no. 2446. (www.peacenews.info/issues/2446/244620.html – last reviewed January 2008.)
14. B'Tselem. "Israeli Civilians Killed by Palestinians in the Occupied Territories." (www.btselem.org/english/Statistics/Casualties.asp – last reviewed April 2008.)
15. Author Norman Finkelstein states in his book *Beyond Chutzpah* that "beginning September 2000, the ratio of Palestinians to Israelis killed was 20:1." B'Tselem reports that, since 2000, more than 4,100 Palestinian homes were demolished either for "punishment," because "built without permits," or for "military purposes" or "clearing operations." (www.btselem.org/english/Publications/Summaries/200411_Punitive_House_Demolitions.asp – last reviewed April 2008.)
16. Department of State. 01/02/2006. (http://uscode.house.gov/download/pls/22C38.txt- last reviewed January 2008.)

4—LEBANON

1. Wadih Sa'adeh. "The Dead Are Sleeping." Sa'adeh was born in a peaceful north Lebanon village, Shabtin, and was about 12 years old when he moved to Beirut. He emigrated to Australia in November 1988 due to the war in Lebanon.
2. "What Good Is This Revenge?" *Time.* January 11, 1982. (www.time.com/time/magazine/article/0,9171,925188,00.html - last reviewed January 2008.)
3. United Nations Relief and Works Agency. Lebanon Refugee Camp Profiles. (www.un.org/unrwa/refugees/lebanon.html – last reviewed January 2008.)
4. Chris McGreal. "Capture of Soldiers Was an 'Act of War' Says Israel." *Guardian* (U.K.). July 13, 2006. (www.guardian.co.uk/frontpage/story/0,,1819122,00. html – last reviewed January 2008.)
5. Lebanon under Siege. Presidency of the Council of Minister – Higher Relief Council. (www.lebanonundersiege.gov.lb/english/F/Main/index.asp? – last reviewed April 2008.)
6. Lara Marlowe. "Grief and Loss Eating into the U.S. Psyche." *Irish Times.* September 16, 2004. (www.ireland.com/focus/uselection2004/features/1091051938820.html – last reviewed January 2008.)

7. Lara Marlowe. "America's Irrational Streak Runs Deep." *Irish Times*. September 18, 2004. (www.ireland.com/focus/uselection2004/features/1091051943673. html – last reviewed January 2008.)
8. Khalil Gibran. "Pity the Nation."
9. Nada Bakri and Hassan M. Fattah. "Clash Pits Hezbollah against Lebanon." *New York Times*. January 24, 2007.
10. Robert Fisk. *The Great War for Civilization*. Knopf, Borzoi Books, 2005.
11. Judith Palmer Harik. *Hezbollah: The Changing Face of Terrorism*. I. B. Tauris, 2004.
12. Fisk. *The Great War for Civilization*.
13. Sara Osseiran, personal conversation with the author. January 2007.
14. Leon Hadar. "Birth Pangs of a New Middle East?" Antiwar.com. July 27, 2006. (www.antiwar.com/orig/hadar.php?articleid=9416 – last reviewed April 2008.)
15. Learn more about SOS Children's Villages: www.soschildrensvillages.org. uk/children-charity.htm (last reviewed January 2008).

5—SYRIA

1. Nizar Qabbani. *Conquering the World With Words*. Qabbani left his life as a Syrian diplomat to become one of the Arab world's greatest poets.
2. "Palestinians on Iraq-Syria border." Reuters AlertNet, citing UNHCR. November 24, 2006. (www.alertnet.org/thenews/newsdesk/UNHCR/ 9e1aa5f6076b98162b12ff3075d76fc1.htm – last reviewed January 2008.)
3. "Lebanese refugees pour across Syrian border." CNN. July 20, 2006. (http:// edition.cnn.com/2006/WORLD/meast/07/20/lebanon.refugees/index.html – last reviewed January 2008.)

6—AFGHANISTAN

1. Mowlana Jalaluddin Rumi. "Remember Me" from *Rumi—In the Arms of the Beloved*. Translated by Jonathan Star. Rumi (his full name means "Love and ecstatic flight into the infinite"), the great spiritual master and poetic genius and founder of the Mawlawi Sufi order, was born in Wakhsh (Tajikistan) in 1207.
2. "Bush Says If Younger, He Would Work in Afghanistan." Reuters. March 13, 2008. (www.reuters.com/article/politicsNews/idUSN133311112008031 3?sid13 – last reviewed April 2008.)
3. Taiseer Alouni. From the film "The Giant Buddas." Directed by Christian Frei. (www.giant-buddhas.com/en/synopsis/ – last reviewed April 2008.)
4. Excerpted from the film *Motherland Afghanistan*, directed by Afghan American Sedika Mojadidi. (www.pbs.org/independentlens/motherlandaf-ghanistan/index.html – last reviewed April 2008.)

5. CIA World Fact Book. (www.theodora.com/wfbcurrent/afghanistan/index. html – last reviewed April 2008.)

6. Personal conversations at anti-war demonstration held in Fayetteville, N.C. March 19, 2004.

7. Daniel Sieberg. "Hijackers Likely Skilled with Fake IDs." CNN. September 21, 2001. (http://archives.cnn.com/2001/US/09/21/inv.id.theft/ – last reviewed April 2008.)

8. For names and details known by FBI: "FBI Announces List of 19 Hijackers." September 14, 2001. (www.fbi.gov/pressrel/pressrel01/091401hj.htm – last reviewed April 2008.)

9. Excerpted from an interview with Robert Darr on Raising Sand Radio, March 2008. Listen to the full interview at www.raisingsandradio.org.

10. Various charitable, non-profit, religious, and educational organizations exempt from some U.S. federal income taxes.

7—UNITED STATES

1. Jack Hirschman. "Path." Hirschman is a social activist, a communist, and a prominent figure in American poetry with a half-century of published work. He is San Francisco's 2006 poet laureate. (www.leftcurve.org/LC28WebPages/Path.html – last reviewed April 2008.)

2. William Shakespeare. "The World Is Too Much With Us; Late and Soon."

3. Operation Iraqi Freedom (OIF) Mental Health Advisory Team (MHAT) Report. December 16, 2003. Chartered by US Army Surgeon General & HQDA G-1. (www-tc.pbs.org/wgbh/pages/frontline/shows/heart/readings/mhat.pdf. See also 2006 Final Report: www.armymedicine.army.mil/news/mhat/mhat_iv/MHAT_IV_Report_17NOV06.pdf – both sites last reviewed April 2008.)

4. "Troops Put Thorny Questions to Rumsfeld." CNN. Thursday, December 9, 2004. (www.cnn.com/2004/WORLD/meast/12/08/rumsfeld.troops/index. html – last reviewed April 2008.)

5. Press Conference by the President. White House Indian Treaty Room. December 20, 2006. (www.whitehouse.gov/news/releases/2006/12/20061220-1.html – last reviewed April 2008.)

6. National Center for PTSD: Fact Sheet. "Comparison for the ICD-10 PTSD diagnosis with the DSM IV criteria." (www.ncptsd.va.gov/ncmain/ncdocs/fact_shts/fs_icd10_ptsd_1.html?opm=1&rr=rr1362&srt=d&echorr=true – last reviewed March 2008.)

7. Leonard Shyles. "The Army's 'Be All You Can Be' Campaign." 1990 Inter-University Seminar on Armed Forces and Society. (http://afs.sagepub. com/cgi/content/abstract/16/3/369 – last reviewed April 2008.)

8. Learn more at GI Rights Hotline, www.girightshotline.org; Truth and Alternatives to Militarism in Education, www.tamewisconsin.org; National Lawyers Guild Military Law Task Force, www.nlgmltf.org. (Last reviewed April 2008.)

9. End Stop Loss Now. (www.endstoploss.com/ – last reviewed March 2008.)

8—WHERE DO WE GO FROM HERE?

1. Testimony of former Specialist Jason Moon on Raising Sand Radio, February 11, 2008. (www.raisingsandradio.org – last reviewed April 2008.)
2. Associated Press. "Reprise of Winter Soldier Anti-War Conference Held Near D.C." *Examiner*. March 15, 2008. (www.examiner.com/a-1280748~Reprise_of_Winter_Soldier_anti_war_conference_held_near_D_C_.html – last reviewed April 2008.)
3. "U.S. Used White Phosphorus in Iraq." BBC News. November 16, 2005. (http://news.bbc.co.uk/2/hi/middle_east/4440664.stm – last reviewed April 2008.)
4. Dahr Jamail's MidEast Dispatches. (http://dahrjamailiraq.com/covering_iraq/archives/commentary/000118.php – last reviewed August 2008.)
5. Sgt. Kevin Benderman. "A Matter of Conscience." Antiwar.com. January 18, 2005. (www.antiwar.com/orig/benderman.php?articleid=4455 – last reviewed April 2008.)
6. Gareth Porter of Inter Press Service, four decades after My Lai, obtained an original copy of Directive 525-3, issued by General Westmoreland and stating that once the "free fire zones" were established, "anybody who remained had to be considered an enemy combatant," and operations in those areas "could be conducted without fear of civilian casualties." The directive made it clear that humane treatment of civilians did not apply to those who had been under long-term Communist rule. A key point in the directive said, "Specified strike zones should be configured to exclude populated areas, except those in accepted VC bases."

    The term "accepted VC bases" referred to large parts of South Vietnam, including Son My village (My Lai). In his memoirs published in 1976, General Westmoreland wrote that, once the "free-fire zones" were established, "anybody who remained had to be considered an enemy combatant," and operations in those areas "could be conducted without fear of civilian casualties."

    Westmoreland was even more explicit in a visit to a unit of the 101st Airborne Division called the Tiger Force in Quang Ngai province in 1967. As recounted by members of the Tiger Force who were present, Westmoreland told them, "[I]f there are people who are out there—and not in the camps—they're pink as far as we're concerned. They're Communist sympathizers. They were not supposed to be there." "My Lai Probe Hid Policy that Led to Massacre." Inter Press Service. March 17, 2008. (www.ipsnews.net/news.asp?idnews=41608 – last reviewed April 2008.)
7. Dr. Stanley Milgram. *Obedience to Authority: An Experimental View.* The Milgram experiment, conducted at Yale University, was a seminal series of social psychology experiments that measured the willingness of study participants to obey an authority figure who instructed them to perform acts that conflicted with their personal conscience.
8. Paul Meadlo. (www.law.umkc.edu/faculty/projects/ftrials/mylai/myl_bmeadlo.htm – last reviewed March 2008.)
9. Christopher Buchanan. *Frontline.* "The Soldier's Heart." (www.pbs.org/wgbh/pages/frontline/shows/heart/lucey/ – last reviewed April 2008.)

10. Erik Eckholm. "Army Contract Official Critical of Halliburton Pact Is Demoted." *New York Times*. Monday, August 29, 2005. (www.nytimes. com/2005/08/29/international/middleeast/29halliburton.html?scp=1&sq=A rmy+Contract+Official+Critical+of+Halliburton+Pact+Is+Demoted&st=nyt – last reviewed April 2008.)

11. Seymour M. Hersh. "The General's Report: How Antonio Taguba, who investigated the Abu Ghraib scandal, became one of its casualties." *The New Yorker*. June 25, 2007. (www.newyorker.com/reporting/2007/06/25/070625fa_fact_hersh?currentPage=1 – last reviewed April 2008.)

12. Raising Sand Radio. "Iraq Veterans against War (IVAW, Olympia, WA Chapter)." March 2007. (Archived at www.radio4all.net/index. php?op=program-info&program_id=22064 – last reviewed March 2008.)

13. "Lieutenant Watada's War Against the War." *The Nation*. June 26, 2006. (www.thenation.com/doc/20060626/brecherwebvideo – last reviewed April 2008.)

14. Executive Government. "Mary A. Wright's resignation letter." March 19, 2003. (www.govexec.com/dailyfed/0303/032103wright.htm – last reviewed April 2008.)

15. Richard Boudreaux. "Israel Criticized For Cluster Bombs." *The Los Angeles Times*. February 1, 2008. (www.commondreams.org/archive/2008/02/01/6786/ – last reviewed April 2008.)

16. Nir Rosen, interviewed on *Democracy Now!* April 1, 2008. (www. democracynow.org – last reviewed April 2008.)

17. Eric Boehlert. "Rush's Forced Conscripts." Salon.com. February 4, 2008. (http://dir.salon.com/story/news/feature/2004/05/26/rush_limbaugh/ – last reviewed April 2008.)

18. "It's Not about Us; This Is War!" *The Rush Limbaugh Show*. May 4, 2004. (www.salon.com/politics/war_room/2004/05/06/limbaugh/ – last reviewed April 2008.)

19. Thomas Ricks. "Slayings of 4 Soldiers' Wives Stun Ft. Bragg; Husbands Alleged to Have Committed Killings; 3 Suspects Were in Special Operations in Afghanistan." *Washington Post*. July 27, 2002. (www.washingtonpost. com/ac2/wp-dyn/A7848-2002Jul26?language=printer – last reviewed March, 2008.)

20. Stephen Foley. "Traumatised Veterans 'Have Killed 120 in U.S.'" *The Independent* (UK). January 14, 2008. (www.commondreams.org/archive/2008/01/14/6364/ – last reviewed April 2008.)

21. Andrew J. Bacevich. "The Failure of an All-Volunteer Military." *The Boston Globe*. January 21, 2007. (www.boston.com/news/globe/editorial_opinion/oped/articles/2007/01/21/the_failure_of_an_all_volunteer_military/ – last reviewed March 2008.)

22. *Good Morning America*. ABC News. March 18, 2003.

23. Lt. Col. Dave Grossman. *On Killing: The Psychological Cost of Learning to Kill in War and Society*. Bay Books, 1996.

24. Mark Benjamin. "Iraq Sticker Shock." Salon.com. January 1, 2006. (www. salon.com/news/feature/2006/01/11/iraq_cost/ – last reviewed April 2008.) See also: Greg Jaffe. "As Benefits For Veterans Climb, Military Spending Feels Squeeze Congress's Generosity May Hurt Weapons, Other Programs."

Wall Street Journal. January 25, 2005. (http://americansforsharedsacrifice.
org/David_Chu.htm – last reviewed December 2007.)

25. "Projecting the Costs to Care for Veterans of U.S. Military Operations in
Iraq and Afghanistan." Congressional Budget Office Testimony. Statement
of Matthew S. Goldberg, Deputy Assistant Director for National Security
testimony to Congressional Budget Office. Before the Committee on Veterans'
Affairs, U.S. House of Representatives. October 17, 2007. (www.cbo.gov/
ftpdoc.cfm?index=8710 – last reviewed December 2007.)

26. Matt Kelley. "U.S. Soldiers' Suicide Rate Up in Iraq." *Associated Press.*
January 14, 2004.

27. "Army Suicides Hit Highest Level Since 1993." *Associated Press.* April 21,
2006. (www.msnbc.msn.com/id/12428185 – last reviewed January 2008.)

28. "CBS News Investigation Uncovers A Suicide Rate For Veterans Twice That
Of Other Americans." CBS. November 13, 2007. (www.cbsnews.com/
stories/2007/11/13/cbsnews_investigates/main3496471.shtml – last reviewed
March 2008.)

29. Jeremy Scahill. *Blackwater: The Rise of the World's Most Powerful Mercenary
Army.* Nation Books, 2007.

30. Rowan Wolf. "So-called Military Contractors Lean More Towards 'Military'
than 'Contractor.'" August 29, 2007. (www.bestcyrano.org/avenger212/?p=86
– last reviewed April 2008.)

31. Testimony by Captain Luis Carlos Montalvan at Winter Soldier Hearings,
March 14, 2008. Listen to audio interview on Raising Sand Radio. (www.
raisingsandradio.org – last reviewed March 2008.)

32. "Letter from Birmingham Jail." African Studies Center, University of
Pennsylvania. April 16, 1963. (www.africa.upenn.edu/Articles_Gen/Letter_
Birmingham.html – last reviewed April 2008.)

33. Hersh. "The General's Report." *Op. cit.*

34. Prof. Philip Zimbardo, interviewed on Raising Sand Radio. (www.raising-
sandradio.org – last reviewed April 2008.)

35. "Report of the Independent Panel to Review DoD Detention Operations."
August 2004. (www.prisonexp.org/pdf/SchlesingerReport.pdf – last reviewed
April 2008.)

36. Dr. Philip Zimbardo. *The Lucifer Effect: Understanding How Good People
Turn Evil.* Random House, 2007.

37. *Ibid.*

38. "Officer's Abu Ghraib Conviction Tossed Out: Military's Action Brings
Complaints of Whitewash in Prisoner Abuse Case." *Associated Press.*
January 10, 2008. (www.msnbc.msn.com/id/22594842/ – last reviewed April
2008.)

9—JUST THE FACTS

1. Elisabeth Sköns. Stockholm International Peace Research Institute—SIPRI,
2007. (http://yearbook2007.sipri.org/video/pc-elisabeth – last reviewed April
2008.)

2. Joseph Stiglitz interview on "Democracy Now!" April 9, 2008. (www.democracynow.org/2008/2/29/exclusive_the_three_trillion_dollar_war – last reviewed April 2008.)
3. "One In Five Iraq and Afghanistan Veterans Suffer from PTSD or Major Depression." RAND Corporation Press Release. April 17, 2008. (http://rand.org/news/press/2008/04/17/ – last reviewed April 2008.)
4. "War, War, What Is It Good For? Defense Industry Stocks." *Seeking Alpha*. January 26, 2007. (www.seekingalpha.com/ – last reviewed April 2008.)
5. Jad Mouawd. "Exxon Sets Profit Record: $40.6 Billion Last Year." *The New York Times*. February 2, 2008. (www.nytimes.com/2008/02/02/business/02oil.html?st=cse&sq=Exxon+Posts+Record+Profits+on+Oil+Prices&scp=3 – last reviewed April 2008.)
6. Food Research and Action Center. "Food Stamp Participation in April 2008 Hits Record Highs." (www.frac.org/html/news/fsp/2008.04_FSP.htm – last reviewed August 2008.)
7. Helen Benedict. "The Private War of Women Soldiers." Salon.com. March 7, 2007. (www.salon.com/news/feature/2007/03/07/women_in_military/ – last reviewed April 2008.)
8. Kim Curtis. "Women Sue U.S. Marine Corps Over Alleged Recruiter Rapes." Associated Press. March 8, 2006. (www.truthout.org/cgi-bin/artman/exec/view.cgi/58/18256 – last reviewed April 2008.)
9. John Broder and James Risen. "Contractor Deaths in Iraq Soar to Record." *New York Times*. May 19, 2007. Numbers according to government figures and dozens of interviews. (www.nytimes.com/2007/05/19/world/middleeast/19contractors.html?_r=2&hp&oref=slogin&oref=slogin – last reviewed April 7, 2008.)
10. Numbers from Pentagon and Department of Veterans Affairs obtained by Veterans for Common Sense and Freedom of Information Act.
11. Transcribed excerpt from Donald Rumsfeld on *Fox News*, November 2, 2003. (www.foxnews.com/story/0,2933,101956,00.html – last reviewed April 2008.)
12. Jonathan Steele and Suzanne Goldenberg. "What is the real death toll in Iraq?" *The Guardian*. March 19, 2008. (www.guardian.co.uk/world/2008/mar/19/iraq – last reviewed April 2008.)
13. Neil Munro and Carl M. Cannon. "Data Bomb." *National Journal*. Friday, January 4, 2008. (http://news.nationaljournal.com/articles/databomb/index.htm – last reviewed April 2008.)
14. Steele and Goldenberg, "What is the real death toll in Iraq?" *Op. cit.*
15. Kim Sengupta. "Five Years After Fall of Baghdad, All-Day Curfew Is Imposed." *The Independent* (UK). April 10, 2008. (www.independent.co.uk/news/world/middle-east/five-years-after-fall-of-baghdad-allday-curfew-is-imposed-807020.html – last reviewed April 2008.)

Index

Compiled by Sue Carlton